Budget
of the U. S. Government

Fiscal Year 2011

Office of Management and Budget
www.budget.gov

THE BUDGET DOCUMENTS

Budget of the United States Government, Fiscal Year 2011 contains the Budget Message of the President, information on the President's priorities, budget overviews organized by agency, and summary tables.

Analytical Perspectives, Budget of the United States Government, Fiscal Year 2011 contains analyses that are designed to highlight specified subject areas or provide other significant presentations of budget data that place the budget in perspective. This volume includes economic and accounting analyses; information on Federal receipts and collections; analyses of Federal spending; information on Federal borrowing and debt; baseline or current services estimates; and other technical presentations.

The *Analytical Perspectives* volume also contains supplemental material with several detailed tables, including tables showing the budget by agency and account and by function, subfunction, and program, that is available on the Internet and as a CD-ROM in the printed document.

Historical Tables, Budget of the United States Government, Fiscal Year 2011 provides data on budget receipts, outlays, surpluses or deficits, Federal debt, and Federal employment over an extended time period, generally from 1940 or earlier to 2011 or 2015.

To the extent feasible, the data have been adjusted to provide consistency with the 2011 Budget and to provide comparability over time.

Appendix, Budget of the United States Government, Fiscal Year 2011 contains detailed information on the various appropriations and funds that constitute the budget and is designed primarily for the use of the Appropriations Committees. The *Appendix* contains more detailed financial information on individual programs and appropriation accounts than any of the other budget documents. It includes for each agency: the proposed text of appropriations language; budget schedules for each account; legislative proposals; explanations of the work to be performed and the funds needed; and proposed general provisions applicable to the appropriations of entire agencies or group of agencies. Information is also provided on certain activities whose transactions are not part of the budget totals.

AUTOMATED SOURCES OF BUDGET INFORMATION

The information contained in these documents is available in electronic format from the following sources:

Internet. All budget documents, including documents that are released at a future date, spreadsheets of many of the budget tables, and a public use budget database are available for downloading in several formats from the Internet at *www.budget.gov/budget*. Links to documents and materials from budgets of prior years are also provided.

Budget CD-ROM. The CD-ROM contains all of the budget documents in fully indexed PDF format along with the software required for viewing the documents. The CD-ROM has many of the budget tables in spreadsheet format and also contains the materials that are included on the separate *Analytical Perspectives* CD-ROM.

For more information on access to electronic versions of the budget documents (except CD-ROMs), call (202) 512-1530 in the D.C. area or toll-free (888) 293-6498. To purchase the budget CD-ROM or printed documents call (202) 512-1800.

GENERAL NOTES

1. All years referenced for budget data are fiscal years unless otherwise noted. All years referenced for economic data are calendar years unless otherwise noted.

2. Detail in this document may not add to the totals due to rounding.

U.S. GOVERNMENT PRINTING OFFICE
WASHINGTON 2010

For sale by the Superintendent of Documents, U.S. Government Printing Office
Internet: bookstore.gpo.gov Phone: toll free (866) 512-1800; DC area (202) 512-1800
Fax: (202) 512-2104 Mail: Stop IDCC, Washington, DC 20402-0001

ISBN 978-0-16-084795-0

Table of Contents

THE BUDGET MESSAGE OF THE PRESIDENT

To the Congress of the United States:

We begin a new year at a moment of continuing challenge for the American people. Even as we recover from crisis, millions of families are still feeling the pain of lost jobs and savings. Businesses are still struggling to find affordable loans to expand and hire workers. Our Nation is still experiencing the consequences of a deep and lasting recession, even as we have seen encouraging signs that the turmoil of the past 2 years is waning. Moving from recession to recovery, and ultimately to prosperity, remains at the heart of my Administration's efforts. This Budget provides a blueprint for the work ahead.

But in order to understand where we are going in the coming year, it is important to remember where we started just 1 year ago. Last January, the United States faced an economic crisis unlike any we had known in generations. Irresponsible risk-taking and debt-fueled speculation—unchecked by sound oversight—led to the near-collapse of our financial system. Our Gross Domestic Product (GDP) was falling at the fastest rate in a quarter-century. Five trillion dollars of Americans' household wealth had evaporated in just 12 weeks as stocks, pensions, and home values plummeted. We were losing an average of 700,000 jobs each month, equivalent to the population of the State of Vermont. The capital and credit markets, integral to the normal functioning of our economy, were virtually frozen. The fear among economists—from across the political spectrum—was that we risked sinking into a second Great Depression.

Immediately, we undertook a series of difficult steps to prevent that outcome. We acted to get lending flowing again so that businesses could get loans to buy equipment and ordinary Americans could get financing to buy homes and cars, go to college, and start or run businesses. We enacted measures to foster greater stability in the housing market, help responsible homeowners stay in their homes, and help to stop the broader decline in home values. To achieve this, and to prevent an economic collapse that would have affected millions of additional families, we had no choice but to use authority enacted under the previous Administration to extend assistance to some of the very banks and financial institutions whose actions had helped precipitate the turmoil. We also took steps to prevent the rapid dissolution of the American auto industry—which faced a crisis partly of its own making—to prevent the loss of hundreds of thousands of additional jobs during an already fragile time. Many of these decisions were not popular, but we deemed them necessary to prevent a deeper and longer recession.

Even as we worked to stop the economic freefall and address the crises in our banking sector, our housing market, and our auto industry, we also began attacking the economic crisis on a broader front. Less than 1 month after taking office, we enacted the most sweeping economic recovery package in history: the American Recovery and Reinvestment Act. The Recovery Act not only provided tax cuts to small businesses and 95 percent of working families and provided emergency relief to those out of work or without health insurance; it also began to lay a new foundation for long-term economic growth and prosperity. With investments in health care, education, infrastructure, and clean energy, the Recovery Act both saved and created millions of jobs and began the hard work of transforming our economy to thrive in the modern, global marketplace and reverse the financial decline working families experienced in the last decade. Because of these and other steps, we can safely say we have avoided the depression many feared, and we are no longer facing the potential collapse of our financial system. But our work is far from complete.

First and foremost, there are still too many Americans without work. The steps we have taken have helped stop the staggering job losses we were experiencing at the beginning of last year. But the damage has been done. More than seven million jobs were lost since the recession began 2 years ago. This represents not only a terrible human tragedy, but also a very deep hole from which we have to climb out. Until our businesses are hiring again and jobs are being created to replace those we have lost—until America is back at work—my Administration will not rest and this recovery will not be finished.

That is why this Budget includes plans to encourage small businesses to hire as quickly and effectively as possible, to make additional investments in infrastructure, and to jump-start clean energy investments that will help the private sector create good jobs in America.

Long before this crisis hit, middle-class families were under growing strain. For decades, Washington failed to address fundamental weaknesses in the economy: rising health-care costs, a growing dependence on foreign oil, and an education system unable to prepare our children for the jobs of the future. In recent years, spending bills and tax cuts for the wealthy were approved without paying for any of it, leaving behind a mountain of debt. And while Wall Street gambled without regard for the consequences, Washington looked the other way.

As a result, the economy may have been working very well for those at the very top, but it was not working for the middle class. Year after year, Americans were forced to work longer hours and spend more time away from their loved ones, while their incomes flat-lined and their sense of economic security evaporated. Beneath the statistics are the stories of hardship I've heard all across America. For too many, there has long been a sense that the American dream—a chance to make your own way, to support your family, save for college and retirement, own a home—was slipping away. And this sense of anxiety has been combined with a deep frustration that Washington either didn't notice, or didn't care enough to act.

Those days are over. In the aftermath of this crisis, what is clear is that we cannot simply go back to business as usual. We cannot go back to an economy that yielded cycle after cycle of speculative booms and painful busts. We cannot continue to accept an education system in which our students trail their peers in other countries, and a health-care system in which exploding costs put our businesses at a competitive disadvantage and squeeze the incomes of our workers. We cannot continue to ignore the clean energy challenge and stand still while other countries move forward in the emerging industries of the 21st Century. And we cannot continue to borrow against our children's future, or allow special interests to determine how public dollars are spent. That is why, as we strive to meet the crisis of the moment, we are continuing to lay a new foundation for the future.

Already, we have made historic strides to reform and improve our schools, to pass health insurance reform, to build a new clean energy economy, to cut wasteful spending, and to limit the influence of lobbyists and special interests so that we are better serving the national interest. However, there is much left to do, and this Budget lays out the way ahead.

Because an educated workforce is essential in a 21st Century global economy, we are undertaking a reform of elementary and secondary school funding by setting high standards, encouraging innovation, and rewarding success; making the successful Race to the Top fund permanent and opening it up to innovative school districts; investing in educating the next generation of scientists and engineers; and putting our Nation closer to meeting the goal of leading the world in new college graduates by 2020. Moreover, since in today's economy learning must last a lifetime, my Administration will reform the job-training system, streamlining it and focusing it on the high-growth sectors of the economy.

Because even the best-trained workers in the world can't compete if our businesses are saddled with rapidly increasing health-care costs, we're fighting to reform our Nation's broken health insurance system and relieve this unsustainable burden. My Budget includes funds to lay the groundwork for these reforms—by investing in health information technology, patient-centered research, and prevention and wellness—as well as to improve the health of the Nation by increasing the number of primary care physicians, protecting the safety of our food and drugs, and investing in critical biomedical research.

Because small businesses are critical creators of new jobs and economic growth, the Budget eliminates capital gains taxes for investments in small firms and includes measures to increase these firms' access to the loans they need to meet payroll, expand their operations, and hire new workers.

Because we know the nation that leads in clean energy will be the nation that leads the world, the Budget creates the incentives to build a new clean energy economy—from new loan guarantees that will encourage a range of renewable energy efforts and new nuclear power plants to spurring the development of clean energy on Federal lands. More broadly, the Budget makes critical investments that will ensure that we continue to lead the world in new fields and industries: doubling research and development funding in key physical sciences agencies; expanding broadband networks across our country; and working to promote American exports abroad.

And because we know that our future is dependent on maintaining American leadership abroad and ensuring our security at home, the Budget funds all the elements of our national power—including our military—to achieve our goals of winding down the war in Iraq, executing our new strategy in Afghanistan, and fighting al Qaeda all over the world. To honor the sacrifice of the men and women who shoulder this burden and who have throughout our history, the Budget also provides significant resources, including advanced appropriations, to care for our Nation's veterans.

Rising to these challenges is the responsibility we bear for the future of our children, our grandchildren, and our Nation. This is an obligation to change not just what we do in Washington, but how we do it.

As we look to the future, we must recognize that the era of irresponsibility in Washington must end. On the day my Administration took office, we faced an additional $7.5 trillion in national debt by the end of this decade as a result of the failure to pay for two large tax cuts, primarily for the wealthiest Americans, and a new entitlement program. We also inherited the worst recession since the Great Depression—which, even before we took any action, added an additional $3 trillion to the national debt. Our response to this recession, the Recovery Act, which has been critical to restoring economic growth, will add an additional $1 trillion to the debt—only 10 percent of these costs. In total, the surpluses we enjoyed at the start of the last decade have disappeared; instead, we are $12 trillion deeper in debt. In the long term, we cannot have sustainable and durable economic growth without getting our fiscal house in order.

That is why even as we increased our short-term deficit to rescue the economy, we have refused to go along with business as usual, taking responsibility for every dollar we spend, eliminating what we don't need, and making the programs we do need more efficient. We are taking on health care—the single biggest threat to our Nation's fiscal future—and doing so in a fiscally responsible way that will not add a dime to our deficits and will lower the rate of health-care cost growth in the long run.

We are implementing the Recovery Act with an unprecedented degree of oversight and openness so that anyone anywhere can see where their tax dollars are going. We've banned lobbyists from serving on agency advisory boards and commissions, which had become dominated by special interests. We are using new technology to make Government more accessible to the American people. And last year, we combed the budget, cutting millions of dollars of waste and eliminating excess wherever we could—including outdated weapons systems that even the Pentagon said it did not want or need.

We continued that process in this Budget as well, streamlining what does work and ending programs that do not—all while making it more possible for Americans to judge our progress for themselves. The Budget includes more than 120 programs for termination, reduction, or other savings for a total of approximately $23 billion in 2011, as well as an aggressive effort to reduce the tens of billions of dollars in improper Government payments made each year.

To help put our country on a fiscally sustainable path, we will freeze non-security discretionary funding for 3 years. This freeze will require a level of discipline with Americans' tax dollars and a number of hard choices and painful tradeoffs not seen in Washington for many years. But it is what needs to be done to restore fiscal responsibility as we begin to rebuild our economy.

In addition to closing loopholes that allow wealthy investment managers to not pay income taxes on their earnings and ending subsidies for big oil, gas, and coal companies, the Budget eliminates the Bush tax cuts for those making more than $250,000 a year and devotes those resources instead to reducing the deficit. Our Nation could not afford these tax cuts when they passed, and it cannot afford them now.

And the Budget calls for those in the financial sector—who benefited so greatly from the extraordinary measures taken to rescue them from a crisis that was largely of their own making— to finally recognize their obligation to taxpayers. The legislation establishing the Troubled Asset Relief Program (TARP) included a provision requiring the Administration to devise a way for these banks and firms to pay back the American taxpayer. That is why in this Budget we have included a fee on the largest and most indebted financial firms to ensure that taxpayers are fully compensated for the extraordinary support they provided, while providing a deterrent to the risky practices that contributed to this crisis.

Yet even after taking these steps, our fiscal situation remains unacceptable. A decade of irresponsible choices has created a fiscal hole that will not be solved by a typical Washington budget process that puts partisanship and parochial interests above our shared national interest. That is why, working with the Congress, we will establish a bipartisan fiscal commission charged with identifying additional policies to put our country on a fiscally sustainable path—balancing the Budget, excluding interest payments on the debt, by 2015.

This past year, we have seen the consequences of those in power failing to live up to their responsibilities to shareholders and constituents. We have seen how Main Street is as linked to Wall Street as our economy is to those of other nations. And we have seen the results of building an economy on a shaky foundation, rather than on the bedrock fundamentals of innovation, small business, good schools, smart investment, and long-term growth.

We have also witnessed the resilience of the American people—our unique ability to pick ourselves up and forge ahead even when times are tough. All across our country, there are students ready to learn, workers eager to work, scientists on the brink of discovery, entrepreneurs seeking the chance to open a small business, and once-shuttered factories just waiting to whir back to life in burgeoning industries.

This is a Nation ready to meet the challenges of this new age and to lead the world in this new century. Americans are willing to work hard, and, in return, they expect to be able to find a good job, afford a home, send their children to world-class schools, receive high-quality and affordable health care, and enjoy retirement security in their later years. These are the building blocks of the middle class that make America strong, and it is our duty to honor the drive, ingenuity, and fortitude of the American people by laying the groundwork upon which they can pursue these dreams and realize the promise of American life.

This Budget is our plan for how to start accomplishing this in the coming fiscal year. As we look back on the progress of the past 12 months and look forward to the work ahead, I have every confidence that we can—and will—rise to the challenge that our people and our history set for us.

These have been tough times, and there will be difficult months ahead. But the storms of the past are receding; the skies are brightening; and the horizon is beckoning once more.

BARACK OBAMA

THE WHITE HOUSE,
FEBRUARY 1, 2010.

RESCUING THE ECONOMY

When the President took office on January 20, 2009, the economy was on the brink of a potentially severe depression. Real GDP fell at a 5.4 percent annual rate in the fourth quarter of 2008 and at a 6.4 percent annual rate in the first quarter of 2009 (see Figure 1, Real GDP).

Employment, which had been falling by less than 150,000 jobs per month before September 2008, declined by an average of 622,000 jobs per month from October through March. Altogether, in the fourth quarter of 2008, the country lost 1.7 million jobs—the largest quarterly decline since the end of World War II and a number only to be exceeded by the next quarter, when 2.1 million jobs were lost (see Figure 2, Nonfarm Payroll Employment). By January 2009, the underemployment rate, which measures all those out of work or underemployed for economic reasons, rose to 14 percent. Consumer confidence plummeted. Housing starts hit a record low, and the number of homes in foreclosure grew significantly. As financial markets collapsed, Americans lost their jobs, and the economy shrank, household net worth fell from the third quarter of 2007 to the first quarter of 2009 by $17.5 trillion or 26.5 percent, which is the equivalent to more than one year's GDP.

This decline was not simply the result of a normal downturn in the business cycle; indeed, the more fundamental cause was a meltdown in our credit and capital markets precipitated by a perfect storm of excessive risk-taking, inadequate disclosure, non-existent or myopic oversight, market gatekeepers compromised by conflicts of interest, and irresponsible lending to hundreds of thousands of Americans. Through sophis-

ticated financial engineering, these bad loans made their way onto the books of some on Wall Street, and were then sold to investors all over the world. Once the real estate market cooled, loans defaulted at alarming rates, and the credit boom unraveled.

The resulting collapse laid low some of the most prominent financial institutions in the American economy, wiped out trillions of dollars in wealth and retirement savings, and created a level of uncertainty that brought our financial system to the brink of collapse. A lack of confidence in the economy and in the financial system effectively froze the credit markets, preventing businesses from expanding, and families from financing a new home or college education; and caused massive job loss and economic contraction.

The Administration, consequently, entered office facing twin trillion-dollar deficits. The first was the gap between what the economy could be producing and what it was producing; this GDP gap totaled $1 trillion for 2009, or approximately 7 percent of the economy. The second was the budget deficit, estimated to be $1.3 trillion on the day the President took office, or 9.2 percent of GDP. And the budget deficit over the following decade—driven by the previous Administration's decisions not to offset three large domestic initiatives (the tax cuts of 2001 and 2003, as well as the Medicare prescription drug benefit) and the effects of the economic collapse and the efforts needed to combat it—produced this historically large 10-year deficit, totaling more than $8 trillion.

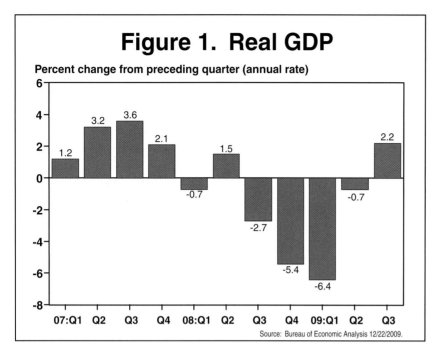

Figure 1. Real GDP

Percent change from preceding quarter (annual rate)

Source: Bureau of Economic Analysis 12/22/2009.

after taking office, the American Recovery and Reinvestment Act (the Recovery Act) to create and save jobs, as well as transform the economy to compete in the 21st Century.

The Recovery Act contains three parts. Approximately one-third—or $288 billion—is dedicated to tax cuts for small businesses and 95 percent of working families. Another third—or $224 billion—is for emergency relief for those who have borne the brunt of the recession; for example, more than 17 million Americans benefited from extended or increased unemployment benefits and health insurance was made 65 percent less expensive for laid-off workers and their families who rely on COBRA. In addition, aid to State and local governments helped them to close budget shortfalls, saving the jobs of hundreds of thousands of teachers, firefighters, and police officers. The final third is for investments to create jobs, spur economic activity, and lay the foundation for future sustained growth.

Facing this economic crisis, the Administration moved swiftly to take a series of extraordinary, but necessary, steps to pull the economy back from the brink. Because of these efforts, the immediate crisis has passed, the economy is on the path toward recovery, and we are laying a new foundation for long-term economic growth.

Jumpstarting the Economy: The American Recovery and Reinvestment Act

When the Administration took office, it became clear that there was a substantial shortfall between what the economy could produce and what it was producing. Economists across the spectrum agreed that substantial steps needed to be taken to bolster macroeconomic demand, jumpstart economic activity, and break a potentially vicious recessionary cycle. With traditional monetary policy levers largely exhausted, the Administration moved rapidly to sign into law, just 28 days

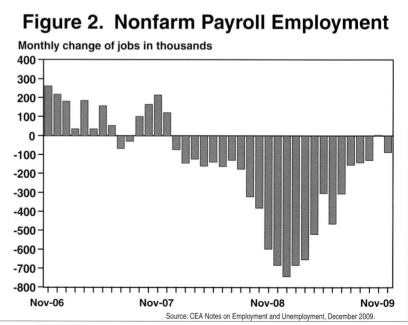

Figure 2. Nonfarm Payroll Employment

Monthly change of jobs in thousands

Source: CEA Notes on Employment and Unemployment, December 2009.

The Administration committed itself to implementing the Recovery Act with unprecedented accountability and transparency. In addition to an independent Recovery Board to monitor the program, the Act required recipients of Recovery funds to report quarterly on the amount of monies spent, the status of each project, the number of jobs created and/or saved, and other relevant details. This information is available for public scrutiny on the *Recovery.gov* website.

The effects of the Recovery Act on families, businesses, and the economy as a whole have been significant. In the 10 months since the Recovery Act was signed into law, the Administration cut taxes for 95 percent of working families through the Making Work Pay Tax Credit, which amounted to $37 billion in tax relief for 110 million working families over that time period. To help prevent cuts to Medicaid programs across the country, more than $40 billion was disbursed. Also, nearly $60 billion in funding for education was provided which helped to create or save more than 300,000 education jobs nationwide.

To create jobs now and build the infrastructure needed to support the jobs of the 21st Century, the Recovery Act already has funded more than 12,000 transportation construction projects nationwide, ranging from highway construction to airport improvement projects; begun or accelerated work at more than 50 Superfund sites from the Environmental Protection Agency's National Priority List; and started more than 2,000 construction and improvement projects at over 350 military facilities nationwide. To build America's competitiveness in the emerging industries of tomorrow, the Administration has made multi-billion dollar investments in innovation, science, and technology including: $2.4 billion in grants to companies and educational institutions in over 20 States to fund 48 new advanced battery manufacturing, transportation electrification, and electric drive vehicle projects that will help power the next generation of advanced vehicles; $3.4 billion in grants to private companies, utilities, manufacturers, and cities to fund smart energy grid projects that will support tens of

thousands of jobs and benefit consumers in 49 States; and more than $5 billion in grants to fund 12,000 cutting-edge medical research projects at research and educational institutions in every State across the country.

It is worth noting that in several cases, the Government Accountability Office has found that Recovery Act projects are coming in under budget, allowing funds to support more projects, assist more communities, and help create more jobs. For instance, the Federal Aviation Administration (FAA) initially committed $1.1 billion to 300 airport improvement projects; since those projects have come in $200 million below estimate, the FAA can now fund an additional 60 airport projects. Similarly, Department of Defense construction contracts are coming in about 12 percent under-budget, representing hundreds of millions of dollars in savings that will fund additional projects and further spur economic growth.

All told, as of the end of November 2009, about 50 percent of Recovery Act funds—or $395 billion—has been either obligated or is providing assistance directly to Americans in the form of tax relief. By design, the bulk of the remaining 50 percent of Recovery Act funds will be deployed in the coming months of 2010 and during the beginning of 2011 to support additional job creation when our economy continues to need a boost. Many of the programs slated to receive additional funding in the near future are those with significant promise of job creation. These include more than $7 billion in broadband expansion, approximately $8 billion in funds to lay the foundation for a high-speed rail network, and continued funding for other transportation projects. All told, the Recovery Act is on track to meet the goal of disbursing 70 percent of its funds in the first 18 months of its life.

Taken together, the fiscal relief, tax cuts and other direct assistance, and funding of critical infrastructure projects have had a substantial effect on the economy. Following implementation of the Recovery Act, the trajectory of the economy changed dramatically. Government and private-sector estimates suggest that the Recovery Act added two to three percentage points to real GDP growth in the second quarter of 2009, and three to four percentage points to growth in the third quarter of that year. Considering that real GDP growth for the third quarter of 2009 was 2.2 percent, many independent experts and forecasters agree that all the economic growth in that quarter was attributable—either directly or indirectly—to the Recovery Act.

In addition, there is evidence that the Recovery Act helped prevent the unemployment rate from climbing even higher over the past year. The Council of Economic Advisers (CEA), Congressional Budget Office (CBO), and private forecasters estimate that the Recovery Act increased employment relative to what would have occurred without the Act by between 900,000 and 1.5 million jobs over the second and third quarters of 2009.

Health Insurance Reform

As part of the Recovery Act, the Administration made a down payment on one of the most important unmet challenges facing the Nation and burdening the economy: the rising costs of health care.

Health care is consuming an ever-increasing amount of our Nation's resources: in 1970, health care expenditures were 7 percent of GDP; as of 2008, they exceeded 16 percent; and at this rate are projected to hit 20 percent by 2017. For individuals with health insurance, there is a strain on their family budgets. In fact, the past decade saw dramatic increases in premiums that far outstripped gains in wages. Not only is this burden felt directly when these bills are due, but it also is felt indirectly as take-home pay is constrained by these increasing health insurance costs. Moreover, many with insurance run the risk that when they need care, their coverage could be dropped; that if they leave their job, they will not be able to find affordable coverage or any coverage at all because of a pre-existing condition; or that they will be forced into bankruptcy due to huge un-

paid medical bills. Finally, those without any health insurance present both a moral burden and real financial cost on us all as every time an uninsured person walks into an emergency room because there is nowhere else to turn, a hidden tax is imposed on other citizens as premiums go up. For State governments, these rising costs crowd out expenditures on other vital services such as higher education and law enforcement.

While the United States spends more per capita on health care than any other developed nation, it is not always clear that we are receiving better care. On many metrics, other developed nations surpass us on health outcomes. In addition, several academic studies suggest that we spend as much as $700 billion a year on health care that does little or nothing to improve patients' health. Wide variation in health care practices among regions, States, cities, and even among health care providers within these localities generates significant differences in health outcomes and costs—with the high-cost medical centers not necessarily generating better outcomes than the lower-cost ones.

Recognizing that the current situation is not sustainable for families, businesses, and the Nation as a whole and that our long-term fiscal and economic health depend on bringing down the costs of health care, the President launched a health insurance reform effort last year.

First, in the Recovery Act itself, the Administration included funding critical to transforming the health care system into one that delivers better care, not just more care. Specifically, it included a program to spur an effort to computerize Americans' health records in five years, and do so in a way that rigorously protects patient privacy and helps to reduce health care costs in the long run. Because in so many areas of medical care, providers lack basic data on which interventions work and which do not, the Act provided $1.1 billion for patient-centered health research. And since chronic diseases that are manageable and preventable contribute disproportionately to poor health and rising costs, the Administration made an unprecedented $1 billion investment in prevention and wellness interventions.

Second, working with the Congress, the Administration has brought the Nation closer to health insurance reform than ever before. The bills passed by both chambers of Congress will give Americans with health insurance the stability and security they need by protecting consumers from being denied coverage based on pre-existing conditions or seeing it dropped or diluted once one falls ill. The legislation creates a health insurance exchange to increase consumer choice and provide affordable coverage for individuals and small businesses, and expands coverage to more than 30 million Americans. It will reduce the growth of health care costs for American families, seniors, and businesses. The bills also include important reforms that will end insurer abuses, hold insurance companies accountable, and enhance consumer rights. They include overdue reforms of the health care delivery system that will strengthen Medicare and improve quality of care for all Americans. And they put in place mechanisms to keep the system dynamic and responsive to changing market conditions.

Finally, the legislation meets the President's standard of changing the way Washington is doing business by paying for major new initiatives so they do not add to our Nation's debt. Indeed, the legislation meets the President's demand that health care reform not add to budget deficits in the first 10 years (and, in fact, it reduces them), and of reducing deficits thereafter. Deficit neutrality is accomplished by relying on tangible, accountable savings—as scored by the independent CBO—to pay for health insurance reform, such as savings from Medicare and revenue measures. The legislation also includes potentially more important cost-savings from transforming the health care delivery system, which will undoubtedly help to improve our long-term fiscal standing—even if it is challenging to quantify by precisely how much.

Fiscally-responsible health insurance reform is a critical part of the recovery of the Nation's economy. Our fiscal future is so dominated by

health care that if we can slow the rate of cost growth by just 15 basis points per year (0.15 percentage points per year), the savings on Medicare and Medicaid alone would equal the impact from eliminating Social Security's entire 75-year shortfall. Undertaking health insurance reform at this moment is an important step toward putting the country on a more solid foundation for economic growth.

Reviving the Financial System and Critical Sectors of the Economy

Along with reviving macroeconomic demand, the Administration was forced to take extraordinary, and sometimes understandably unpopular, steps to help revive the credit and capital markets and restore trust in the financial system. At the beginning of 2009, the financial system was extremely fragile. The viability of major financial institutions remained in doubt and vital aspects of the financial system were deeply impaired—preventing the flow of credit that small firms need to grow and families need to buy a home or car, attend college, or start a business. With the risk that inaction could lead to an even deeper downturn, the Administration implemented a plan to restore financial stability that, in conjunction with fiscal stimulus, has helped to stabilize financial markets and the economy and pull the financial system back from the brink of systemic collapse.

Financial Stabilization

Upon taking office, the Administration undertook a comprehensive, forceful, and sustained commitment to stabilize the financial system, assist in the cleanup of legacy assets, jumpstart the provision of new credit for households and businesses, and support distressed housing markets. The Administration's Financial Stability Plan helped to shore up confidence in our financial institutions and markets, while mobilizing private capital—especially in the wake of the "stress test" conducted of major financial institutions. The Administration also redirected the focus of the

Figure 3. TARP Investments in Banks

(In billions of dollars)

	Commitments			
	Pre-Jan 20th	Jan 20-Present[1]	Total[2]	Repayments
Existing Programs:				
Large Banks[3]	230	2	232	114
Small Banks[4]	9	5	14	2
Total	239	7	246	116
Common Equity and Other Regulatory Capital Raised by the Largest Banks Since "Stress Test" Results Were Announced in May				114

[1] Estimates as of December 9, 2009.

[2] Estimates may not sum to total due to rounding.

[3] CPP, AGP, TIP. Large banks are defined as banks with total assets of over $10 billion.

[4] CPP.

Source: Department of the Treasury.

Troubled Asset Relief Program (TARP) from large financial institutions to households, small banks, and small businesses (see Figure 3, TARP Investments in Banks). Indeed, since the President took office, only $7 billion in TARP funds have been provided to banks—much of it to smaller institutions—while major banks subject to the "stress test" have raised more than $140 billion in high-quality capital from the private sector.

As financial markets have stabilized and private capital has replaced Government capital, many of the initial programs created under TARP have become unnecessary, and institutions have begun to repay Federal money deployed through TARP programs. As of December 31, 2009, Treasury received $165 billion in TARP repayments, and taxpayers also have received about $17 billion in interest, dividends, and capital gains through the sale of warrants.

At the height of the crisis, the Treasury guaranteed that Americans would get back at least what they had invested in money market funds that participated in its temporary guarantee program. The program achieved its purpose, and it was terminated in September 2009. Not only did it not cost the taxpayers a dime; it earned them $1.2 billion in fees.

As we move from rescue to recovery and as financial stabilization funds are being repaid,

the Administration has developed a four-step exit strategy for modifying TARP to assist in rebuilding of the economy. First, we will continue winding down or terminating many of the Government programs put in place to address the crisis—a process that already is well underway. Second, we will limit future commitments to preserving home ownership, stimulating credit for small businesses, and supporting securitization markets which facilitate consumer and small business loans that promote job creation and economic growth. Third, beyond these limited new commitments, we will not use remaining stabilization funds unless necessary to respond to an immediate and substantial threat to the economy stemming from financial instability. Fourth, we will continue to carefully manage the equity investments acquired during this extraordinary period in a cost-effective manner, while protecting taxpayers and unwinding those investments as soon as practicable.

Housing

The steps taken to stabilize housing markets and help distressed homeowners represent another important element of the Administration's policy response. For the thousands of responsible homeowners who are facing foreclosure or are at risk of losing their homes, the Administration undertook a number of efforts to help them. On

February 18, 2009, the Administration announced the Homeowner Affordability and Stability Plan, a broad set of programs designed to stabilize the U.S. housing market and keep millions of homeowners in their homes.

First, the Administration took action to stabilize the housing market, in part by making mortgages more affordable. Continued support for Fannie Mae and Freddie Mac and the Treasury's Mortgage Backed Securities (MBS) purchase program, along with $1.1 trillion in MBS purchases by the Federal Reserve, have helped to keep interest rates at historic lows (see Figure 4, Conventional 30-year Mortgage Rate). More than 3 million Americans have taken advantage of these lower rates in 2009 to save money through refinancing. In addition, the Federal Housing Administration has increased its market presence significantly to enable many Americans to purchase homes.

Second, the Administration is working to provide increased access to financing for State and local housing finance agencies, which provide sustainable homeownership and rental resources, for working Americans in all 50 States. In addition, the $8,000 first-time homebuyer tax credit has helped hundreds of thousands of Americans purchase homes. The Recovery Act also supported the Low Income Housing Tax Credit market by creating an innovative Treasury Tax Credit Exchange Program and providing gap financing through the Department of Housing and Urban Development's Tax Credit Assistance Program. In combination, these programs are estimated to provide over $5 billion in support for affordable rental housing. In addition, the Recovery Act provided $2 billion in support for the Neighborhood Stabilization Program,

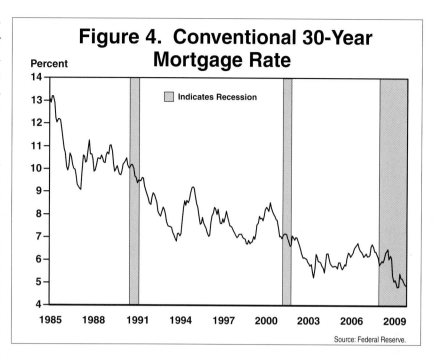

which is designed to rebuild value in areas hardest hit by foreclosures; this amount is on top of the $4 billion provided for the program in the Housing and Economic Recovery Act of 2008.

Third, the Administration initiated the Home Affordable Modification Program (HAMP), which provides eligible homeowners the opportunity to

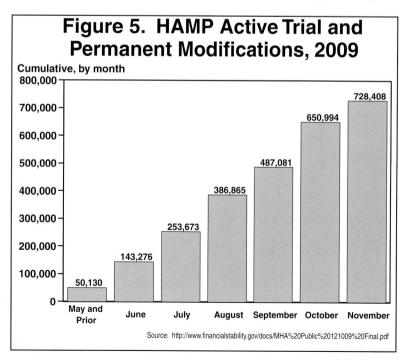

significantly reduce their monthly mortgage payment, remain in their homes, and prevent avoidable foreclosures (see Figure 5, HAMP Active Trial and Permanent Modification). Through November 2009, more than 725,000 borrowers are in active modifications, saving an average of more than $550 a month on their monthly mortgage payments. Servicers report that more than 1 million borrowers have received offers to begin trial modifications. HAMP is designed to offer a second chance to as many as 4 million borrowers by the end of 2012, averaging more than 20,000 trial modifications started per week. To facilitate this and other efforts, the Administration is working to improve the application process, develop operational measurements to hold servicers accountable for their performance, and enhance borrower resources to provide direct access to tools and housing counselors. Finally, the Administration is working with homeowners to help them through the process of converting temporary modifications into permanent ones.

More work needs to be done, and there are still market risks. But there are clear signs that our efforts are having an impact. We will continue to monitor this key component of the economy and work to keep responsible homeowners in their homes.

Automobile Industry

The freezing up of the credits markets in the fall of 2008 made it hard for many households to finance the purchase of motor vehicles. This difficulty, exacerbated by the rapid deterioration in the broader economy, led to reduced demand for motor vehicles, causing considerable financial stress to automobile companies, particularly General Motors (GM) and Chrysler. Without Government intervention, GM and Chrysler would have liquidated, causing widespread and devastating effects throughout the auto industry. Importantly, the repercussions of such liquidations could have included immediate and long-term damage to the U.S. manufacturing/industrial base, a significant increase in unemployment with direct harm to those both directly and indirectly related to the auto sec-

tor, and further damage to our financial system, since automobile financing constitutes a material portion of overall financial activity. Facing what risked becoming the last straw for an economy already severely weakened, the President made the difficult decision to offer assistance to the auto industry in an effort to prevent a further economic meltdown that could have hurt millions of families.

However, the President's offer of financial assistance was coupled with a requirement that GM and Chrysler develop serious restructuring plans that would address prior business failings and put the companies on a path to financial viability without Government assistance. After rejecting GM and Chrysler's initial plans and requiring all stakeholders to make additional sacrifices, the Administration accepted new restructuring plans from these two manufacturers.

In exchange for the assistance provided, the Government obtained from GM $8.8 billion in debt obligations and preferred stock along with a 60.8 percent share of the common equity in the new GM. From Chrysler, the Government obtained a $7.1 billion debt security note and 9.9 percent of Chrysler's common stock. In November 2009, GM announced that it would begin repaying the U.S. Treasury faster than anticipated, and made its first $1 billion repayment in December 2009.

To further assist the auto industry as well as the economy as a whole, the Administration also launched the Car Allowance Rebate System (CARS)—or "Cash for Clunkers"—program to accelerate demand for new automobiles. The program, signed into law by President Obama on June 24, provided bonuses of $3,500 to $4,500 to buyers who traded in automobiles with mileage ratings of 18 miles per gallon or below, if they purchased a new car or truck with improved mileage ratings. The Cash for Clunkers program boosted auto sales by nearly 500,000 units between July and August 2009, adding about $3.5 billion to the GDP. The CEA estimates that because of the program, employment in the second half of 2009 was about 70,000 job-years higher than it would otherwise have been. As an additional benefit, the program accelerated the replacement of high-polluting "clunker" motor vehicles with cleaner, higher-efficiency vehicles (see Figure 6, U.S. Light Motor Vehicle Sales).

Figure 6. U.S. Light Motor Vehicle Sales

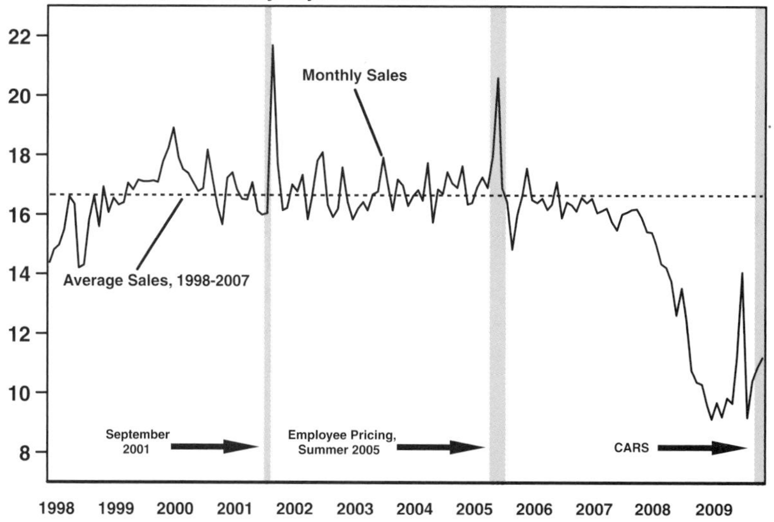

Source: Department of Commerce (Bureau of Economic Analysis) and CEA Report on Economic Impact of CARS.

While there is more to be done to assure financial stability, these steps have allowed us to move from the rescue phase to the next phase of rehabilitation and rebuilding. Even as we roll back emergency measures that are no longer needed, the Administration remains steadfast in its commitment to preserve the stability of the financial system. Some Government programs will stay in place to serve as a bulwark against unforeseen events and to provide confidence in our financial markets. Overall, however, the Administration believes that we are past the point of having to provide emergency relief, and looks forward to recouping the costs of these extraordinary efforts.

Rising to the Challenges Ahead

As a result of our steps to support the financial system, confidence has improved, credit is easing, and the economy is growing. Moreover, the Government is exiting from its emergency financial policies, and taxpayers are being repaid. Indeed, the ultimate cost of those policies is likely to be significantly lower than previously expected. The Administration now estimates that TARP will cost about $117 billion—$224 billion less than was projected in the 2010 Mid-Session Review (see Figure 7, Costs of Troubled Asset Relief Program Actions). For example, we now expect that there will be a positive return on $248 billion of investments in

Figure 7.   Costs of Troubled Asset Relief Program Actions (Excluding Debt Service) [1]

(In billions of dollars)

TARP Actions	2010 MSR		2011 Budget		Change from 2010 MSR to 2011 Budget	
	TARP Obligations	Subsidy Cost	TARP Obligations	Subsidy Cost	TARP Obligations	Subsidy Cost
Equity Purchases	383.7	158.1	344.1	55.9	−39.6	−102.2
Structured & direct loans and asset-backed security purchases	330.5	133.6	148.6	25.0	−181.9	−108.6
Guarantees of troubled asset purchases [2]	12.5	−0.8	5.0	−3.0	−7.5	−2.2
Home Affordable Modification Program (HAMP)	50.0	50.0	48.8	48.8	−1.2	−1.2
Total	**776.7**	**340.9**	**546.4**	**126.7**	**−230.3**	**−214.2**
Memorandum:						
Deficit impact before administrative costs and interest effects [3]		340.9		116.8		−224.1

1 Total reflects estimated lifetime TARP obligations and costs through 2020.

2 The 2010 MSR reflected total face value of guarantees of $419 billion. The 2011 Budget reflects the actual face value of $301 billion.

3 The 2011 Budget total dficit impact includes interest on downward reestimates of $9.9 billion.

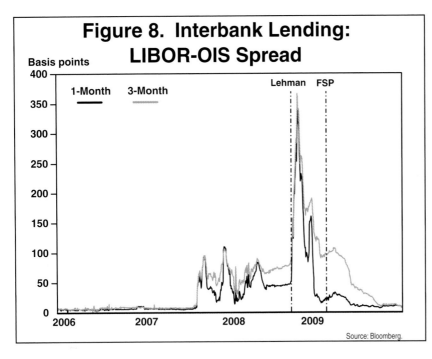

Figure 8. Interbank Lending: LIBOR-OIS Spread

Source: Bloomberg.

banks, about two-thirds of which have already been repaid over the past year.

Confidence in the stability of our financial markets and institutions has improved dramatically over the past year. Interbank lending rates, which reflect stress in the banking system, have returned to levels associated with more stable times. For example, the spread of one-month LIBOR to the overnight index swap—a measure of liquidity in the banking system—has fallen from a peak of about 340 basis points in October 2008 to roughly 10 basis points today (see Figure 8, Interbank Lending: LIBOR-OIS Spread). Credit-default swap spreads for financial institutions, which measure investor confidence in their health, have also fallen significantly. An aggregate measure of credit-default swaps for the largest U.S. banks reached over 450 basis points in October 2008; it is roughly 100 basis points today (see Figure 9, Credit-Default Swap Spreads for Financial Institutions).

As borrowing costs have come down, businesses have raised substantial capital from private sources. Corporations have raised more than $900 billion in investment-grade debt and in excess of $100 billion in high-yield debt this past year. While much of the new issuance early this year was supported by Government guarantees, in recent months private investors have funded most new corporate debt without public support: only 14 percent was guaranteed in October, whereas nearly 50 percent of new issuance was guaranteed by the Government in January 2009. The U.S. banking system is much better capitalized today than it was at the height of the crisis. Since the announcement of the stress test results, the largest banking institutions have raised over $140 billion in high-quality capital and over $60 billion in non-guaranteed unsecured debt in the private markets. Banks have used private capital to repay TARP preferred equity, allowing TARP to fulfill its function as a bridge to private capital.

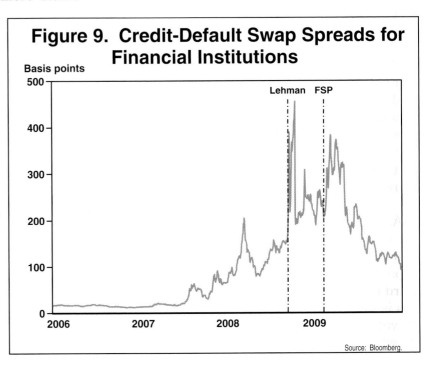

Figure 9. Credit-Default Swap Spreads for Financial Institutions

Source: Bloomberg.

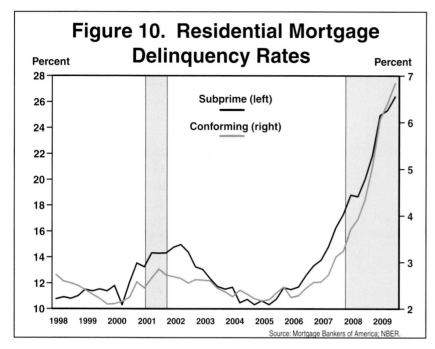

Figure 10. Residential Mortgage Delinquency Rates

Source: Mortgage Bankers of America; NBER.

The market for municipal bonds is also recovering from the financial crisis. The Recovery Act included an innovative new tool for municipal financing, Build America Bonds, which are taxable bonds for which Treasury pays a 35 percent direct subsidy to the issuer to offset borrowing costs. Build America Bonds are now providing State and local governments with access to low-cost financing that is providing them with a much needed economic boost.

Housing markets likewise are showing some signs of stabilizing, and wealth is recovering; these real improvements in individual-level finances should stimulate consumer spending, which is a vital component to American economic growth. For example, household net worth increased by $2 trillion in the second quarter of 2009, the first increase since the second quarter of 2007.

As credit conditions have improved and with the macroeconomic boost of the Recovery Act, the economy has started to grow again. The economy expanded at an annual rate of 2.2 percent in the third quarter of 2009, and the Blue Chip consensus is for 4 percent growth in the fourth quarter. Private economists generally expect moderate growth over the next year, and in line with their

estimates the Budget assumes that the economy will grow by an annual rate of 3.0 percent in 2010, and accelerate to approximately 4.25 percent annually over 2011 to 2013.

While the economy has turned a corner, there are still significant challenges that must be addressed.

Home foreclosure and delinquency rates remain too high (see Figure 10, Residential Mortgage Delinquency Rates), placing enormous pressure on American families and homeowners. Bank lending continues to contract overall, although the pace of contraction has moderated and some categories of lending are growing again. For example, commercial and industrial loans contracted at an annual rate of 27 percent in the third quarter, but 16 percent since then. Such loans are particularly important for small businesses, which generally cannot raise money by issuing debt in securities markets. Without access to capital, business expansion and job creation will be limited.

Perhaps the biggest challenge facing the economy, as we move from rescue to recovery, is the weak labor market. Far too many workers who would rather be earning a paycheck are on unemployment, left worrying about how to pay their mortgage or the rent, keep their health insurance, and continue to provide for their families. In November 2009, the unemployment rate fell to 10 percent and payrolls increased—for the first time since 2007—by 4,000 jobs. In December the unemployment rate remained constant at 10 percent, with a loss of 85,000 jobs. The fact that a single month of job gains, followed by a steady unemployment rate, is seen as progress points to the severe job loss the economy had experienced over the course of the recession (see Figure 11, Initial Claims for Unemployment Insurance).

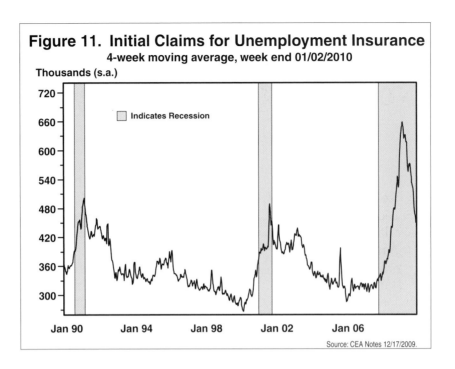

Figure 11. Initial Claims for Unemployment Insurance
4-week moving average, week end 01/02/2010

Source: CEA Notes 12/17/2009.

The typical progression in a recovery is, first, that worker productivity increases as firms try to do more with their existing staff. Then, the number of hours worked increases for already employed workers as the economy picks up. Finally, as growth is sustained, companies begin hiring again. There are signs that this process is beginning to happen with this recovery as well. In the third quarter of 2009, non-farm business sector labor productivity increased by 8.1 percent on an annualized basis, the largest gain in productivity since the third quarter of 2003. There are signs that hours worked began to rebound in the fourth quarter of 2009. And hiring of temporary workers—a reliable leading indicator of full-time hiring—increased substantially in the fourth quarter as well.

Unfortunately, the progression to consistent and substantial job growth is not coming soon enough. Sparking job creation in the private sector is an urgent priority, one reflected throughout the Budget and in the policies put forth by the Administration. Americans are willing to work hard, and in return, they expect to be able to find a good job, afford a home, send their kids to a good school, receive high-quality and affordable health care, and enjoy retirement security in their later years. These are the building blocks of the middle class that makes America strong, and together they constitute the new foundation we seek for our economy. Our challenge is to put politics aside and take the steps now that will deliver on this promise for all Americans now and in generations to come.

REVIVING JOB CREATION AND LAYING A NEW FOUNDATION FOR ECONOMIC GROWTH

The economy has been rescued from disaster, and is on the road to recovery. We are no longer facing the potential collapse of our financial system, and the country has avoided the depression many feared just a year ago. Our economy is growing; our markets are returning to functionality; and some of the losses of the past year have been restored. These indicators may be heartening to economists, but they are cold comfort to the millions who are out of work, communities that have seen industries downsized and factories shuttered, and the cities and towns who are finding it hard to provide services to their residents.

There are 7 million fewer jobs today than when the recession began in December 2007. The immediate effects of being unemployed are felt deeply by the unemployed and their families: bills that are not paid, college tuition payments that are not sent, and homes that are no longer affordable. Moreover, there is growing evidence that unemployment has a lasting effect on these workers' children too. A range of studies have found that having a parent experience unemployment is closely tied with whether you graduate from high school, whether you go to college, whether you get a job after college, and how much you get paid in that job. And the effect is persistent—with higher high school dropout rates and lower college enrollment rates evident even years later. For those in college and graduating into a recession, studies suggest that it leads to depressed wages in the first year of employment and for years to come. There is also evidence that unemployment has a lasting negative effect on community and civic engagement, not only among the jobless but among their neighbors as well.

We cannot sit idly by and allow a generation of Americans to be knocked off course just as they are ready to come into their own. We cannot be content with a recovery that is felt on Wall Street, but not on Main Street. And we cannot be satisfied with business as usual, returning to an economy of boom and bust, easy credit, and reckless actions that only works for the wealthiest and the well-connected. We must lay a new foundation in which innovation and job creation are nurtured, the middle class is strengthened, and economic opportunity is available to all. Doing that entails using this moment of economic recovery to rebuild our Nation and transform our economy so that we can compete and thrive in the decades ahead.

Investing in Job Creation

In the short-term, it is critical that we take steps to jumpstart job creation so that the nascent economic recovery is one that lifts American workers and families. Looking to the future, we know that in the high-tech, interdependent economy of the 21st Century, two of the most precious resources for any nation are the know-how and creativity of its people. Basic research across the sciences leads to discoveries and technologies that create whole industries, thousands of businesses, and millions of jobs. From bio-technology to information technology, we have seen that happen in our own time. Yet this is not the moment to rest on our past accomplishments; we must support invention and innovation today so that our scientists, engineers, and entrepreneurs can grow these businesses of tomorrow.

At the same time, we need to recognize that our economy is strongest when we tap the potential of all its participants. Small businesses, which over the past 15 years have created roughly 65 percent of all new private sector jobs in America, are critical to the future of our economy. We need to create the conditions whereby if you have a good idea and the drive to act on it, you can open your own store or start your own company. Economic growth and job creation also must not be limited to our cities and suburbs; rural America too must be able to provide jobs and economic opportunities to its residents. Hard-working young people in small towns across America should be able to find good jobs and promising opportunities at home. Moreover, we need to recognize that competitive, high-performing regional economies are essential to a strong national economy. That's why the President announced a broad-based initiative to review how Federal policies impact local communities and to better target and coordinate resources across agencies to promote job creation, environmental sustainability, and broad-based economic growth. Finally, all Americans should be able to balance the needs of their careers and their families and retire with security. To foster job growth across the economy, the Budget will:

Spur Job Creation. While we are no longer hemorrhaging jobs at the rate we were last year, unemployment is still unacceptably high. Looking to the future, the investments made in the Budget in education, clean energy, infrastructure, and in several other areas will lay a new foundation for economic growth and job creation. But in the short term, it is clear that the some targeted measures are required to spur private sector job creation. The Administration will work with the Congress to implement a jobs creation package along the lines the President announced in December of 2009. It will include immediate steps to help small businesses grow and hire, to upgrade and build infrastructure, and create jobs through energy efficiency and clean energy investments. In addition, to help those most affected by the recession, the Budget will extend emergency assistance to seniors and families with children, Unemployment Insurance benefits, COBRA

tax credits, and relief to States and localities to prevent layoffs.

Provide Small Businesses Access to Credit. One of the biggest challenges facing the country as we recover from the economic crisis is giving small businesses access to credit. That is why the Budget provides funds to support $17.5 billion in SBA 7(a) loan guarantees that will help small businesses operate and expand. The Budget also supports $7.5 billion in guaranteed lending for commercial real estate development and heavy machinery purchases; $3 billion in Small Business Investment Company debentures to support new businesses and new jobs through early-stage and mezzanine small business financing; and $25 million in direct microloans, for intermediaries to provide small loans to emerging entrepreneurs and other promising, but "un-bankable," borrowers. In addition, the Budget proposes to significantly increase the maximum loan sizes on SBA loans, including an increase from $2 million to $5 million for 7(a) business loans, to further improve small business access to credit.

Refocus Troubled Asset Relief Program (TARP) Funds to Assist Small Businesses. As we move from rescue to recovery and financial stabilization funds are being repaid, the Treasury is redirecting TARP to focus on preserving homeownership and supporting small business lending. The Treasury is working with the Small Business Administration to refocus funds on a special initiative that—with the support of new legislation—is designed to encourage widespread participation by small banks in increasing lending to small businesses in their communities. The Administration has also announced a TARP program to increase small business lending in hard-hit areas by providing lower cost capital to Community Development Financial Institutions.

Eliminate Capital Gains Tax on Investments in Small Businesses. Opening up one's own business is a critical part of the American dream; it is a hallmark of our economy's vitality and an important creator of jobs. To create an incentive for long-term investments in the small business sector, the Budget eliminates capital gains taxes on long-term investments in many small businesses. The American Recovery and Reinvestment Act (Recovery Act) temporarily increased the exclusion to 75 percent. The Budget proposes to raise this exclusion to 100 percent, meaning that no income tax whatsoever would be paid on these investments in our Nation's small businesses.

Extend the Making Work Pay Tax Cut. The Recovery Act created the Making Work Pay tax credit, a refundable income tax credit, which offsets the Social Security payroll tax on up to the first $6,450 of earnings for about 95 percent of all American workers. This helps small business owners struggling to meet expenses, and will put needed money in the pockets of families struggling to make ends meet and cover their costs. As part of its plan to restore health to the economy, the Budget proposes to extend the Making Work Pay tax cut for one year.

Promote American Exports to Fuel Economic Growth. A key component of stable, long-term economic growth is opening up foreign markets to American goods and services. The Budget provides $534 million, a 20-percent increase, to the Commerce Department's International Trade Administration, to promote exports from small businesses, help enforce free trade agreements with other nations, eliminate barriers to sales of U.S. products, and improve the competitiveness of U.S. firms. The Budget also provides funding to the Export-Import Bank to expand U.S. small business use of the Bank's financial export assistance. In addition, the Budget supports expanded action by the Department of Agriculture to overcome sanitary and phyto-sanitary public health and related technical barriers to trade and to assist overseas market development activities, and provides funds to better protect U.S. intellectual property rights overseas.

Invest in Science Research and Development. Investment in science and basic research is critical to long-term economic growth. That's why the Budget invests $61.6 billion in civilian research and development, an increase of $3.7 billion, a 6.4 percent increase, and an amount

that continues the commitment to double funding for three key basic research agencies—the National Science Foundation, the Department of Energy's Office of Science, and the National Institute of Standards and Technology. This funding includes $1.8 billion for research in basic energy sciences to discover novel ways to produce, store, and use energy to address energy independence and climate change and $300 million for the Advanced Research Projects Agency-Energy, to accelerate game-changing energy technologies in need of rapid and flexible experimentation or engineering. The Budget includes increased funding for research to help create the foundation for the industries and jobs of the future, such as nano-manufacturing, advanced robotics, and new tools for the design of biological systems.

Increase Funding for Biomedical Research. To accelerate progress in biomedical research, the Budget continues to support research both on the campuses of the National Institutes of Health (NIH) and for approximately 300,000 scientists and other research personnel at institutions across the country. Investments will focus on priority areas including genomics, translational research, science to support health care reform, global health, and reinvigorating the biomedical research community. The Budget also includes $6,036 million to continue to expand research related to cancer, and $143 million to expand research related to Autism Spectrum Disorders. Finally, under the President's Executive Order and subsequent NIH Guidelines for Human Stem Cell Research, NIH approved 40 responsibly-derived stem cell lines—nearly double the previous number of lines available—for path-breaking research. Additionally, NIH will pursue the discovery, development, and pre-clinical testing of novel compounds for the prevention and treatment of symptoms associated with Alzheimer's disease.

Reinvigorate Space Science and Exploration. Leaving the boundaries of our planet has helped to spur innovation and push the boundaries of scientific knowledge across many fields. Recognizing the importance of space science and exploration, the Administration is proposing to cancel the National Aeronautics and Space

Administration's (NASA's) Constellation program—which is based largely on existing technologies and was over budget, behind schedule, and lacking in innovation—and replace it with a bold, new approach to human space flight that embraces commercial industry, forges international partnerships, and invests in the building blocks of a more capable approach to space exploration. This includes: research and development to support future cost-effective, heavy-lift rocket systems; a vigorous new technology development and test program that aims to increase the capabilities and reduce the cost of future exploration activities; and the development of precursor robotic exploration missions to scout locations and demonstrate technologies to increase the safety and capability of future human missions and provide scientific dividends. To support this effort, the Budget adds $6 billion to NASA's budget over the next five years.

Enhance Regional Economic Competitiveness. Competitive, high-performing regional economies are essential to national growth. The Budget supports growth strategies based on stronger regional clusters of economic activity through funding across many agencies. The Budget provides $75 million in regional planning and matching grants within the Commerce Department's Economic Development Administration to support the creation of regional innovation clusters. The SBA will support enhanced small business participation in clusters by awarding competitive grants to promote greater coordination of resources. Recognizing that labor markets are typically regional, yet the workforce system is designed around State and local boundaries, the Department of Labor's Workforce Innovation Fund will support these efforts by facilitating regional collaboration and close linkages with employers so that relevant training leads to good jobs.

Foster Job Creation and Economic Growth in Rural America. The country as a whole cannot prosper if we do not tap the potential of all Americans—including those who call rural America home. That's why the Budget includes several investments to promote economic growth and job

creation in rural communities. First, to support the Rural Innovation Initiative, the Department of Agriculture (USDA) plans to set aside funding to foster rural revitalization through a competitive grant program. Second, the Budget supports local and regional food systems through many USDA programs including the Business and Industry guaranteed loan program and the Federal State Marketing Improvement Program. Third, the Budget funds a variety of USDA renewable energy programs including support for bio-refineries to utilize advanced biomass crops, research designed to create cellulosic and other advanced biofuels, and assistance to help transition fossil fuel-dependent electric utilities to renewable energy—all of which can help a clean energy economy take root in rural America. In addition, the Administration proposes more than $700 million to restore ecosystems and manage public lands, which will increase employment in rural areas, produce new sources of renewable energy, and develop recreational opportunities, including fishing and hunting, for local residents and tourists. Finally, the Budget fully funds the Voluntary Public Access and Habitat Incentive Program, which encourages private landowners to voluntarily open their land to the public for hunting and fishing.

Aid Working Adults in Caring for Their Families. In today's economy, working Americans struggle to find time and money to provide their children and their own parents with the care they deserve. That is why the Budget provides tax relief of up to $2,100—an increase of $900 relative to current law—for middle-class families to pay for the costs of caring for a child or a relative. The Budget also provides a $1.6 billion increase in child care funding for working families with low incomes—not only extending the funding provided in the Recovery Act, but also providing new funding for new slots. In addition, the Budget includes $103 million for the Administration on Aging's Caregiver Initiative, which will help family caregivers better manage their multiple responsibilities and help seniors and people with disabilities live in the community for as long as possible.

Help Americans Prepare for a Secure Retirement. Too many families have seen their IRAs and their 401(k)s lose value during the recent downturn, and far too many lack retirement savings at all. The Budget includes a series of steps to shore up saving including enhancing transparency and consumer protections, requiring employers who do not offer a retirement plan to give employees the option of making deposits into retirement accounts, doubling the small employer pension plan startup credit for firms that establish a retirement plan, expanding the Saver's Credit, and reducing barriers to saving for recipients of means-tested programs.

Revitalize Distressed Urban Neighborhoods. The Budget reflects an integrated and performance-driven approach to distressed urban neighborhoods, where the challenges tied to jobs, education, public safety, and other needs intersect and compound each other. The Budget includes $250 million for the Department of Housing and Urban Development's (HUD's) Choice Neighborhoods program, which will target neighborhoods anchored by distressed public or assisted housing with physical and social revitalization grounded in promising, measurable, and evidence-based strategies. Choice Neighborhoods also will coordinate with the Department of Justice, which is requesting $40 million for targeted, innovative programs to assist neighborhoods and has a variety of other programs to prevent gang violence and assist prisoners re-integrate into the job market and community life. The Budget also includes $2.5 billion for health centers to provide affordable high-quality primary and preventive care to underserved populations, including the uninsured.

Promote Responsible and Affordable Homeownership. The President's Budget proposes important reforms to the Federal Housing Administration's (FHA's) core mortgage finance programs, including its widely used single-family mortgage insurance product. These reforms will protect taxpayers by replenishing the FHA's capital reserves, while continuing to promote affordable homeownership and support the recovery of the housing market, which is central to the broader economic recovery. At the same time, these changes will better manage credit risk to the Federal taxpayer. In addition, the Budget supports increased funds for housing counseling. To mitigate the threat of foreclosure for responsible homeowners, the Administration is continuing to implement the Home Affordable Mortgage Program, which will commit up to $50 billion through the Department of the Treasury along with approximately $25 billion through the Government-Sponsored Enterprises. These funds will offer relief to an estimated 3 to 4 million at-risk homeowners struggling to make their mortgage payments, while preventing communities from suffering the spillover effects of foreclosures. Treasury is also implementing the recently extended and expanded homebuyer tax credit, which supports demand for home sales in markets nationwide.

Building the Infrastructure for Job Creation

For too long, our Nation avoided making the necessary investments in the roads, bridges, levees, waterways, communications networks, and transit systems needed to keep pace with the times. Outdated infrastructure burdens our communities in a number of ways: longer commutes, businesses choosing to locate elsewhere including overseas, and growth and job creation held back. Through the Recovery Act, we made the largest investment in our Nation's infrastructure since President Eisenhower called for the creation of the national highway system half a century ago. In just 10 months since it became law, the Act funded—for example—more than 12,000 transportation projects, and more than 500 new or improved waste and water systems in rural America. This year, funds from the Act will help bring broadband Internet access to remote corners of our country, lay the foundation for a high-speed rail network, and jump-start innovative transportation projects through competitive awards. In the 2011 Budget, the Administration will:

Create a National Infrastructure Innovation and Finance Fund. The Budget includes $4 billion to create a National Infrastructure Innovation and Finance Fund to invest in projects of regional or national significance. This marks an important departure from the Federal Government's traditional way of spending on infrastructure through grants to specific States and localities. The Fund will allocate resources based on demonstrable merit and analytical measures of performance. The Fund will provide planning, feasibility, and analytical capacity to help sponsors identify high-value projects from around the country and then carefully select the most worthwhile projects.

Expand Access to Broadband. During 2011, the Department of Commerce and USDA will focus on administering the $7.2 billion program to expand broadband deployment, as well as programs to improve broadband adoption and data collection, which were funded by the Recovery Act. In addition, the Budget expands access to broadband services by offering $418 million in USDA loans and grants to move rural communities into the modern information economy.

Invest in a Smart, Energy-Efficient, and Reliable Electric Grid. The Budget continues to support modernization of the Nation's electric grid by investing in the research, development, and demonstration of smart-grid technologies that will spur the Nation's transition to a smarter, stronger, more efficient, and reliable electric system. The end result will promote energy- and cost-saving choices for consumers, increase efficiency, and foster the growth of renewable energy sources like wind and solar. In addition, the Budget supports the Power Marketing Administrations' ability to reliably operate, maintain, and rehabilitate the Federal hydropower and transmission systems.

Support Clean Water Infrastructure Investments. The 2011 Budget requests $3.3 billion for the Clean Water and Drinking Water State Revolving Funds (SRFs). The Federal SRF funding provides grants to States for low-interest loans to communities through a combination of Federal capitalization, State matches, State leveraging, interest, and loan repayments. Since loan interest and principal payments are returned to the program, the SRFs continue to generate funding for new loans even without continued Federal funding. For 2011, the Environmental Protection Agency proposes a new approach to helping small drinking water systems, as well as reforms to improve the long-term financial, managerial, and environmental sustainability of the SRFs.

Reform Surface Transportation Programs and Put the System on a Viable Financing Path. Surface transportation programs are at a crossroads. The current framework for financing and allocating surface transportation investments is not financially sustainable, nor does it effectively allocate resources to meet our critical national needs. The Administration recommends extending the current authorization through March 2011, during which time it will work with the Congress to reform surface transportation programs and put the system on a viable financing path. Careful consideration is needed to design a Federal surface transportation program that leads to higher-performing investments, increases people's transportation options, and makes our economy more productive. Further, the Federal program must generate the best investments to reduce congestion and improve safety. To do so, the Administration seeks to integrate economic analysis and performance measurement in transportation planning so that taxpayer dollars are better targeted and spent.

Establish a New Federal Transit Safety Program. Unlike other mode of transportation, closed-system rail transit services (generally, metro area subways and light rail systems) are not overseen by Federal safety regulators, but rather are subject to review by a patchwork of State safety organizations. Recent deadly accidents—including tragedies in Washington D.C., Boston, and San Francisco—underscore the need for common nationwide safety standards and for Federal enforcement of these standards. The Budget includes $30 million for a new transit safety oversight program within the Federal Transit Administration (FTA). This will enable

FTA to implement a comprehensive safety oversight strategy, as proposed in legislation.

Modernize the Air Traffic Control System. The Budget provides $1.14 billion, more than a 30-percent increase from 2010, for the Next Generation Air Transportation System, the Federal Aviation Administration's long-term effort to improve the efficiency, safety, and capacity of the aviation system. The 2011 Budget will help move from a national ground-based radar surveillance system to a more accurate satellite-based surveillance system; aid in the development of more efficient routes through the airspace; and fund improvements in aviation weather information.

Sustain Multi-Year Support for High-Speed Rail. Building on the historic $8 billion down payment provided through the Recovery Act, the President's Budget includes $1 billion for high-speed rail, which supports the President's five-year, $5 billion pledge from the 2010 Budget. High-speed rail promises to give the traveling public a practical alternative to flying or driving, particularly where there is congestion in the skies and on the roads. With trains efficiently connecting city and business centers, travelers would enjoy a new level of convenience not available in most parts of the country today. The Administration is dedicated to working with States and project sponsors to identify high-speed rail projects that will provide the greatest transportation, social, and environmental benefits, while maximizing the return on taxpayer dollars.

Invest in America's Water Resources Infrastructure. It is critical that sound investments be made in the Nation's water resources infrastructure to assure the safe and reliable operation and maintenance of key facilities of the Army Corps of Engineers and Bureau of Reclamation. The Administration will allocate funds to those ongoing commercial navigation and flood and storm damage reduction projects with the highest economic and environmental returns while achieving public safety objectives for communities. Resources are also focused on the restoration of significant ecosystems and initiatives that would allow greater conservation of water in the West. The Budget also emphasizes a new direction for water infrastructure projects by updating the 25-year-old procedures for planning future Federal water resources infrastructure projects to incorporate modern planning procedures and methods, assure adequate consideration of ecosystem values, and promote non-structural solutions. In addition, the Corps of Engineers is updating its estimates of the benefits and costs of its ongoing construction projects to help assure that funding decisions are based on the most current information available on the return to the Nation of these investments. The Administration also intends to develop a set of water resources reforms for the Corps of Engineers for consideration as part of the next Water Resource Development Act legislation.

Educating a Workforce for the Jobs of the 21st Century

From unlocking the cures of tomorrow to creating clean energy industries, from growing our economy and creating jobs to securing our Nation in the years to come, there is one constant in addressing these challenges: they all depend on having a highly-educated workforce. More than ever before, success in the global economy and among the nations of the world is rooted in providing a world-class education to all our children. It is a fundamental element of the new foundation we must lay for our economy.

The Administration made a significant down payment in our schools and schoolchildren through the Recovery Act by including the largest one-time investment in education in our Nation's history. The Recovery Act saved and created hundreds of thousands of education-related jobs during a time of acute State budget shortfalls. It also included a $4 billion Race to the Top fund, a competitive source of education funding and one of the largest investments in reforming our Nation's schools in history. At the same time, the Recovery Act made significant investments in expanding early childhood programs, addressed college affordability by expanding Pell Grants and the American Opportunity Tax Credit, and enhanced job training and referrals for the millions of workers coming through the doors of the Nation's one-stop career centers. Building on these commitments, the Budget proposes to:

Reform Elementary and Secondary School Funding by Setting High Standards, Encouraging Innovation, and Rewarding Success. The Budget supports the Administration's new vision for the Elementary and Secondary Education Act (ESEA). The reauthorized law would encourage States to adopt higher, clearer standards that set the expectation that every student will graduate from high school ready for college and a career. The new law would support dramatic improvements in the quality of assessments to measure complex skills and help teachers identify and respond to students' strengths and needs. The reauthorization would also recognize and reward schools for helping students make important gains, even if they are not yet at grade-level, and offer new flexibility for successful States and districts to pursue new solutions to help all students meet high standards. At the same time, the law would require vigorous efforts to turn around persistently low-performing schools, applying comprehensive strategies that put children first. In support of these efforts, the Budget provides a $3 billion increase in funding for K-12 education programs authorized in the ESEA and the Administration will request up to $1 billion in additional funding if the Congress successfully completes a fundamental overhaul of the law. Together, these measures would represent the largest funding increase for ESEA programs ever requested.

Expand the Race to the Top and Open the Competition to School Districts. The $4 billion Race to the Top, created by the Recovery Act, began a competition among States to spur systemic and innovative reform across four areas: supporting high academic standards; improving teacher effectiveness and distributing effective teachers more equitably; using data to improve achievement; and turning around low-performing schools. Not all States will receive Race to the Top grants, but the competition itself has galvanized key stakeholders across the Nation to

reform State laws and to develop new plans for lifting student achievement. The Budget provides $1.35 billion to continue the President's Race to the Top challenge and to expand the competition from States to school districts that are ready for comprehensive reform.

Increase the Number of Effective Teachers and Principals. Great teachers are the key to a high-quality education. Increasing the number of great teachers, especially in disadvantaged schools, will require major new efforts to help all teachers improve their skills; recognize and reward excellence in the classroom; and help struggling teachers improve or, if need be, exit the classroom. Today, taxpayers invest nearly $3 billion a year in a teacher quality block grant that heavily supports investments with little evidentiary support or impact on increasing learning. As part of the overhaul of ESEA, the Administration will require States taking formula funds to develop the preconditions for an effective human capital system, beginning with strong evaluation systems. At the same time, the Administration will invest $950 million in a new competitive fund for States and districts that supports bold approaches to recruiting, developing, retaining, and rewarding more effective teachers and principals, particularly in the lowest-performing schools. The Administration is also investing $405 million to support successful and innovative pathways into teaching and school leadership.

Invest in Supports for Student Success, Including Promise Neighborhoods. Students need to be safe and healthy, and they need a complete education that extends beyond the traditional hours. As part of a $1.8 billion investment in the Supporting Student Success initiative, the Budget funds comprehensive supports so that students are mentally and physically healthy and ready to learn. The Budget provides $210 million for Promise Neighborhoods, modeled after the Harlem Children's Zone, that aim to improve college enrollment rates by combining vigorous school reform with strong family supports and effective community services across an entire neighborhood. The initiative also reforms the 21st Century Community Learning Centers program to focus funding on models that redesign and extend the school day, week or year to provide additional time for students to engage in academic activities, additional time for enrichment activities, and time for educators to collaborate and improve instruction.

Grow High-Performing Charter Schools and Other Innovative Public Schools. Effective charter schools have achieved impressive results in closing achievement gaps. The Budget will invest $490 million to grow these schools and other autonomous public schools that achieve results, develop new approaches, and give parents more choices. The Budget will support new options for students to transfer to high-performing public schools, support successful magnet schools, and require States and districts accepting these funds to create the conditions for effective schools to grow and ineffective schools to be restructured or shut down.

Expand and Reform Early Childhood Education. Quality early education is an investment that pays off for years by preparing the youngest children for a lifetime of learning. To this end, the Administration has provided the funds to nearly double the number of children served by Early Head Start and expand Head Start. The Budget continues the Recovery Act expansions in these programs while focusing their new funds in 2011 on improving program outcomes. And the Budget provides a historic $1.6 billion increase in child care funding that can support not only an expansion in slots, but also an improvement in quality, safety, and outcomes. Finally, the Budget supports pending legislation that will establish a new Early Learning Challenge Fund administered by the Department of Education and the Department of Health and Human Services (HHS), to help States improve the quality of early childhood programs.

Increase Pell Grants and Put Them on a Firm Financial Footing. Pell Grants have helped millions of Americans afford college, yet in recent decades, growth in their value has fallen far behind the growth in college costs. The Recovery Act and 2009 appropriations bill increased the maximum Pell Grant by more than $600 for a total award of $5,350, and the maximum award will increase to $5,550 in 2010. The Budget proposes to make that increase permanent and put them on a path to grow faster than inflation every year. The Budget also addresses a second concern: Pell Grants currently function much like an entitlement, yet they are funded through an annual appropriations process that can fall behind actual demand for the grants. The Budget proposes to make Pell Grant funding mandatory so that adequate Pell Grant funding is available every year.

Expand Financial Aid for Students and Reduce the Burden of Student Loans. The Budget supports legislation that has passed the House of Representatives and is pending in the Senate that would reform student lending to eliminate tens of billions of dollars in wasteful subsidies to financial institutions, and instead provide loans directly to students more efficiently and reliably by hiring private and non-profit companies through competitive contracts. This measure would then use the savings to make historic investments in increasing college access and success (as well as in early childhood education). In addition to expanded Pell Grants and a simplified student aid system, the legislation includes a new American Graduation Initiative that will strengthen and support America's community colleges, focus on college completion, and help graduate 5 million more students by 2020. Moreover, the Budget proposes an effort to assist overburdened student loan borrowers by reducing monthly payments and shortening the repayment period so that these borrowers will pay only 10 percent of their discretionary income in loan repayments and can have their remaining debt forgiven after 20 years.

Reform the Job-Training System to Encourage Innovation and Empower Workers. Our job-training system is critical to giving all workers the opportunity to succeed in a changing economy, yet too often workers looking for good training cannot find it. As a complement to reauthorization of the Workforce Investment Act (WIA), the Budget increases total funding for major funding streams, including a $101 million increase targeted to youth. But because reform is essential and the current system's fragmentation must end, the Budget also sets aside $261 million in the Department of Labor and $60 million in the Department of Education for innovation funds. They will support competitive grants for the most promising, research-based strategies, including regional approaches and sectoral partnerships for adults and the combination of summer or year-round employment with education for youths. The Departments will cooperate in the administration of the innovation grants as a part of a Workforce Innovation Partnership that will create new incentives for States to break down silos, streamline service delivery, and eliminate duplication. The Partnership will be supported by new cross-program waivers, which will be accompanied by new tools for measuring program performance and sharing information with both policymakers and customers. Finally, the Budget targets high-growth sectors of the economy and workers often left behind through $85 million for green job training and $40 million for transitional jobs programs.

Restructure Narrow and Constrained Education Programs Into Broad and Flexible Competitions that Fund What Works. The Department of Education funds dozens of programs that narrowly limit what States, districts, and schools can do with funds. Some of these programs have little evidence of success, while others are demonstrably failing to improve student achievement. The President's Budget eliminates six discretionary programs and consolidates 38 K-12 programs into 11 new programs that emphasize using competition to allocate funds, giving communities more choices around activities, and using rigorous evidence to fund what works. The Administration will make sure that, under these competitions, there is equitable geographic distribution of funds nationwide, including to rural communities. Building on the Recovery Act, the Administration proposes $500 million to expand the Investing in Innovation Fund, which will expand proven models—and fund and evaluate promising ones—for achieving student success. Finally, the Budget dedicates

funds for the rigorous evaluation of education programs so that we can scale up what works and eliminate what does not.

Creating the Clean Energy Economy of Tomorrow

From the consumer who sees the costs of filling his gas tank or heating her home go up, to the scientists who track how climate change is affecting our planet, we all know that we cannot afford to maintain our reliance on oil and other fossil fuels to power our economy. Failure to act jeopardizes our Nation's security, our economy, and our future. That is why in the Recovery Act, the Administration invested more than $90 billion in clean energy technologies to begin the transformation of the economy. Building on this, the President worked with foreign leaders at the Copenhagen climate change talks in December 2009, where for the first time in history, all of the leaders of the world's major economies came together to accept their responsibility to take action to confront the threat of climate change. The international negotiations made a strong step towards the commitments and the transparency necessary to work together to solve this global challenge.

As we work to slow climate change internationally, we also must continue our efforts to build a clean energy economy here at home. Doing so has the potential to create millions of new jobs, which cannot be shipped overseas, in the new industries of the future. Around the globe, countries and companies see the job-creating potential of clean energy and are moving aggressively to lead the way. Our challenge is to be at the head of that pack. If we lead the way in developing clean energy, we will grow our economy, create new jobs, and leave a stronger and more secure country to our children. To bring about this transformation, the Administration will:

Undertake a Comprehensive Approach to Transform Our Energy Supply and Slow Global Warming. The Administration will work to enact and implement a comprehensive market-based policy that will reduce greenhouse gas emissions in the range of 17 percent in 2020 and more than 80 percent by 2050. Businesses will have the flexibility to seek out the most profitable and least costly ways of achieving greenhouse gas emission reductions, from making investments in energy efficiency and low-carbon or zero-carbon fuels to offsetting their emissions through agricultural activities that remove carbon dioxide from the atmosphere, and developing export markets for American clean energy technologies through investments in emission offset activities abroad. The policy will address the needs of vulnerable families, communities, and businesses to facilitate the transition to a clean energy economy. To prepare for the reduction in emissions, the Government will invest in climate registries to account for greenhouse gas emissions; implement regulations that improve energy efficiency, lower energy bills, and reduce emissions; plan for the effects of a changing climate in the stewardship of our natural resources; and undertake the research and development of next-generation energy technologies that will promote our energy and climate security.

Develop the Market for Clean Energy Technologies. The Budget substantially expands support for construction of new nuclear power plants by increasing the Department of Energy loan guarantees authority for such projects by $36 billion, to a total of $54.5 billion, and provides credit subsidy funding of $500 million to support $3 to $5 billion of loan guarantees for energy efficiency and renewable energy projects. The loan guarantee program will encourage new nuclear facilities and a range of renewable energy projects that reduce greenhouse gases and pollutants, while simultaneously creating jobs and contributing to long-term economic growth. The Budget also supports research, development, and demonstration activities to accelerate deployment and commercialization of nuclear power, carbon capture and storage, renewable energy, and energy efficiency technologies. To reduce greenhouse gas emissions in developing countries, the United States will help them adopt clean energy technologies and low-carbon development strategies.

Spur Investment in Domestic, Clean Energy Manufacturing. The Section 48(c) Advanced Energy Manufacturing Tax Credit was created by the Recovery Act to spur private investment in facilities that manufacture advanced energy technologies in fields like renewable energy, energy storage, advanced energy transmission, energy conservation, and greenhouse gas emissions abatement. The program provides a 30 percent tax credit to qualified investments in new, expanded, or re-equipped advanced energy manufacturing projects, allocating a total of $2.3 billion to clean energy manufacturers. The Budget expands this successful program, providing an additional $5 billion to provide this tax credit to many more advanced energy manufacturing projects. This will help spur private investment in clean energy manufacturing and create jobs, helping to lay the groundwork for American leadership in the new clean energy economy.

Advance the Development of Carbon Capture and Storage Technologies. The Budget supports a balanced research and development portfolio of carbon capture and storage technologies. The $545 million in funding provided in the 2011 Budget for fossil energy climate change technology will help reduce greenhouse gas emissions by focusing resources to develop carbon capture technologies with broad applications to advanced power systems, existing power plants, and industrial sources.

Eliminate Funding for Inefficient Fossil Fuel Subsidies. As we work to create a clean energy economy, it is counterproductive to spend taxpayer dollars on incentives that run counter to this national priority. To further this goal, the Budget eliminates tax preferences and funding for programs that provide inefficient fossil fuel subsidies that impede investment in clean energy sources and undermine efforts to deal with the threat of climate change. We are eliminating 12 tax breaks for oil, gas, and coal companies, closing loopholes to raise nearly $39 billion over the next decade.

Boost Development of Clean Energy on Federal and Tribal Land. Already, public lands and offshore resources managed by the Federal Government constitute about one-third of the domestic supply of fossil fuel resources. The Administration will promote the development of clean, renewable energy on Federal lands. To that end, the Budget adds $14 million—on top of $50 million in 2010 increases—to build agency capacity to review and permit renewable energy projects on Federal lands. This includes conducting the environmental evaluations and technical studies needed to spur development of renewable energy projects, assessing available alternative resources, and mitigating the impacts of development. In addition, the Administration is assisting Indian Tribes in overcoming the unique hurdles in developing renewable resources on Native American lands. Up to 15 percent of our potential wind energy resources are on Native American land, and the potential for solar energy is even higher.

Invest in the Understanding of Climate Change and Its Impacts. While climate policies are developed and investments in clean energy technologies are made, investments to understand the impacts of climate change are also crucial. Coastal areas, floodplains, and water systems will all be affected by the changing climate, and it is vital that we understand the potential effects of climate change so businesses, farmers, ranchers, and the entire Nation can prepare for them now. That is why the Budget invests $2.6 billion to deepen our understanding of climate change and its impact. The United States also will take prompt, substantial action to help the least developed and most vulnerable countries adapt and build resilience to the impacts of climate change.

Providing More Health Security and Bringing Down Its Cost

One of the biggest drains on the future growth of our economy is skyrocketing health care costs. For families who have health insurance, years of premiums that far and away out-paced income gains have taken their toll on family budgets. For businesses, rising health care costs hurt their competitiveness. For the Federal Government, there is no greater threat to our long-term fiscal future than the current rate of health care cost growth. That is why the President laid out a strategy in the 2010 Budget to reform health care in a fiscally responsible way and has worked closely with the Congress to bring about this long overdue change. At this writing, we are closer to health insurance reform than ever before. The bill before Congress will empower Americans who are insured with cost and quality information about doctors and hospitals and give them the stability and security they deserve by ending many discriminatory and capricious insurance industry practices; expand coverage to more than 30 million Americans who lack insurance, improving health and in some cases saving lives; cut waste and reform how medicine is practiced so that we get better quality care; and do this all without adding a dime to the deficit and while reducing the rate of health care cost growth over time. To lay the groundwork for these reforms and to improve the health of the Nation, the Budget will:

Build on Health Information Technology (IT) Adoption Momentum. Digitizing the health care sector is a critical part of creating a health care system that is more effective and efficient. The Budget includes $110 million for continuing efforts to strengthen health IT policy, coordination, and research activities. Combined with the Recovery Act's Federal grant and incentive programs designed to assist providers with adoption and meaningful use of electronic health records, these efforts will improve the quality of health care while protecting privacy and security of personal health information.

Increase Investment in Patient-Centered Health Research. To get the best care, doctors and patients need to know what works and what doesn't. The Budget includes $286 million for research that compares the effectiveness of different medical options, building on the expansion of this research begun under the Recovery Act. Disseminating the results of this research is expected to lead to higher quality, evidence-based medicine, arming patients and physicians with the best available information to allow them to choose the medical option that will work the best for them.

Bolster Prevention and Wellness Activities. The Budget bolsters core prevention activities by expanding community health activities, strengthening the public health workforce, and enhancing surveillance and health statistics to improve detection and monitoring of chronic disease and health outcomes. The Budget funds a new effort in as many as 10 of the largest cities in the United States to reduce the rates of morbidity and disability due to chronic disease through effective policy and environmental change strategies. The Budget also supports a new health prevention workforce to improve capacity of State and local health departments, as well as investments to improve the health and wellness of the Federal workforce.

Expand Affordable High-Quality Primary and Preventive Care. The Budget includes $2.5 billion for health centers to provide affordable high-quality primary and preventive care to underserved populations, including the uninsured. This will allow health centers to continue to provide care to the 2 million patients added through Recovery Act funding and support approximately 25 new health center sites. The Budget also includes funding to expand the integration of behavioral health with primary health care, enhancing the availability and quality of addiction care.

Combat Childhood Obesity. Nearly one-third of children in America are now overweight or obese, and our Nation now spends $150 billion a year treating obesity-related diseases, or nearly 10 percent of all medical spending. To improve children's access to healthy meals and help to reduce childhood obesity rates, the Budget proposes investing an additional $1 billion per year as part of the reauthorization of the school meals program and other child nutrition programs. The Administration also will take steps to bring

grocery stores and other healthy food retailers to "food desert" communities.

Fund Innovative Efforts to Improve Services for Seniors and People with Disabilities. The Budget includes new Medicare and Medicaid demonstration projects that evaluate reforms to provide higher quality care at lower costs, improve beneficiary education and understanding of benefits offered, and better align provider payments with costs and outcomes. Special emphasis will be placed on demonstrations that improve care coordination for beneficiaries with chronic conditions, that better integrate Medicare and Medicaid benefits, and that provide higher value for dollars spent. The Budget will also support the Year of Community Living Initiative to promote collaboration between HHS and HUD to expand access to housing and community supports to enable people with disabilities to live in the community, as opposed to in institutional settings.

Fight Waste and Abuse in Medicare, Medicaid, and the Children's Health Insurance Program (CHIP). Reducing fraud, waste, and abuse is an important part of restraining spending growth and providing quality service delivery to beneficiaries. In November 2009, the President signed an Executive Order to reduce improper payments by boosting transparency, holding agencies accountable, and creating incentives for compliance. This Budget puts forward a robust set of proposals to strengthen Medicare, Medicaid, and CHIP program integrity efforts, including proposals aimed at preventing fraud and abuse before they occur, detecting it as early as possible when it does occur, and vigorously enforcing all penalties and recourses available when fraud is identified. It proposes $250 million in additional resources that, among other things, will help expand the Health Care Fraud Prevention and Enforcement Action Team (HEAT) initiative, a joint effort by the Departments of Health and Human Services and Justice. As a result, the Administration will be better able to minimize inappropriate payments, close loopholes, and provide greater value for beneficiaries and taxpayers.

Improve the Access to, and Quality of, Health Care in Rural Areas. The Budget includes $79 million for an initiative to strengthen regional and local partnerships among rural health care providers, increase the number of health care providers in rural areas, and improve the performance and financial stability of rural hospitals.

Increase the Number of Primary Health Care Providers. The Budget invests $169 million in the National Health Service Corps (NHSC) to place providers in medically underserved areas to improve access to needed health care services. Under the NHSC, primary health professionals—such as physicians, nurse practitioners, and dentists—agree to serve in a medically underserved community in exchange for having a portion of their student loans paid off. In 2011, the requested increase will add nearly 400 NHSC clinicians to the more than 8,100 that will be providing essential primary and preventive care services in health care facilities across the country.

Expand and Focus HIV/AIDS Treatment, Care, and Prevention Activities. The Budget expands access to HIV/AIDS prevention and treatment activities consistent with the President's pledge to develop a National HIV/AIDS Strategy that will focus on reducing HIV incidence, increasing access to care and optimizing health outcomes, and reducing HIV-related health disparities. The Budget focuses HIV testing among high-risk groups, and increases resources for the Ryan White program to support the care and treatment needs for persons living with HIV/AIDS who are unable to afford health care and related support services. The Budget aims to reduce HIV-related health disparities by expanding HIV/AIDS medical services within populations disproportionately affected by the epidemic. The Budget also enhances funding for collaboration and integration activities to improve overall health outcomes for those with HIV/AIDS and co-infections with tuberculosis, hepatitis, or sexually transmitted diseases.

Continue Efforts to Increase Access to Health Care for American Indians and Alaska Natives (AI/ANs). The Budget includes $4.4 billion for the Indian Health Service (IHS) to expand investments initiated in 2010. Increases for IHS will strengthen existing Federal, tribal, and urban programs that serve 1.9 million AI/ANs at approximately 600 facilities nationwide, and will expand access to Contract Health Services to cover health care services provided outside of the Indian health system when services are not available at IHS-funded facilities. The Budget will also fund staff and operating costs at new and expanded facilities to increase access to health care services and enhance the Indian health system. The efforts supported in the Budget to expand health services in Indian communities also include an analysis of how IHS can improve distribution of resources throughout the Indian health system.

Keeping America Safe and Maintaining Our Global Leadership

Just as a strong economy bolsters our standing in the world and enhances our national security, strong global leadership helps protect the American people while allowing the United States to thrive in an interdependent, global economy. The economic and financial crises of the past year demonstrated how market problems in one nation can affect businesses the world over and how inextricably linked the world's economies are. That's why we needed other major economies to join with the United States in taking action to stimulate economic demand. And that's why the President worked with G-20 nations to agree to continue their cooperation as the global economy recovers in order to reduce the likelihood of a future crisis, and to build a "Framework for Strong, Sustainable and Balanced Growth."

Over the past year, the President has worked to repair our alliances and restore America's standing in the world. His effort has been driven by the fact that we face a range of global challenges that demand global action—from disrupting, dismantling, and defeating al Qaeda to stopping the spread of nuclear weapons and strengthening global health. In the last year, the President has taken a number of steps to meet these challenges while restoring American leadership. He has built new partnerships, and used all elements of American power to increase the pressure on al Qaeda worldwide. He laid out a plan to responsibly end the war in Iraq. He put forward a new strategy—with additional resources—to succeed in Afghanistan, and rallied NATO allies and partners to join us in committing additional resources. He signed executive orders that required the closure of the detention facilities at Guantanamo Bay, established a special task force to review detainee policy, and closed all CIA detention facilities as well as required all interrogations to follow the procedures of the Army Field Manual. And the President put forward a global agenda to stop the spread of nuclear weapons, reduce nuclear stockpiles, and to secure all loose nuclear materials from terrorists within four years.

Building on these efforts, the Budget invests in all elements of our national power: diplomacy, economic development and other foreign assistance, our Nation's armed forces, and intelligence. In addition, recognizing the extraordinary commitment and sacrifice of our men and women in uniform, the Administration continues its efforts to support servicemembers and their families and to provide our veterans with the support and resources that they deserve. Specifically, the Administration will:

Support Missions in Afghanistan, Pakistan, and Iraq. In the coming months, 30,000 additional troops will deploy to Afghanistan while U.S. combat forces continue drawing down in Iraq, consistent with the U.S. commitment for all U.S. troops to withdraw from Iraq by the end of 2011. As U.S. forces leave Iraq, the Administration will fund assistance to the Iraqi government and fund security and logistic support for U.S. civilians deployed around the country. To address the costs of increasing military and intelligence operations in Afghanistan and Pakistan while drawing down in Iraq, the Administration is requesting $33.0 billion for the Department of Defense (DOD) in 2010

supplemental funding on top of the $129.6 billion already provided, and a total of $159.3 billion for DOD's 2011 overseas contingency operations activities. The Budget also requests $4.5 billion in 2010 supplemental funding and $11.6 billion in 2011 for Department of State activities in these countries. In particular, funding for Afghanistan and Pakistan increases assistance and civilian personnel, and provides additional resources for governance, reconstruction, and other development activities to counter extremists' influence. The Budget also increases security assistance for Pakistan and for the Afghan Security Forces. In an effort to be as transparent as possible about future costs, the Budget includes placeholder estimates of $50 billion per year for 2012 and beyond. These estimates do not reflect any policy decisions about specific military or intelligence operations, but are only intended to indicate that some as yet unknown costs are anticipated.

Strengthen Homeland Security. As the failed attack on Christmas Day 2009 reminded us, al Qaeda and like-minded terrorists still seek to harm the American people. That is why the Budget continues important investments in our homeland defenses that are targeted to meet priority needs. The Budget, for example, increases funding for the Transportation Security Administration by 9 percent: to fund checkpoint and baggage screening equipment that will replace magnetometers with up to 1,000 new Advanced Imaging Technology screening systems for passengers; more accurate and efficient in-line baggage screening; additional international Federal Air Marshals; and more than 2,000 Transportation Security Officers to operate new screening equipment, employ enhanced screening techniques, and handle canine teams. The Administration also is requesting funds for 300 new Customs and Border Protection officers for passenger and cargo screening at ports of entry, additional new intelligence officers, and expanded pre-screening operations at foreign ports. Finally, the Budget will strengthen the early detection and reporting of terrorists and other threats and will continue the expansion of the Administration's efforts to target and remove criminal aliens.

Stand by Our Nation's Troops and Their Families. The strength of our troops relies on the stability of the families that support them, and the Budget supports these military families as our servicemembers answer our country's call to service. First, the Budget includes funding for a 1.4 percent basic pay raise that will keep military pay increases in line with those in the private sector. Second, the Budget also includes an average housing allowance increase of 4.2 percent, as well as a variety of monthly special skill-based payments, enlistment and reenlistment bonuses, and other benefits. Third, the Budget invests in Coast Guard-owned family housing to help alleviate housing shortages. Fourth, the Administration increases funding for family support programs by over 3 percent above the 2010 enacted level. This includes $1.3 billion (an increase of $87 million over the 2010 enacted level) to expand availability for affordable, high-quality child care services; $1.9 billion ($37 million over the 2010 enacted level) for expanded counseling and assistance services to help families meet the challenges brought on by repeated deployments and family separations; and $84 million (an increase of $12 million over the 2010 enacted level) for enhanced career and educational opportunities for military spouses through tuition assistance and Federal internship programs.

Increase Funding for the Department of Defense. Giving our military the material and support they need to accomplish their missions is the least we can do, given the sacrifices they make. The Administration requests $548.9 billion, an increase of $18.2 billion, or 3.4 percent, over the 2010 enacted level of $530.8 billion. This will provide our troops with the most effective and modern equipment possible and the support they need.

Prevent the Proliferation of Nuclear Weapons. Following on the vision the President outlined this past year, the Budget funds significant steps that will help stop the spread of nuclear weapons and seek the goal of a world without them. The Administration requests $2.7 billion—a 26-percent increase over the 2010 enacted level—for the Department of Energy's De-

fense Nuclear Nonproliferation program. Robust funding is also requested for nonproliferation efforts across the Government, and especially in the Intelligence Community and the Departments of Defense, State, Homeland Security, and Justice. These agencies will lead international efforts to secure all vulnerable nuclear material around the world in four years; deter and interdict the trafficking of nuclear material; and strengthen international nonproliferation treaties, regulatory controls, and safeguards. As the United States reduces the role of nuclear weapons in the national security strategy, this Budget fully funds efforts to maintain a safe, secure, and effective arsenal.

Care for Wounded, Ill, and Injured Servicemembers. Last year, DOD added 18 more Warrior-in-Transition Complexes at posts around the world as part of its efforts to care for the health of the men and women who serve. The Budget sustains ongoing efforts to provide high-quality medical care to servicemembers, their families, and retirees. This includes support for wounded warrior transition units and centers of excellence in vision, hearing, traumatic brain injury, and other areas to continuously improve the care provided to wounded, ill, and injured servicemembers.

Increase Funding for the President's Global Health Initiative. The Administration will build on its commitment to save millions of lives while strengthening the public health infrastructure that can help disease from crossing borders—including our own. The Budget includes increased funding to combat the HIV/AIDS crisis by focusing on increasing treatment and expanding access to prevention; ramping up maternal and child health programming to reduce mortality of mothers and children under five and decrease the prevalence of malnutrition; expanding investments in family planning activities, malaria, tuberculosis, and neglected tropical diseases; and strengthening local health systems to enhance capacity and long-run sustainability. Alongside our multilateral partners, the United States will continue to provide global leadership to fulfill our shared responsibility and our common promise to improve the health of the world's poorest populations.

Fight Global Hunger and Expand Food Security Efforts. The Budget increases funding for agricultural development as part of a multi-year plan to lift a significant number of people out of poverty and reduce malnutrition for millions of children under five years old by 2015. The Budget provides assistance to countries that commit to address their internal food security needs and provides a significant contribution to a new multi-donor facility administered by the World Bank. The Budget also maintains strong support for food aid and other humanitarian assistance.

Increase the Number of Peace Corps Volunteers. The Administration funds the second year of the President's initiative to significantly increase the number of Peace Corps volunteers, and puts the Peace Corps on track to grow by 50 percent so it reaches 11,000 volunteers by 2016.

Continue Advance Appropriations for Department of Veterans Affairs (VA) Medical Care. The 2011 Budget requests $50.6 billion in advance appropriations for the VA medical care program so that care for the Nation's veterans is not hindered by budget delays. This funding will enable the Department to have timely and predictable funding from year to year, ultimately making it easier for veterans to rely on accessible VA care.

Enroll More than 500,000 Previously Ineligible Veterans into VA Health Care by 2013. Last year, for the first time since January 2003, non-disabled veterans with moderate income were made eligible for VA health care. The President's Budget allows for the continued enrollment of more than 500,000 moderate-income veterans into the VA health care system by 2013 while maintaining high-quality and timely care for the lower-income and disabled veterans who also rely on VA.

Boost Compensation to Military Disability Retirees. For the first time, highly-disabled veterans who are medically retired from service will be eligible for concurrent receipt of disability benefits from the VA in addition to DOD retirement benefits. Previously, these benefits were offset. All medically retired servicemembers will be eligible for concurrent receipt of VA and DOD benefits by 2015.

Respond to the Unique Needs of Today's Veterans. Today's veterans have different needs due to their experiences in service, the composition of the armed forces, and the unique challenges that many face. Recognizing that, the Budget strengthens VA's ability to provide veterans the best possible care for Post-Traumatic Stress, Traumatic Brain Injury, and other mental health conditions by investing $5.2 billion in specialized care, and increases collaboration between joint DOD and VA programs that target psychological health. To combat homelessness among veterans, the Budget expands collaborative partnerships with local governments, non-profit organizations, and the Departments of Housing and Urban Development, Justice, and Labor. And responding to the growing number of women veterans, the Budget provides funding for their unique needs, from an appropriate environment of care to specialized medical and counseling services.

Improve Quality of Health Care Through Electronic Records for Our Troops and Veterans. Too often, important patient information is unavailable to VA health care providers, yet that information was acquired by doctors and hospitals that may have treated the veteran while still in uniform. That is why the VA and DOD are jointly implementing the Virtual Lifetime Electronic Record, which will enable VA to maintain a complete health record for each veteran and to deliver care and benefits to veterans with increased efficiency and improved accuracy. The President's Budget also invests over $200 million in automated processing to directly improve the accuracy and timeliness of veterans benefits, particularly disability compensation and the new Post-9/11 GI Bill benefit.

RESTORING RESPONSIBILITY

Laying a new foundation for economic growth and prosperity for working families will take a change in policies and programs to unleash the creativity and hard work of the American people. But to prevent our country from backsliding into the irresponsibility of the past, we need to change how Washington works. We have seen the consequences of fiscal recklessness, of tolerance for programs that no longer work or are outdated, and of a government that is most open to those with access and influence. The deficits, wasted resources, and special treatment squandered funds that could have been used to help Americans gain or retain a foothold in the middle class and enjoy what every family wants: a good job, a roof over their heads, excellent schools for their children, affordable and high-quality health care, and a secure retirement.

Over the past year, the Administration has begun the hard work of changing Washington. On his first full day in office, the President issued an Executive Order that: prohibits executive branch employees from accepting gifts from lobbyists; closes the revolving door between Government and the private sector that had given the latter undue influence; requires that Government hiring be based on competence and qualifications and not political connections; and orders every one of his appointees to sign a pledge abiding by these tough new rules. As the Administration undertook its efforts to rescue the economy, it issued restrictions on lobbying for financial stabilization and American Recovery and Reinvestment Act (Recovery Act) funds. In addition, the President also banned lobbyists from serving on agency advisory boards and commissions, bodies which had become dominated by special interests.

Believing that sunlight is the best disinfectant, the Administration opened up the doors of Government to the scrutiny of the American people. The President signed an Executive Order expanding public access to presidential records, decided voluntarily to disclose the names of visitors to the White House, and used new media technologies—from video feeds at previously closed-door meetings to web chats with high-ranking officials—to let the American people monitor the Government at work and interact with its leaders. In implementing the Recovery Act, the Administration continues to insist on an unprecedented level of transparency so that Americans can see where Recovery dollars are going as they are spent and the effect they are having. In addition, the Administration launched a comprehensive Open Government Initiative that is breaking down long-standing barriers between the American people and their Government. This drive to a more open government is speeding information to citizens, saving taxpayers' dollars, and erasing frustrating red tape.

While the economic crisis forced the President to add temporarily to an already record-setting deficit, he laid out a commitment to cut in half the deficit he inherited upon taking office. Moreover, he did so while being open and honest about our fiscal situation. The Administration's first Budget eliminated previous budget gimmicks that would have made the 10-year deficit number $2.6 trillion smaller. Instead, the President insisted on presenting an honest budget to the American people. Thus, the 2010 Budget—for example—accounted for the costs of wars in Iraq and Afghanistan and provided a 10-year look into the future rather than a five-year one and acknowledged the full costs associated with preventing the Alternative Minimum Tax from taxing more middle-class families. This same desire to evaluate Government performance accurately also motivated the Administration's line-by-line review of the Federal budget for programs that were ineffective, duplicative, or obsolete. Working with the military leadership and Secretary of Defense Gates, the President identified billions of dollars in defense savings for this year, canceling the new presidential helicopter and additional F-22 fighter jets.

The Administration also undertook a comprehensive effort to reform Government contracting—ending unjustified sole-source and cost-reimbursement contracts and pursuing other steps that will save $40 billion a year by 2011—and the President issued an Executive Order cracking down on the $100 billion in improper payments that go out from the Government.

The President also made a major change in the way Washington has done business in recent years by demanding that all entitlement and tax legislation be fully paid for (with the exception of temporary measures to address the economic crisis). He put this into practice, for instance, by insisting on fiscally-responsible health reform that not only did not add a dime to our deficits, but also reduced the rate of health care cost growth—the main driver of our long-term fiscal future. Finally, the President has championed Pay-As-You-Go legislation, which would require the Congress to fully offset the costs of any entitlement increases or tax cuts by finding savings elsewhere—helping to make this change in practice the law of the land.

Taken together, these steps to streamline what works and eliminate what doesn't, to open government to the American people, and to end special interest access are critical to instilling a new sense of responsibility for taxpayer dollars, rebuilding the connection between Americans and their Government, and putting the Nation back on a fiscally responsible path.

Restoring Fiscal Discipline

When the President took office he faced a deficit of $1.3 trillion for that first fiscal year, a far cry from the budget surpluses predicted at the start of the previous administration. Since the 2010 Budget was released in February of 2009, unfavorable economic conditions and technical re-estimates have worsened the deficit outlook by $2 trillion through 2019—the equivalent of 1 percent of GDP per year—with a deterioration of about $200 billion in 2015 alone.

Looking out over the next decade, we are $12 trillion deeper in debt than we were in 2001 because of three specific developments. The national debt is $7.5 trillion larger by the end of this decade because of the failure to pay for two large tax cuts, primarily for the wealthiest Americans, and a new entitlement program. An additional $3 trillion in debt is the result of inheriting the worst recession since the Great Depression. Our response to this recession, the Recovery Act, which has been critical to restoring economic growth, added an additional $1 trillion to the debt—only 10 percent of the total.

Now, as we turn the corner from rescuing the economy to rebuilding it, it's time to once again take responsibility for our fiscal future. While it's essential that we do not stifle the momentum of our recovery from the current recession, we also cannot adequately grow the economy and spur job creation in the long term if we allow these deficits to persist. That is why, as the economy recovers, the Administration will take the steps necessary to restore discipline to our Nation's finances to put our country on firm fiscal footing. The Administration will:

Freeze Non-Security Discretionary Spending for the Next Three Years. Over the past year, an extraordinary surge in tax cuts and Federal spending helped stimulate macroeconomic demand and bring the economy back from the brink of a second Great Depression. Expanding the short-term deficit during a moment of economic crisis is widely recognized as necessary by economists from across the ideological spectrum. Nonetheless, the ramifications of the large deficits we inherited and the response that was required to stop the economic freefall has repercussions both in the near term and in years to come in the form of higher debt and interest payments. As the economy recovers, we need to rebalance our spending priorities. That is why the President is proposing a three-year freeze in non-security discretionary funding in this year's Budget.

Establish a Bipartisan Fiscal Commission. To help put our Nation on a sustainable fiscal path, the Administration will work to create a fiscal commission charged with identifying policies to improve the fiscal situation in the medium term and to achieve fiscal sustainability over the long run. Specifically, the Commission is charged with balancing the budget excluding interest payments on the debt by 2015. The result is projected to stabilize the debt-to-GDP ratio at an acceptable level once the economy recovers. The magnitude and timing of the policy measures necessary to achieve this goal are subject to considerable uncertainty and will depend on the evolution of the economy. In addition, the Commission will examine policies to meaningfully improve the long-run fiscal outlook, including changes to address the growth of entitlement spending and the gap between the projected revenues and expenditures of the Federal Government.

Require the Financial Services Industry to Pay Back Taxpayers. The assistance given the financial services industry to weather the crisis of the past year represented an extraordinary step that no one wanted to take, but that was necessary to prevent deeper pain to the economy. Yet the largest Wall Street firms have been both the source of extraordinary costs throughout the economy due to their excessive risk-taking, and the beneficiaries of the extraordinary measures taken to prevent a deeper financial crisis. While the expected cost of the TARP program has fallen by $224 billion since the 2010 Mid-Session Review to about $117 billion, shared responsibility requires that the largest financial firms pay back the taxpayer as a result of the extraordinary

action taken. Congress recognized that when it wrote the legislation authorizing TARP by requiring the President to propose a way for the financial sector to pay back taxpayers so that not one penny of TARP-related debt is passed on to the next generation. The Administration is therefore calling for a Financial Crisis Responsibility Fee on the largest Wall Street and financial firms that will last at least 10 years, but longer if necessary, to compensate taxpayers fully for the extraordinary support they provided. This fee would be limited to financial firms with over $50 billion in assets. As it would be based on an institution's size and exposure to debt, it would also further the Administration's financial reform goals by providing a check against the risky behavior that contributed to this crisis.

Close the Carried Interest Loophole for Wealthy Investment Managers. The Administration supports reforming our tax code to ensure that the income earned by investment managers is treated the same way as income earned by middle-class families. Currently, a loophole in our tax system allows some investment managers to cut their tax bills by more than half by treating their earned income as capital gains—which is taxed at a 15 percent rate, far less than the marginal tax rate that would otherwise apply. By closing this loophole, we will recognize the "carried interest" earned by these investment managers for what it is—ordinary income that should be taxed at ordinary income tax rates. This measure would raise $24 billion over the next 10 years.

Allow the Bush Tax Cuts for Households Earning More Than $250,000 to Expire. In the last Administration, those at the very top enjoyed large tax breaks and income gains while almost everyone else struggled and real income for the middle class declined. Our Nation cannot afford to continue these tax cuts, which is why the President supports allowing those tax cuts that affect families earning more than $250,000 a year to expire and committing these resources to reducing the deficit instead. This step will have no effect on the 98 percent of all households who make less than $250,000.

Reduce the Itemized Deduction Write-off for Families with Incomes over $250,000. Currently, if a middle-class family donates a dollar to its favorite charity or spends a dollar on mortgage interest, it gets a 15-cent tax deduction, but a millionaire who does the same enjoys a deduction that is more than twice as generous. By reducing this disparity and returning the high-income deduction to the same rates that were in place at the end of the Reagan Administration, we will raise $291 billion over the next decade.

Reform the Taxation of International Income and Eliminate Other Corporate Loopholes. The American corporate tax code is riddled with inefficiencies and loopholes, including the fact that it allows companies to indefinitely defer the payment of U.S. taxes on foreign income while immediately benefiting from the tax deductions associated with these activities. It also allows many companies to take advantage of transfer pricing to shift income earned in the United States to lower-tax countries. The Budget will reform and end these practices.

Eliminate Funding for Inefficient Fossil Fuel Subsidies. As we work to create a clean energy economy, it is counterproductive to spend taxpayer dollars on incentives that run counter to this national priority. To further this goal and reduce the deficit, the Budget eliminates tax preferences and funding for programs that provide inefficient fossil fuel subsidies that impede investment in clean energy sources and undermine efforts to deal with the threat of climate change. We are eliminating 12 tax breaks for oil, gas, and coal companies, closing loopholes to raise nearly $39 billion over the next decade.

Recommit to Cutting the Deficit in Half by the End of the President's First Term. Even though he entered office facing an historic economic and financial crisis, the President committed his Administration to cutting the deficit he inherited upon taking office in half by the end of his first term. Since then, it has become clear that the recession was worse than anyone thought

at the beginning of 2009, costing the Government even more in assistance and lost revenue. Nonetheless, the President remains committed to cutting in half by the end of his first term the deficit he inherited on January 20, 2009.

Streamlining What Works, Eliminating What Doesn't

Now more than ever, it's critical that taxpayer dollars are not wasted on programs that do not work, are duplicative, or are out-of-date. Allowing taxpayer dollars to be wasted in this way is an irresponsible use of funds and an irresponsible abuse of the trust the American people put in its elected leaders. Instead of accepting business as usual, we need to streamline programs that work and fix or eliminate those that do not. We need to instill a new responsibility for taxpayer dollars, and modernize government to deliver better services to the American people for less. To accomplish this, the Administration will:

Terminate or Consolidate Outdated or Ineffective Programs. Too often programs and practices persist because of inertia. The President sought to change this mentality by having his Administration conduct a line-by-line review of the Federal budget. In his first Cabinet meeting, he challenged the assembled agency heads to find at least $100 million in collective cuts to their administrative budgets, separate and apart from those identified in the 2010 Budget. They responded by identifying 77 cost-saving measures—amounting to $243 million in savings through 2010. In addition, as part of the 2010 Budget, the President identified 121 programs for reduction, termination, and other savings amounting to $17 billion in savings. While recent administrations have seen between 15 to 20 percent of their proposed cuts approved by the Congress, this year we were able to see 60 percent become law. Building on that, the President is proposing more than 120 savings proposals totaling approximately $23 billion.

Freeze Pay and Eliminate Bonuses for Senior Political Appointees. The Administration values the essential work of our talented Federal employees, but at a time when millions of Americans are without work and millions more are going without bonuses and raises, the Federal Government too must cut back. Last year, the President ordered a freeze of White House senior staff pay. And for 2011, the Administration proposes to extend this pay freeze to all senior political appointees throughout the Federal Government and continue the policy of no bonuses for all political appointees.

Reduce Improper Payments. Each year, taxpayers lose billions of dollars in wasteful, improper payments by the Federal Government to individuals, organizations, and contractors who inadvertently or deliberately overbill the Government. In 2009, the Administration was able to identify improper payments totaling $100 billion—a figure driven by improved detection and the significant increase in Federal outlays associated with the economic downturn and recovery. In response, agencies will be implementing an Executive Order the President signed at the end of 2009 to rein in improper payments. First, we will bring more transparency to these errors by creating an online dashboard of key indicators and statistics so that the public can access information on improper payments, view payment error rates by agency and program, and see a list of the most egregious actors. Second, we will hold agencies accountable for reducing improper payments while maintaining program access, through—among other steps—designating one Senate-confirmed appointee to be accountable to the President for meeting improper payment reduction targets and consolidating program integrity activities. Third, we will provide incentives for States, agencies, and recipients to report and reduce payment errors by using rewards—such as allowing States that reduce improper payments—to recoup more Federal grant dollars to cover administrative expenses, and use punishments, such as financial penalties on contractors who do not timely disclose an improper payment Lastly, the Administration is launching the Partnership Fund for Program Integrity Innovation, an initiative which focuses on improving service delivery, payment accuracy, and administrative efficiency in Federal assistance programs while reducing access barriers for beneficiaries.

Cut Waste in Contracting. Since 2002, Federal spending on contracts has more than doubled to more than $500 billion. From 2002 to 2008, the value of contracts awarded without full and open competition increased by 129 percent—from $82 billion to $188 billion. The President has charged Federal departments and agencies with saving $40 billion annually by 2011 through terminating unnecessary contracts, strengthening acquisition management, ending the overreliance on contractors, and reducing the use of high-risk contracts. In the first year of this effort, agencies have identified more than $19 billion of savings in 2010—on track to meet the $40 billion target. In 2011, the Administration will work with agencies on furthering their contracting reform efforts so that the $40 billion target is met. In addition, we will explore ways to gain additional savings through leveraging the purchasing power of the Federal Government. We are also making significant investments in the acquisition workforce to make sure agencies have adequate capacity to oversee and manage contracts—and ultimately to save money and provide better services to the American people. The Department of Defense also will further reduce its use of high-risk contracts by 9 percent and take steps to ensure that military requirements for weapons are reasonable, program costs and schedules are realistic, and acquisition funding is stable.

Increase Accountability in, and Reduce the Number of, Earmarks. For too many years, the use of earmarks went virtually unchecked. Projects were inserted into legislation without any scrutiny or identifiable sponsor. Billions of taxpayer dollars were spent without examination by any committee or either branch of Congress. In 2007 and 2008, the Congress worked to end these abusive practices. Anonymous earmarks were eliminated and replaced with transparency measures so people can see who is spending their tax dollars and why. Yet, even with the changes, earmark overuse and abuse have continued. The

President has put forward core principles for significant earmark reform: earmarks must have a legitimate public purpose and be subject to public scrutiny; members of Congress must disclose publicly their earmark requests; and any earmark for a for-profit private company should be subject to the same competitive bidding requirements as other Federal contracts. The 2010 appropriations bills showed progress, with earmarks reduced in cost by more than 23 percent or more than $3 billion. The Administration will continue to work with the Congress to reduce earmark overuse and abuse.

Rigorously Evaluate Program Performance. In order to drive evidence-based decisions about what works and what doesn't, the Administration is aggressively expanding its program evaluation efforts. In response to the Office of Management and Budget (OMB) guidance, 17 agencies submitted a total of 61 specific proposals ranging from new efforts to evaluate the efficacy of new investments in early childhood education to a proposal to determine which approaches to foreign assistance are most effective in reducing poverty in poor countries. In the Budget, the Administration will fund 23 of the most promising new program evaluations and strengthen evaluation capacity in other agencies. All major evaluations planned or underway will be posted online from the time they are started, so that agencies cannot hide negative findings.

Close the Technology Gap. Twenty years ago, when people came to work for the Government, they had access to the world's best technology. Today, Government employees often have better technology at home than at work. The Federal Government spends tens of billions of dollars on information technology (IT), but fragmentation, poor project execution, and the drag of legacy technology has not delivered the productivity and performance gains to government that are found when IT is deployed effectively in the private sector. Under the leadership of the Federal Chief Information Officer, the Administration is continuing its efforts to close the gap in effective technology use between the private and public sectors. Specifically, the Administration

will continue to roll out less intensive and less expensive cloud-computing technologies; reduce the number and cost of Federal data centers; and work with agencies to reduce the time and effort required to acquire IT, improve the alignment of technology acquisitions with agency needs, and hold providers of IT goods and services accountable for their performance.

Centralize Provision of Information Technology Services for Non-Military Agencies. As technology and IT management practices continue to evolve rapidly, it is critical that the Government is able to adapt to these changes to achieve greater efficiency and effectiveness. Following examples set by the Department of Defense (DOD), several State governments, and best practices in private industry, the Administration will establish one or more efficient, centralized IT service providers for non-military agencies. Centralizing Federal IT services will reduce duplicative and wasteful spending; reduce facility space usage; increase security; improve service delivery; and reduce energy consumption. It is projected that this approach could prevent billions in increased costs across the Federal Government over the next few years.

Hold Agency Leaders Accountable for Specific Goals. Government leaders must make hard choices about the priorities that matter most to the American people and then do what it takes to deliver on those objectives. This has historically been difficult, however, because senior political leaders tend to focus on policy development rather than on management and implementation. To encourage senior leaders to deliver results against the most important priorities, the Administration launched the High-Priority Performance Goal initiative. Building on this effort in the 2011 Budget, the Administration is requiring agency heads to commit to a limited number of priority goals that matter to the public. The goals must have ambitious targets to be achieved within 24 months without the need for new resources or legislation, and have well-defined, outcomes-based measures of progress. OMB will work with agencies to help them to achieve their goals and spread this management approach throughout their organizations.

Revamp the Federal Hiring Process. High-performing companies and other forward-looking employers view their people as their key asset and are constantly re-evaluating and improving their approaches to attracting, motivating, and developing the best talent. However, the Federal hiring process currently takes over 150 days on average and requires far too many steps involving many different people. Often, government loses top talent to faster moving competitors. In the past year, most agencies have ended the "black box" of the Federal hiring process by notifying applicants of their status online at four steps in the process. To fix the hiring process, OMB and the Office of Personnel Management have initiated an effort to streamline hiring to achieve major reductions in the hiring times by the end of 2010. Going forward, we plan to increase the quality of applicants through innovative recruitment strategies, improved assessments of applicants, and proposing necessary regulatory and legislative changes to further streamline hiring processes while continuing to rely on the merit-based hiring system that has served the country so well.

Eliminate Unneeded Federal Real Estate from the Government Books. The Government Accountability Office in January 2003 identified Federal real property as a high-risk area of concern because of long-standing problems with excess and underutilized property, deteriorating facilities, unreliable real property data, over-reliance on costly leasing, and building security challenges. While the Government has made some progress to address these chronic challenges, the changes have been slow primarily because the Federal real property portfolio is based on an outmoded, outdated business model. Across the Government, billions of dollars in physical assets are not needed but remain on the Government's hands. The Administration will pursue expanding the authority of agencies to retain sales proceeds while also proposing a five-year pilot to expedite the sale of real property by streamlining the process for select asset sales.

Opening Government Up to the American People

The President has been clear from day one in office: the Federal Government must break down the barriers between it and the people it is supposed to serve. Through an unprecedented Open Government Directive, he put transparency, participation, and collaboration at the center of the Government's operations. In response, every Cabinet agency, along with the White House, has taken a range of steps to open government up to the American people. These include the release of information, such as the White House visitor logs; efforts to get citizen input and comment on executive orders; and the use of online technologies so the public can ask questions of their Government leaders. In addition, the Administration has moved affirmatively to reduce special interest influence on the Federal Government through, for example, restrictions on lobbying related to the Recovery Act and financial stabilization efforts and a ban on lobbyists serving on agency advisory boards and commissions, bodies which had become dominated by special interests.

Transparency not only strengthens the bond between citizens and their Government, it also boosts performance by strengthening accountability, supporting the identification of effective practices, stimulating idea flow, and motivating better performance. Online posting of performance data—including agency goals, performance trends, improper payments and IT projects—represents an important step toward creating a culture of accountability in government. Openness also can improve the quality of the services delivered to citizens. Transparent processes allow citizens to offer feedback on service quality to make government better, improving satisfaction levels. To further open up the government to the American people, the Administration will:

Publish More Government Information Online. To increase accountability, promote informed participation by the public, and create economic opportunity, each Cabinet-level and independent agency is working to make openness standard. Timely publication of information is an essential component of transparency. Through the *Data.gov* portal—launched in May 2009 with just 47 sets of data—the public now can identify, examine, download, and cross-analyze more than 118,000 Government data sets. In 2011, the Government will expand *Data.gov* with previously unpublished, high-priority information, offered in open formats. Federal departments and agencies also will create open Government websites to serve as a gateway for access to their transparency activities.

Update Regulations to Allow the Use of New Technologies. Improvements in technology, in many places, have outpaced the regulations put in place to govern its use. In some cases, those regulations never anticipated the advances made. In response, OMB, in consultation with the Chief Technology Officer, will review Government-wide information policies, such as the Paperwork Reduction Act and the Federal cookies policy, which may need updating or clarifying to allow agencies to utilize new technologies that fully promote open government.

Launch New Tools to Track Regulations. The Federal regulatory process is opaque, yet critically important to the economy and lives of Americans. Greater transparency will help to break down barriers to participation in the government and understanding of its actions. The Administration will launch a new regulation tracking portal to make it easier to track specific regulations under review—where they are in the process, what the key deadlines are, and when the review will be completed. The public also will be able to track rules in the aggregate by agency, to see which have been identified as economically significant, and to link to sites where comments can be offered to help shape the final rule.

Make It Easier to Track How Taxpayer Dollars Are Spent. For too long, Americans have been in the dark about how their tax dollars are spent. They pay their taxes, but have no clear, concise way to track how and where the money is spent and what it accomplishes. The Administration is committed to pulling back the curtain on Government spending and will launch a new tracking tool with daily updates that will provide citizens with the ability to see aggregate spending by agency and also by geographic area. A new search engine will allow the public to customize their information by location, by agency, or by timeframe. This innovative development will allow people to have a greater understanding of how their Government works, and hold officials accountable for responsible spending decisions.

Create an Online Citizen Engagement Platform. With the growing number of social media tools available, citizens are demanding more engagement with their Government in new, innovative ways. The Citizen Engagement Platform (CEP), a joint collaboration between the General Service Administration and OMB, will increase the Government's ability to interact and collaborate with citizens and provide a simple, cost-effective vehicle for agencies to access tools and guidance to be successful in those endeavors. The CEP will build on pilots launched last year by continuing to identify new technology applications to enable intra-agency and interagency collaboration and create a coordinated process for identifying tools and eliminating the redundant work presently carried out by agencies implementing new social media tools.

DEPARTMENT OF AGRICULTURE

Funding Highlights:

- Promotes economic and job creation opportunities for rural America by focusing on five core areas: access to broadband services, innovative local and regional food systems, renewable energy programs, climate change, and rural recreation.

- Provides $7.6 billion for the Special Supplemental Nutrition Program for Women, Infants, and Children (WIC) to serve all eligible individuals.

- Provides $10 billion over 10 years for a strong Child Nutrition and WIC reauthorization.

- Provides $50 million for a new "Healthy Food Financing Initiative" to bring grocery stores and other healthy food retailers to underserved communities.

- Provides $429 million, the highest funding level ever, for competitive grants through the Agriculture and Food Research Initiative.

- Refocuses Forest Service resources to support watershed and ecosystem improvement efforts.

- Supports the Department's effort to reduce foodborne illnesses from products inspected by USDA.

- Funds several important conservation efforts such as improving water quality, restoring and protecting almost 200,000 additional acres of wetlands, and reducing nutrient loading in the Chesapeake Bay.

- Enhances the Department's efforts to promote U.S. agricultural exports by increasing assistance to develop and maintain overseas markets and reduce foreign trade barriers and other practices that hinder agricultural exports.

- Targets farm payments to those who need—and can most benefit from—assistance, and reforms the crop insurance program by renegotiating the Government's agreement with crop insurance companies.

The U.S. Department of Agriculture (USDA) provides leadership on issues related to food, agriculture, rural development, and natural resources based on sound public policy, the best available science, and efficient management. USDA focuses on further developing alternative markets for agricultural products and activities, providing financing needed to help expand job opportunities and improve housing, utilities, and infrastructure in rural America. The Department also works to enhance food safety by taking steps to reduce the prevalence of food-

45

borne hazards, improve nutrition and health by providing food assistance and nutrition education and promotion, support international agricultural and economic development, and manage and protect America's public and private lands by working cooperatively with other levels of government and the private sector. The President's Budget provides $26 billion in discretionary budget authority to support this important mission.

Supports Growth and Job Creation in Rural America. The President's Budget supports USDA's Rural Innovation Initiative, which is designed to promote economic opportunity and job creation in rural communities. To support this innovative approach, USDA plans to set-aside roughly 5 percent of the funding from approximately 20 existing programs and allocate these funds competitively among regional pilot projects tailored to local needs and opportunities. This targeting effort will allow USDA to prioritize areas with the greatest need and potential by encouraging comprehensive and innovative approaches to foster rural revitalization.

The Budget also helps lay the foundation for job creation and expanded economic opportunities throughout rural America by:

- Expanding access to broadband services by offering $418 million in loans and grants to transition rural communities into the modern information economy.

- Nurturing local and regional food systems and expanding access to healthy foods for low-income Americans in rural and urban food deserts.

- Funding a variety of renewable energy programs across the Department, including support for biorefineries to utilize advanced biomass crops, research designed to create cellulosic and advanced biofuels, and assistance to help transition fossil fuel-dependent electric utilities to renewable energy. Taken together, these programs support the USDA's effort to help America in achieving energy independence and reducing greenhouse gas emissions.

- Supporting the President's climate change policy by promoting activities including carbon sequestration, renewable energy, and water conservation. In addition, the Budget supports a science-based, risk-management approach to mitigate the effects of climate change by stressing forest and watershed resiliency designed to minimize the loss of large carbon sinks.

- Developing rural recreation and employment opportunities, including fishing and hunting for local residents and tourists by proposing more than $700 million to restore and manage public lands. The Budget also fully funds the Voluntary Public Access and Habitat Incentive Program, which encourages private landowners to voluntarily open their land to the public for hunting and fishing.

Strengthens Nutrition Assistance and Promotes Healthy Eating. At a time of continued need, the President's Budget provides $8.1 billion for discretionary nutrition program supports, which is a $400 million increase over the 2010 enacted level. Funding supports 10 million participants in the WIC program, which is critical to the health of pregnant women, new mothers, and their infants. The Budget also supports a strong Child Nutrition and WIC reauthorization package so that schoolchildren have access to healthy meals and to help fulfill the President's pledge to end childhood hunger. The Budget provides $10 billion over 10 years for program reforms aimed at improving program access, establishing high standards for the nutritional quality of food available in school, exploring new strategies for reducing hunger and improving children's food choices, and strengthening program management.

Responds to the Needs of Low-Income Americans. The President continues to support the nutrition provisions incorporated in the American Recovery and Reinvestment Act (ARRA). Participants in the Supplemental Nutrition Assistance Program (SNAP) will continue to receive enhanced benefits at an average value of about $20 per person per month. The Budget also proposes to extend the ARRA provision in SNAP that temporarily eliminates the time limits for certain working-age, low-income adults without dependents for an additional fiscal year. This extension helps remove access barriers to SNAP and increase food purchasing power among some of the hardest-to-reach populations.

Increases Funding for the Agriculture and Food Research Initiative. The Budget provides $429 million, the largest funding level ever, for competitive peer-reviewed research grants through the Agriculture and Food Research Initiative. This increase is designed to foster a more robust research program within USDA with special emphasis related to the following five core areas: climate change, bioenergy, childhood obesity, world hunger, and food safety.

Focuses Forest Restoration Resources. The President's Budget focuses Forest Service resources to support more watershed and ecosystem improvement efforts based upon a variety of management actions, including mechanical removal of timber, road decommissioning, and wildlife habitat improvement. The Budget adopts an ecosystem-based approach to forest management that focuses on enhancing forest and watershed resiliency, preventing the loss of large carbon sinks, and maintains jobs. To address the need to protect forest resources and wildlife habitat in an era of global climate change, the Budget establishes a pilot program for long-term, landscape scale restoration activities that emphasize resiliency, health, and sustainable economic development.

Budgets Responsibly for Wildfires. The Budget fully funds the 10-year average cost of fire suppression and includes a $282 million discretionary funding reserve to be used only when the $1.2 billion in appropriated 10-year average funding is exhausted. The Budget also prioritizes hazardous fuels reduction activities in the wildland-urban interface where they are most effective—particularly in communities that are on track to meet Firewise standards, have identified acres to be treated in Community Wildfire Protection Plans (or the equivalent), and have made

an investment in implementing local solutions to protection against wildland fire.

Enhances Food Safety. The President's Budget takes important steps to improve the safety of the Nation's supply of meat, poultry, and processed egg products and works to make certain that these products are wholesome and accurately labeled and packaged. Consistent with the recommendations of the President's Food Safety Working Group, the Budget supports increasing regulatory testing and baseline studies and strengthening USDA's Public Health Epidemiology Program to support the inter-agency Federal-State Foodborne Disease Outbreak Response Team. These efforts will contribute toward a reduction in foodborne illness and improvements in public health and safety.

Supports Conservation on Private Lands. The Budget will accelerate the protection of our natural resources by strategically targeting funding to high priority program areas. This includes funding the Wetlands Reserve Program at a level to enable the restoration and protection of almost 200,000 additional acres of wetlands, providing over $1.2 billion for the Environmental Quality Incentives Program to help farmers comply with regulatory requirements and protect natural resources, providing a 67 percent increase in funding over the 2010 enacted level to reduce nutrient loading in the Chesapeake Bay, and enrolling 12 million acres into the Conservation Stewardship Program to improve water quality and enhance energy efficiency. The Budget also provides funding to support the installation of high-impact targeted conservation practices on 1.5 million acres in priority landscapes, including the Bay-Delta region in California and the Upper Mississippi.

Promotes Agricultural Exports. The Budget includes $54 million in discretionary funding to enhance USDA's efforts to promote the export of U.S. agricultural products. This funding will double the Department's cost-share assistance to agricultural trade associations in support of overseas market development activities, such as technical assistance and market research ($35 million); increase exporter assistance, in-country market promotions, and trade enforcement activities to remove non-tariff trade barriers, such as unwarranted sanitary and phytosanitary standards placed on U.S. commodities by other countries ($10 million); and double a grant program to assist U.S. specialty crop producers in overcoming sanitary, phytosanitary, and other technical barriers to trade ($9 million).

Reforms Farm Payments and Delivery of Crop Insurance. The Budget proposes to limit farm subsidy payments to wealthy farmers by reducing the cap on direct payments by 25 percent and reducing the Adjusted Gross Income (AGI) payment eligibility limits for farm and non-farm income by $250,000 over three years. The Farm Bill currently precludes an individual or an entity from receiving any benefit in a year where their non-farm AGI exceeds $500,000 and precludes receipt of any direct payments when their farm

AGI exceeds $750,000. This proposal would allow USDA to target payments to those who need and can benefit from them most, while at the same time preserving the safety net that protects farmers against low prices and natural disasters. The Budget also includes a proposal that will save billions of dollars by reforming how the Federal Government administers the crop insurance program. Crop insurance companies currently benefit from huge windfall profits due to the structure and terms of the Government's contract with the companies, called the Standard Reinsurance Agreement (SRA). Through the SRA renegotiation process, which will occur in 2010, USDA will pursue reforms to the financial terms in the SRA that will allow the Department to offer the same program benefits to farmers and ranchers with significantly reduced costs—saving $8 billion over 10 years.

Department of Agriculture
(In millions of dollars)

	Actual 2009	Estimate 2010	Estimate 2011
Spending			
Discretionary Budget Authority:			
Commodities and International	3,240	4,253	4,099
Rural Development	2,597	2,983	2,646
Forest Service	4,757	5,316	5,377
Conservation	968	1,009	964
Food and Nutrition Service	7,300	7,880	8,132
Research	2,648	2,846	2,723
Marketing and Regulatory Programs	2,012	2,095	2,057
Central Administration	510	636	663
Subtotal, excluding items below	24,032	27,018	26,661
Receipts	−58	−70	−71
Legislative proposal, Rural Housing receipts	—	—	−7
Mandatory savings proposals	—	—	−812
Total, Discretionary budget authority	23,974	26,948	25,771
Memorandum:			
Budget authority from American Recovery and Reinvestment Act	*6,892*	*—*	*—*
Budget authority from supplementals	*1,366*	*400*	*—*

Department of Agriculture—Continued

(In millions of dollars)

	Actual 2009	Estimate	
		2010	2011
Total, Discretionary outlays	25,063	28,402	27,143
Memorandum: Outlays from American Recovery and Reinvestment Act	*507*	*1,831*	*1,499*
Mandatory Outlays:			
Food and Nutrition Service	66,210	78,406	82,393
Commodity Credit Corporation	11,411	14,224	12,664
Crop Insurance	7,889	6,954	7,555
Natural Resources Conservation Service	1,584	2,124	2,772
Agricultural Marketing Service	1,106	1,276	1,270
Forest Service	816	874	757
Rural Development including liquidating accounts	−152	−933	−2,133
Receipts, reestimates and all other programs	−4,615	−1,980	−132
Total, Mandatory outlays	84,249	100,945	105,146
Memorandum: Outlays from American Recovery and Reinvestment Act	*4,626*	*10,843*	*11,966*
Total, Outlays	109,312	129,347	132,289
Credit activity			
Direct Loan Disbursements:			
Farm Loans	1,825	2,280	1,745
Commodity Credit Corporation	8,291	8,593	8,346
Rural Utilities Service	6,005	8,820	10,836
Rural Housing Service	2,042	4,300	4,116
Rural Business Service	—	1	17
P.L. 480	32	62	—
All other programs..	60	84	80
Total, Direct loan disbursements	18,255	24,140	25,140
Guaranteed Loan Commitments:			
Farm Loans	2,594	2,759	2,439
Commodity Credit Corporation	5,357	5,448	5,500
Rural Utilities Service	5	22	32
Rural Housing Service	14,166	14,200	13,627
Rural Business Service	1,110	2,158	2,275
Total, Guaranteed loan commitments	23,232	24,587	23,873

DEPARTMENT OF COMMERCE

Funding Highlights:

- Invests in American economic competitiveness and job creation by promoting innovation in manufacturing, advancing standards research and technology, protecting intellectual property rights, and deploying broadband.

- Promotes opportunities for American exporters in new markets and reduces barriers to sales abroad.

- Invests in smarter economic development through the promotion of regional innovation clusters.

- Advances climate science and services and supports critical satellite programs to monitor the Earth's weather and climate as well as global sea-level change.

- Implements the President's National Ocean Policy by supporting coastal zone management and marine spatial planning, expanding catch-share based fisheries management, and accelerating research on ocean acidification.

- Invests additional resources to improve economic and household statistics to analyze our economic health more accurately and target Government funds more precisely.

The Department of Commerce (DOC) has a broad mandate to advance economic growth, jobs and opportunities for the American people. It has cross-cutting responsibilities in the areas of trade, technology, entrepreneurship, economic development, environmental stewardship, and statistical research and analysis. To support this important work, the 2011 Budget allocates $8.9 billion to DOC.

Invests in America's Innovation and Competitiveness. The Budget includes $712 million for National Institute of Standards and Technology (NIST) laboratories as part of the President's Plan for Science and Innovation. This funding will support advanced measurement and standards development at NIST that will facilitate

the economy-wide development and adoption of a wide variety of new technologies, ranging from nanotechnology and computer security advances to energy conservation systems. The Budget also provides $80 million for the Technology Innovation Program, which invests in high-impact research that will address critical national needs and advance innovation. The Hollings Manufacturing Extension Partnership will receive $130 million to enhance the competitiveness of the Nation's manufacturers by facilitating the adoption of more efficient manufacturing processes. In addition, the President's Budget gives the U.S. Patent and Trademark Office (USPTO) full access to its fee collections and will strengthen USPTO's efforts to improve the speed and quality of patent examinations through a fee surcharge.

Promotes American Exports. The Budget provides $534 million, a 20-percent increase, to the International Trade Administration (ITA), so it can help launch the National Export Initiative, a broader Federal strategy to increase American exports. ITA will strengthen its efforts to promote exports from small businesses, help enforce free trade agreements with other nations, fight to eliminate barriers to sales of U.S. products, and improve the competitiveness of U.S. firms.

Expands Access to Broadband. Broadband is a central part of the infrastructure necessary for the economy to create jobs and thrive in this century. During 2011, Commerce's National Telecommunications and Information Administration will focus on administering the $4.7 billion program to expand broadband deployment, as well as programs to improve broadband adoption and data collection, which were funded by the American Recovery and Reinvestment Act. The Budget will also achieve savings by eliminating the Public Telecommunications Facilities Program, consolidating support for public broadcasters into the Corporation for Public Broadcasting.

Enhances Regional Economic Competitiveness. Competitive, high-performing regional economies are essential to national growth. The Budget supports growth strategies based on stronger regional clusters of economic activity through funding in the Department's Economic Development Administration (EDA), the Small Business Administration (SBA), as well as the Department of Labor with other agencies in key support roles. As part of the Administration's place-based initiative, the Budget provides $75 million in regional planning and matching grants within EDA to support the creation of Regional Innovation Clusters that leverage regions' competitive strengths to boost job creation and economic growth.

Supports Improvements in Weather Forecasting, Climate Monitoring, Fisheries Management, and Ocean Programs. The Budget maintains continuity of National Oceanic and Atmospheric Administration (NOAA) satellite coverage needed for monitoring weather and climate by providing over $2 billion to fund the development and acquisition of NOAA's polar orbiting and geo-stationary weather satellite systems, satellite-borne measurements of sea level and other climate variables, and other space-based observations. The Budget supports enhancements to climate science and services, including improved modeling and assessments at global and regional levels. The Budget advances the President's National Ocean Policy with funding for coastal zone management and planning, competitive grants in support of regional ocean partnerships, integrated ecosystem assessments, catch-share based fisheries management, and research on ocean acidification.

Strengthens Key Statistical Programs. The Budget provides $1.3 billion to the Census Bureau to process, tabulate, and release 2010 Census data, conduct extensive evaluations of the census, improve the data collection methods of the American Community Survey, and begin a continuous update process of the Census Bureau's geospatial and address data, which is expected to produce long-run cost savings. These initiatives will provide more accurate data for decision-makers at all levels of government and in the private sector. Funds are also provided to prepare for the 2012 Economic and Government Censuses and to improve an important measure of poverty. Finally, the Budget provides additional funding for the Bureau of Economic Analysis to develop new data series on key economic sectors (such as manufacturing and retail trade) and household consumption, income, and expenses. These measures will provide policymakers more timely, detailed, and robust data on the state of the business and household sectors of the economy.

Department of Commerce
(In millions of dollars)

	Actual 2009	Estimate	
		2010	2011
Spending			
Discretionary Budget Authority:			
Departmental Management:			
Salaries and Expenses	53	58	66
Steel Loan Program	—	—	−43
Herbert C. Hoover Building Renovation	5	22	17
Office of the Inspector General	28	27	29
Subtotal, Departmental Management	86	107	69
Economic Development Administration:			
Salaries and Expenses	37	38	40
Economic Development Assistance Programs	221	255	246
Regional Innovation Cluster Initiative (non-add)	—	*50*	*75*
Subtotal, Economic Development Administration	258	293	286
Bureau of the Census:			
Salaries and Expenses	234	259	280
Periodic Censuses and Programs	2,905	6,966	987
Decennial Census (non-add)	*2,689*	*6,751*	*740*
Subtotal, Bureau of the Census	3,139	7,225	1,267
Economics and Statistics Administration	91	97	113
International Trade Administration	420	446	534
Bureau of Industry and Security	84	100	113
Minority Business Development Agency	30	32	32
National Oceanic and Atmospheric Administration:			
Operations, Research, and Facilities	3,130	3,413	3,408
Procurement, Acquisition and Construction	1,242	1,358	2,184
Other Accounts	82	82	−38
Subtotal, National Oceanic and Atmospheric Administration	4,454	4,853	5,554
Patent and Trademark Office:			
Program Level	1,899	1,887	2,322
Fees	−1,901	−2,003	−2,322
Subtotal, Patent and Trademark Office	−2	−116	—
National Institute of Standards and Technology:			
Scientific and Technical Research Services	478	520	587
Industrial Technology Services	170	195	210
Technology Innovation Program (non-add)	*60*	*70*	*80*
Manufacturing Extension Partnership (non-add)	*110*	*125*	*130*
Construction of Research Facilities	172	147	125
Subtotal, National Institute of Standards and Technology	820	862	922

Department of Commerce—Continued
(In millions of dollars)

	Actual 2009	Estimate 2010	Estimate 2011
National Telecommunications and Information Administration:			
Salaries and Expenses	16	20	22
Broadband Technology Opportunities Program Administration	—	—	24
Public Telecomm. and Facilities Planning and Construction	18	20	—
Subtotal, National Telecommunications and Information Administration	34	40	46
All other	−2	−7	−8
Total, Discretionary budget authority	9,412	13,932	8,928
Memorandum:			
Budget authority from American Recovery and Reinvestment Act	*7,845*	*−128*	*—*
Budget authority from supplementals	*40*	*—*	*—*
Total, Discretionary outlays	8,967	13,535	8,953
Memorandum: Outlays from American Recovery and Reinvestment Act	*566*	*2,473*	*2,249*
Mandatory Outlays:			
Digital Television Transition and Public Safety Fund	1,296	506	125
Grants to Manufacturers of Worsted Wool Fabrics:			
Existing law	1	10	5
Legislative proposal	—	—	−5
All other	−101	191	176
Total, Mandatory outlays	1,196	707	301
Total, Outlays	10,163	14,242	9,254
Credit activity			
Direct Loan Disbursements:			
Fisheries Finance Direct Loan Financing account	23	23	23
Total, Direct loan disbursements	23	23	23

DEPARTMENT OF DEFENSE

Funding Highlights:

- Provides $548.9 billion for the Department of Defense base budget in 2011, a 3.4 percent increase over the 2010 enacted level.

- Includes $33.0 billion for a 2010 supplemental request and $159.3 billion for 2011 to support ongoing overseas contingency operations, including funds to execute the President's new strategy in Afghanistan and Pakistan.

- Maintains ready forces and continues efforts to rebalance military forces to focus more on today's wars, and provides capabilities to deter or if necessary engage in future conflicts.

- Continues strong support for our men and women in uniform through a robust benefits package including pay increases that keep pace with the private sector.

- Supports access to medical care to the more than 9.5 million beneficiaries: active military members and their families, military retirees and their families, dependent survivors, and eligible Reserve Component members and families.

- Supports wounded warrior transition units and centers of excellence in vision, hearing, traumatic brain injury, and other areas to continuously improve the care provided to wounded, ill, and injured servicemembers.

- Continues to reform defense acquisition, reducing its use of high-risk contracts related to time-and-materials and labor-hours by 17 percent through the end of 2011, while modernizing key weapons systems to provide our troops with the best technology to meet battlefield needs, and eliminating or reconfiguring lower-priority acquisitions.

- Prioritizes resources by ending or reducing several programs, including the C-17 aircraft, the Joint Strike Fighter Alternate Engine program, the Third Generation Infrared Surveillance program, and the Net-Enabled Command Capability program.

- Supports a reconfigured ballistic missile defense strategy, in line with the President's policy, to better address current threats.

While the U.S. military is addressing ongoing challenges—such as drawing down responsibly in Iraq and carrying out the President's strategy in Afghanistan and Pakistan—the Department of Defense (DOD) is identifying long-term strategic needs and targeting resources toward its highest priorities. These priorities, developed in concert with DOD's Quadrennial Defense Review, include taking care of our men and women in uniform, rebalancing our forces to address both current and future conflicts, and reforming business practices, such as developing and purchasing weapons.

The 2011 Budget for DOD requests an increase of $18.2 billion, or 3.4 percent, from the 2010 enacted level of $530.8 billion. This funding increase allows DOD to address its highest priorities, such as the President's commitment to reform defense acquisition, develop a ballistic missile defense system that addresses modern threats, and continue to provide high quality healthcare to wounded servicemembers. In addition, the Budget will continue to incorporate into the base those items previously funded in emergency supplemental appropriations that should be considered enduring activities that are not driven by specific conflicts.

Supports Missions in Iraq, Afghanistan, and Pakistan (OCO). The President has ordered his military commanders to send an additional 30,000 troops to Afghanistan, which will bring the total number of U.S. forces in Afghanistan to almost 100,000 by 2011. Meanwhile, DOD will continue drawing down its combat forces from Iraq, and all U.S. forces will be withdrawn from Iraq by the end of 2011. To address the costs of increasing military and intelligence operations in Afghanistan and Pakistan and drawing down in Iraq and leaving Iraq's security forces with the minimum essential capabilities to operate after U.S. forces depart, the Administration is requesting $33.0 billion in 2010 supplemental funding on top of the $129.6 billion already provided, and a total of $159.3 billion for its 2011 overseas contingency operations (OCO) activities. In addition to this DOD funding, the supplemental request will also include funding for Department of State activities in 2010. The Budget includes placeholder estimates of $50 billion per year for 2012 and beyond. These estimates do not reflect any policy decisions about specific military or intelligence operations, but are only intended to indicate that some as-yet unknown costs are anticipated.

Maintains Readiness for Today's Challenges. The Administration is committed to providing its service members with the resources needed to be ready to respond to the multiple, complex, and sometimes unconventional threats posed by today's security environment. The Budget includes robust funding for operations and maintenance, covering such crucial activities as training and operations, pay for a high quality civilian workforce, upkeep of equipment and facilities, repair parts, fuel, and supplies.

Supports Our Nation's Troops and Their Families. The Budget continues the Administration's commitment to caring for our Nation's men and women in uniform and promoting the well-being of the families who support them. To meet this objective, the Budget includes funding for a 1.4 percent basic pay raise that will keep military pay increases in line with those in the private sector. In addition to this pay raise, the Budget also includes an average housing increase of 4.2 percent, as well as a variety of monthly special skill-based payments, enlistment and reenlistment bonuses, and other benefits.

The strength of our troops relies on the strength and stability of the families that support them, and the Budget supports these military families as our servicemembers answer our country's call to service. Overall, family support programs grow over 3 percent above the 2010 enacted level. Examples include:

- $1.3 billion, an increase of $87 million over the 2010 enacted level, to expand availability for affordable, high-quality child care services at over 800 child development centers both in the United States and overseas.

- $1.9 billion, $37 million over the 2010 enacted level, for expanded counseling and assistance services, from financial counseling to transition and relocation assistance, to help families meet the challenges brought on by repeated deployments and family separations.

- $84 million, an increase of $12 million over the 2010 enacted level, for enhanced career and educational opportunities for military spouses through tuition assistance and Federal internship programs.

Cares for Wounded, Ill, and Injured Servicemembers. The 2011 Budget sustains ongoing efforts to provide high quality medical care to the over 9.5 million servicemembers as well as military family and retiree beneficiaries. This includes support for wounded warrior transition units and centers of excellence in vision, hearing, traumatic brain injury, and other areas to continuously improve the care provided to wounded, ill, and injured servicemembers, including:

- $30.9 billion overall for medical care, an increase of 5.8 percent over the 2010 enacted level.

- $669 million to provide care for traumatic brain injury and psychological health.

- $250 million for continued support of mental health and traumatic brain injury research, such as the development of tools to detect and treat post-traumatic stress, and enhancements to suicide prevention measures.

- Support for DOD's efforts to update its health information technology infrastructure, while partnering with the Department of Veterans Affairs and the private sector to pursue the Administration's goal of building a Virtual Lifetime Electronic Record to deliver care and benefits to servicemembers and veterans with efficiency and accuracy.

Reforms Acquisition. DOD contracts account for approximately 70 percent of all Federal procurement spending, so DOD reform initiatives are critical to the Administration's efforts to improve Government acquisition. The 2010 Budget took important first steps to reform this process; in 2011, DOD will continue these efforts by terminating or delaying programs that are inadequately justified or not performing well. For example, the Budget ends the C-17 aircraft program because additional aircraft are not needed, saving $2.5 billion. It also eliminates the Joint Strike Fighter Alternate Engine program, saving $465 million, because this program raises logistical, management, and cost concerns. The Budget saves an additional $73 million by terminating the Third Generation Infrared Surveillance program, and instead procuring upgraded Space Based Infrared System Satellites in the future; it saves $8.5 million more by eliminating the Net-Enabled Command Capability program, which has been unable to meet its requirements on schedule. The Department will also further reduce its use of high-risk contracts in areas that relate to time-and-materials and labor hours by 17 percent through the end of 2011, and take steps so that military requirements for weapons are reasonable, program costs and schedules are realistic, and acquisition funding is stable.

Provides Ballistic Missile Defense to Address Modern Threats. The Administration is committed to a robust defense against emerging missile threats by deploying technology that is proven, cost-effective, and adaptable for countering an evolving security environment. Starting in 2011, the new Phased Adaptive Approach will guide missile defense architecture. It will feature incremental deployments of increasingly capable sea- and land-based missile interceptors and a range of sensors in Europe to defend against growing ballistic missile dangers. This phased approach will offer more effective defenses against near-term ballistic missile threats and augment the current defense of the U.S. homeland against long-range ballistic missile threats. It will provide for the defense of U.S. deployed forces, their families, and our Allies in Europe sooner and more comprehensively than the previous program, while reaffirming the U.S. commitment to strengthening NATO and integrating U.S. systems with Allied capabilities and networks.

Modernizes Weapon Systems. A major goal of the Administration is to provide the troops with the most effective and modern equipment possible. To accomplish this, the 2011 Budget continues to develop and procure many advanced weapons systems that support both today's wars and future conflicts. These include: the F-35 Joint Strike Fighter, a new family of ground vehi-cles, new ships such as the next generation ballistic missile submarine, and the P-8 aircraft. The Budget also bolsters capabilities in Unmanned Aerial Vehicles, helicopters, and cyber capabilities and electronic warfare, which are key components in the ongoing task of rebalancing the military to focus on current and emerging threats.

Department of Defense
(In millions of dollars)

	Actual 2009	Estimate	
		2010	2011
Spending			
Discretionary Base budget authority:			
Military Personnel	125,625	134,968	138,541
Operation and Maintenance	179,103	184,488	200,248
Procurement	100,886	104,803	112,873
Research, Development, Test and Evaluation	79,392	80,097	76,131
Military Construction	21,898	21,022	16,924
Family Housing	3,163	2,259	1,822
Revolving and Management Funds	3,155	3,118	2,380
Subtotal, Discretionary Base budget authority	513,222	530,755	548,919
Discretionary Overseas Contingency Operations (OCO) budget authority:			
Enacted	145,741	129,648	—
Requested (2011 includes $254 million in U.S. Coast Guard funding)	—	33,014	159,336
Subtotal, Discretionary OCO budget authority	145,741	162,662	159,336
Total, Discretionary budget authority (Base and OCO)	658,963	693,417	708,255
Memorandum: Budget authority from American Recovery and Reinvestment Act	*7,435*	*—*	*—*
Total, Discretionary Outlays (Base and OCO)	633,797	684,436	714,428
Memorandum: Outlays from American Recovery and Reinvestment Act	*238*	*3,991*	*2,491*
Mandatory Outlays:			
Existing law	2,740	3,605	3,959
Legislative proposal	—	—	408
Total, Mandatory outlays	2,740	3,605	4,367
Total, Outlays	636,537	688,041	718,795

Department of Defense—Continued
(In millions of dollars)

	Actual 2009	Estimate	
		2010	2011
Credit activity			
Total, Direct loan disbursements	172	195	200

NATIONAL INTELLIGENCE PROGRAM

Funding Highlights:

- Strengthens the capabilities of the Nation's intelligence agencies to furnish timely, accurate, and insightful intelligence on the capabilities and intentions of foreign powers, including international terrorist groups.

- Supports the President's strategy in Afghanistan and Pakistan.

- Enhances Federal cybersecurity capabilities to protect a central part of our Nation's and economy's infrastructure.

- Allocates resources in support of a U.S. Government-wide counterterrorism action plan.

The National Intelligence Program (NIP) funds intelligence activities in several Federal departments and the Central Intelligence Agency (CIA). NIP's budget is classified, so the 2011 Budget does not publicly disclose funding requests for intelligence activities. This chapter highlights key NIP-funded activities without detailing funding information.

Strengthens Capabilities of our Nation's Intelligence Agencies. To protect America's national security, the Intelligence Community (IC) provides effective intelligence collection, the analysis of that intelligence, and the production of finished intelligence products. The IC is responsible for timely and effective dissemination of intelligence to those who need it, ranging from the President, to heads of Executive Departments, military forces, and law enforcement agencies. To meet this country's national security challenges, the IC is: strengthening its component agencies' ability to collect intelligence; maintaining the security of Federal cyber networks; and protecting against the threat of in-

ternational terrorism in the United States. The 2011 Budget for NIP supports the Administration's national security objectives and the new National Intelligence Strategy. The Director of National Intelligence, the Director of the CIA, and Department Secretaries with intelligence organizations will use 2011 funds to defeat terrorist networks, prevent the spread of weapons of mass destruction, penetrate and analyze the most difficult targets of interest to U.S. foreign policymakers, and anticipate geopolitical and economic developments of strategic concern.

Supports the President's Strategy in Afghanistan and Pakistan. The Administration will request 2011 funding and supplemental funding for 2010 to cover the costs of global intelligence operations. In particular, the Budget will support the President's strategy in Afghanistan and Pakistan and the additional U.S. forces being deployed there. IC collection and analysis play a key role in informing decision-makers at the strategic level and supporting the war fighter at a tactical level.

61

Enhances Federal Cybersecurity Capabilities. The U.S. information infrastructure—including telecommunications and computer networks and systems, and the data that reside on them—is critical to virtually every aspect of modern life. Threats to our information technology infrastructure endanger our national and economic security and our citizens' privacy and, therefore, are an important policy focus of the Government. In 2009, President Obama directed a comprehensive review to assess U.S. policies and structures for cybersecurity. The 2011 Budget supports actions detailed in the Cyberspace Policy Review and continues activities begun as part of the Comprehensive National Cybersecurity Initiative.

Allocates Resources to Support a Counterterrorism Plan. The National Counterterrorism Center (NCTC) has developed a U.S. Government-wide counterterrorism action plan. This plan lays out broad strategic objectives aligned with policy objectives to guide the overall implementation of this national strategy on counterterrorism. The Administration is committed to integrating mission-based budgeting in the counterterrorism area with the annual budget process and will work with NCTC, IC, and relevant Departments, such as Defense, State, and Homeland Security, to direct resources in support of counterterrorism implementation objectives.

DEPARTMENT OF EDUCATION

Funding Highlights:

- Provides a $3 billion increase in K-12 education programs, plus up to $1 billion in additional funding if Congress successfully completes a fundamental overhaul of the Elementary and Secondary Education Act (ESEA). Together, these measures would represent the largest funding increase for ESEA programs ever requested.

- Supports needed reforms of Federal K-12 programs to promote college- and career-readiness, enhance teacher and principal effectiveness, deliver a rigorous and complete education, improve educational options, and prepare our children for the jobs of the future.

- Provides $1.35 billion to expand Race to the Top for school districts as well as States to carry out systemic reform, and $500 million to continue the Investing in Innovation program to test, validate, and scales up effective approaches to student learning.

- Increases the number, and improves the distribution of, effective teachers and principals, by investing $950 million in competitive grants to States and school districts that build comprehensive systems to recruit, prepare, retain, and reward effective teachers and principals.

- Invests $210 million in Promise Neighborhoods, an initiative that integrates school reform with strong family supports and effective community services across an entire neighborhood, so that youth successfully complete high school and continue on to college.

- Expands educational options and increases access to high-quality schools by investing $490 million to grow effective charter schools and other effective, autonomous public schools that achieve results, develop new approaches, and give parents more choices.

- Consolidates 38 K-12 programs into 11 new programs that emphasize competitive funding, accountability for outcomes and flexibility in approaches, and use of evidence to get results.

- Supports the next generation of scientists and engineers by helping States develop and implement math and science instructional practices that are aligned to rigorous college- and career-ready standards and by supporting districts and nonprofit organizations that develop, implement, and evaluate promising and effective programs.

- Increases aid for needy students, reforms Federal student aid programs, and simplifies the financial aid application process.

- Funds new reforms across the Nation's early learning programs for children birth through age five, so they're prepared to enter kindergarten ready for success.

- Creates a Workforce Innovation Partnership with the Department of Labor to test and validate effective strategies to improve services under the Workforce Investment Act.

The President's Budget proposes a bold strategy to achieve the Department of Education's mission of fostering educational excellence, advancing equity and opportunity, improving student achievement, rewarding successful outcomes, investing in innovation, and preparing our Nation's children for global competitiveness.

Reform Elementary and Secondary School Funding by Setting High Standards, Encouraging Innovation, and Rewarding Success. The Budget supports the Administration's new vision for the Elementary and Secondary Education Act (ESEA). The reauthorized law would encourage States to adopt higher, clearer standards that set the expectation that every student will graduate from high school ready for college and a career. The new law would support dramatic improvements in the quality of assessments to measure complex skills and help teachers identify and respond to students' strengths and needs. The reauthorization would also recognize and reward schools for helping students make important gains, even if they are not yet at grade-level, and offer new flexibility for successful States and districts to pursue new solutions to help all students meet high standards. At the same time, the law would require vigorous efforts to turn around persistently low-performing schools, applying comprehensive strategies that put children first. In support of these efforts, the Budget provides a $3 billion increase in funding for K-12 education programs authorized in the ESEA, including $900 million for School Turnaround Grants, and the Administration will request up to $1 billion in additional funding if Congress successfully completes a fundamental overhaul of the law. Together, these measures would represent the largest funding increase for ESEA programs ever requested.

Expand the Race to the Top, and Open the Competition to School Districts. The $4 billion Race to the Top, created by the American Recovery and Reinvestment Act (Recovery Act), began a competition among States to spur systemic and innovative reform across four areas: supporting high academic standards; improving teacher effectiveness and distributing effective teachers more equitably; using data to improve achievement; and turning around low-performing schools. Not all States will receive Race to the Top grants, but the competition itself has galvanized key stakeholders across the Nation to reform State laws and to develop new plans for lifting student achievement. The Budget provides $1.35 billion to continue the President's Race to the Top challenge and to expand the competition from States to school districts that are ready for comprehensive reform.

Increase the Number of Effective Teachers and Principals. Great teachers are the key to a high-quality education. Increasing the number of great teachers, especially in disadvantaged schools, will require major new efforts to help all teachers improve their skills; recognize and reward excellence in the classroom; and help struggling teachers improve or, if need be, exit the classroom. Today, taxpayers invest nearly $3 billion a year in a teacher quality block grant that heavily supports investments with little evidence of or impact on increasing learning. As part of the overhaul of ESEA, the Administration will require States taking formula funds to develop the preconditions for an effective human capital system, beginning with strong evaluation systems. At the same time, the Administration will invest $950 million in a new competitive fund for States and districts that supports bold approaches to recruiting, developing, retaining, and rewarding more effective teachers, particularly in the lowest-performing schools. The Administration is also investing $405 million in supporting successful and innovative pathways into teaching and school leadership.

Invest in Supports for Student Success. While an isolated schoolhouse with limited hours was adequate in an earlier time, today's competitive global marketplace requires more. Students need to be safe and healthy, and they need a complete education that extends beyond the traditional hours. As part of a $1.8 billion investment in the Supporting Student Success initiative, the Budget funds comprehensive supports so that students are mentally and physically healthy and ready to learn. The initiative also reforms the 21st Century Community Learning Centers program to focus funding on models that redesign and extend the school day, week, or year to provide additional time for students to engage in academic activities, additional time for enrichment activities, and time for educators to collaborate and improve instruction.

Provides Expanded Support for Promise Neighborhoods. As part of a $1.8 billion investment in the Supporting Student Success initiative, the Budget includes dedicated support for Promise Neighborhoods, modeled after the Harlem Children's Zone, which aims to improve college going rates by combining a rigorous K-12 education with a full network of supportive services in an entire neighborhood. This initiative would support comprehensive programs that address the needs of children and youth in a targeted area from before the time they are born to their attendance in college. The core principle behind this initiative is that combining both effective academic programs and strong health and social-service systems can combat the effects of poverty and improve the education and life outcomes of children.

Grow High-Performing Charter Schools and Other Innovative Public Schools. Effective charter schools have achieved impressive results in closing achievement gaps. The Budget will invest $490 million to grow these schools and other autonomous public schools that achieve results, develop new approaches, and give parents more choices. The Budget will support new options for students to transfer to high-performing public schools, support successful magnet schools, and require States and districts accepting these funds to create the conditions for effective schools to grow and ineffective schools to be restructured or shut down.

Restructure Narrow and Constrained Education Programs Into Broad and Flexible Competitions that Fund What Works. The Department of Education funds dozens of programs that narrowly limit what States, districts, and schools can do with funds. Some of these programs have little evidence of success, while oth-

ers are demonstrably failing to improve student achievement. The President's Budget eliminates six discretionary programs and consolidates 38 K-12 programs into 11 new programs that emphasize using competition to allocate funds, giving communities more choices around activities, and using rigorous evidence to fund what works. The Administration will make sure that, under these competitions, there is an equitable geographic distribution of funds nationwide, including to rural communities. Building on the Recovery Act, the Administration proposes $500 million to expand the Investing in Innovation Fund, which will expand proven models—and fund and evaluate promising ones—for achieving student success. Finally, the Budget dedicates funds for the rigorous evaluation of education programs so that we can scale up what works and eliminate what does not.

Expand and Reform Early Childhood Education. Quality early education is an investment that pays off for years to come by preparing the youngest children for a lifetime of learning. The 2011 Budget enables the Administration to build on the expansion to early learning programs made through the Recovery Act, and realize the President's plan to reform early childhood education, promote high standards of quality, and focus on results for children from birth through preschool. In the 2011 Budget, the Administration supports pending legislation that will establish a new Early Learning Challenge Fund administered by the Department of Education and the Department of Health and Human Services to help States improve the quality of early childhood programs to help children enter school ready to succeed.

Invest in the Next Generation of Scientists and Engineers. Our Nation's eighth graders are scoring below their peers from many Asian and European countries, and we are neither adequately closing the achievement gaps in math and science nor providing adequate opportunities for many students from diverse backgrounds. The Budget reflects the Administration's investment in improving science, technology, engineering, and mathematics (STEM) outcomes and creating the next generation of scientists and engineers who can help drive economic growth in the coming decades. The Budget provides $300 million in new grants to States to develop and implement instructional practices and improve teaching and learning in science and math aligned to new high standards. The Budget also dedicates $150 million within the Investing in Innovation Fund to competitive grants for school districts, nonprofits, and other organizations to test, validate, and scale promising strategies to improve teaching and accelerate student learning in STEM subjects. The Department of Education will work with the National Science Foundation and other Federal agencies to identify the most effective interventions that can help States, schools, and teachers improve STEM outcomes.

Increase Pell Grants and Put Them on a Firm Financial Footing. Pell Grants have helped millions of Americans afford college, yet in recent decades, growth in their value has fallen far behind the growth in college costs. The Recovery Act and 2009 appropriations bill increased the maximum Pell Grant by more than $600 for a total award of $5,350, and the maximum award will increase to $5,550 in 2010. The Budget proposes to make that increase permanent and put them on a path to grow faster than inflation every year. The Budget also addresses a second problem: Pell Grants currently function much like an entitlement, yet they are funded through an annual appropriations process that can fall behind actual demand for the grants. The Budget proposes to make Pell Grant funding mandatory so that adequate Pell Grant funding is available every year.

Expand Financial Aid for Students and Make Historic Investments in Improving Education, from Cradle Through College. The Budget supports legislation that has passed the House and is pending in the Senate that would reform student lending to eliminate tens of billions of dollars in wasteful subsidies to banks, and instead, provide loans directly to students on an efficient basis that uses private and nonprofit companies to deliver services. This measure

would then use savings to make historic investments to increase college access and success, and would lay a foundation for success for America's youngest children. In addition to expanded Pell Grants and a simplified student aid system, these investments include a new American Graduation Initiative that will strengthen and support America's community colleges, focus on college completion, and graduate 5 million more students by 2020. Finally, to help graduates overburdened with student loan debt, the Administration will strengthen income-based repayment plans for student loans by reducing monthly payments and shortening the repayment period so that overburdened borrowers will pay only 10 percent of their discretionary income in loan repayments and can have their remaining debt forgiven after 20 years.

Spur Partnership and Innovation in Vocational Rehabilitation and Adult Education. The Budget seeks $60 million in innovation funds to support seamless delivery of services and improved outcomes for people with disabilities and adults seeking basic skills. Under a new Partnership for Workforce Innovation, the Departments of Education and Labor will coordinate their innovation grants and work with other Federal agencies to break down program silos and to build and share evidence of what works.

Evaluate Rigorously Federal Education Programs. The Budget reflects the Administration's commitment to rigorous evaluations that distinguish between what works and what doesn't so we do not waste taxpayer dollars. Compared to two years ago, the current request represents a nearly 20 percent increase in the investment in the development, evaluation, and dissemination of education interventions that increase student learning and achievement through the Institute of Education Sciences. Additional funds will be used to evaluate Federal education programs rigorously, particularly investments launched under the Recovery Act. The increase in education research and evaluation will provide practitioners and policy makers with effective tools for preparing students for success in college and the workforce.

Department of Education
(In millions of dollars)

	Actual 2009	Estimate	
		2010	2011
Spending			
Discretionary Budget Authority:			
Legislative proposal, Elementary and Secondary Education Act:			
College and Career Ready Students [1]	14,492	14,492	14,492
School Turnaround Grants	546	546	900
Race to the Top	—	—	1,350
Investing in Innovation	—	—	500
English Learner Education	730	750	800
Effective Teaching and Learning for a Complete Education	979	920	1,015
College Pathways and Accelerated Learning	51	103	100
Excellent Instructional Teams	3,181	3,505	3,855
Expanding Educational Options	369	409	490
Supporting Student Success	1,795	1,541	1,786
Special Education State Grants [2]	12,319	12,319	12,569
Career and Technical Education Programs	1,272	1,272	1,272
Adult Education State Grants	554	628	612
Workforce Innovation Fund	—	—	60
Federal Student Aid:			
Supplemental Educational Opportunity Grants	757	757	757
Federal Work Study	980	980	980
Higher Education:			
Minority Serving Institutions—Disretionary funding	516	613	642
Minority Serving Institutions—Mandatory funding (non-add)	*278*	*278*	*278*
TRIO programs—Discretionary funding	848	853	853
TRIO programs—Mandatory funding (non-add)	*57*	*57*	*57*
GEAR UP	313	323	323
Student Aid Administration	753	870	1,170
Institute of Education Sciences	617	659	739
All other	5,173	5,241	4,432
Total, Discretionary budget authority [3]	46,245	46,781	49,697
Memorandum:			
Budget authority from American Recovery and Reinvestment Act	*81,124*	*—*	*—*
Total, Discretionary outlays	44,971	46,743	46,740
Memorandum: Outlays from American Recovery and Reinvestment Act	*14,154*	*44,054*	*20,304*
Mandatory Outlays:			
Legislative proposal, Federal Direct Student Loans	–4,263	–6,389	–9,244
Legislative proposal, Federal Family Education Loans	–26,175	–12,649	–106
Legislative proposal, Perkins Loan Program	—	—	–736

Department of Education—Continued
(In millions of dollars)

	Actual 2009	Estimate 2010	2011
Legislative proposal, Federal Pell Grants	14,432	24,076	28,928
Academic Competitive/SMART Grants	607	836	824
Vocational Rehabilitation (VR) State Grants	2,766	2,986	3,080
All other	71	421	1,993
Total, Mandatory outlays	−12,562	9,281	24,739
Memorandum: Outlays from American Recovery and Reinvestment Act	*6,849*	*6,886*	*2,498*
Total, Outlays	32,409	56,024	71,479

Credit activity
Direct Loan Disbursements:

	Actual 2009	Estimate 2010	2011
Historically Black College and University Capital Financing	120	160	186
Federal Direct Student Loans	37,770	67,754	132,427
TEACH Grants	49	52	65
Temporary Student Loan Purchase Authority	62,796	28,456	972
Federal Perkins Loans	—	—	1,355
Total, Direct loan disbursements	100,735	96,422	135,005

Guaranteed Loan Disbursements:

	Actual 2009	Estimate 2010	2011
Federal Family Education Loans	65,346	53,082	—
Total, Guaranteed loan disbursements	65,346	53,082	—

[1] Program level. Budget authority is $2,906 million less than program level in 2009 and $841 million less than program level in 2011.

[2] Program level. Budget authority is $1,736 million less than program level in 2009 and $841 million less than program level in 2011.

[3] Program level. The Budget authority is $4,889 million less than program level in 2009. The 2009 and 2010 discretionary totals do not include mandatory changes enacted in the appropriation bills for those years. The 2011 discretionary total is net of a $597 million rescission of Academic Competitiveness/SMART Grant balances and a $56 million increase over the VR State Grants baseline.

DEPARTMENT OF ENERGY

Funding Highlights:

- Supports high-risk, high-payoff transformational research and development projects with $300 million for the recently established Advanced Research Projects Agency–Energy (ARPA-E).

- Supports and encourages the early commercial deployment of innovative energy technologies with an additional $36 billion in guaranteed loan volume authority for advanced nuclear power plants and an additional $500 million in credit subsidy to support $3 to $5 billion in loan guarantees for innovative energy efficiency and renewable energy projects.

- Provides a 4.6 percent, or $226 million, increase in funding at the Office of Science for basic research and world-leading laboratories to support transformational scientific discoveries and accelerate solutions to our Nation's most pressing challenges.

- Invests $2.3 billion in applied energy research and development to position the United States as the world leader in energy technology that will address climate change, develop new industries, and create new jobs.

- Accelerates the transition to a low-carbon economy through support of development and deployment of clean energy technologies such as solar, biomass, geothermal, wind, nuclear, and low-carbon emission coal power.

- Reduces security risks through major increases in funding for the detection, elimination, and securing of nuclear material and radiological sources worldwide and the maintenance of a safe, secure, and effective nuclear weapons stockpile.

- Continues the Nation's efforts to reduce environmental risks and safely manage nuclear materials.

The President's 2011 Budget provides $28.4 billion for the Department of Energy (DOE) to support scientific innovation, develop clean and secure energy technologies, maintain national security, and reduce environmental risk.

Invests in the Sciences. The 2011 Budget continues the President's Plan for Science and Innovation. The Budget provides $5.1 billion for the Office of Science, including $1.8 billion for basic energy sciences to discover novel ways to produce, store, and use energy. The Budget also expands graduate research fellowship programs that will train students in critical energy-related fields. The 2011 Budget includes $300 million for the Advanced Research Projects Agency-Energy, to accelerate game-changing energy technologies in need of rapid and flexible experimentation or engineering.

Encourages the Early Commercial Use of New, Innovative Energy Technologies that Will Reduce Greenhouse Gas Emissions. The Budget substantially expands support for DOE loan guarantees for innovative energy technologies, by adding $36 billion in new loan authority (for a total of $54.5 billion) for nuclear power facilities and an additional $500 million in credit subsidy to support $3 to $5 billion in loan guarantees for innovative energy efficiency and renewable energy projects. The loan guarantee program also will continue to support a range of commercial renewable energy programs and other facilities that help reduce pollutants and greenhouse gases while simultaneously creating clean energy jobs and contributing to long-term economic growth and international competitiveness.

Invests in Smart, Energy Efficient, and Reliable Electricity Delivery Infrastructure. The Budget continues to support the modernization of the Nation's electric grid, by investing in research, development and demonstration of smart-grid technologies that will spur the transition to a smarter, more efficient, secure and reliable electric system. The end result will promote energy- and cost-saving choices for consumers, reduce emissions, and foster the growth of renewable energy sources like wind and solar. In addition, the Budget supports the Power Marketing Administration to reliably operate, maintain, and rehabilitate the Federal hydropower and transmission systems.

Advances the Development of Carbon Capture and Storage Technologies. The Budget supports a balanced research and development (R&D) portfolio of carbon capture and storage technologies. The $545 million for climate change technology funding provided for Fossil Energy R&D in the 2011 Budget will help reduce greenhouse gas emissions by focusing resources to develop carbon capture technologies with broad applications to advanced power systems, existing power plants, and industrial sources.

Invests in Clean Energy Technologies to Reduce Dependence on Oil and Accelerate the Transition to a Low-Carbon Economy. The Budget provides support for accelerating research, development, demonstration of nuclear technologies, and the commercialization of new nuclear power facilities and various clean energy technologies. Nearly $2.4 billion is provided for energy efficiency and renewable energy programs, an increase of $113 million over the 2010 appropriation, including $302 million for solar energy, $220 million for biofuels and biomass R&D, $325 million for advanced vehicle technologies, and $231 million for energy efficient building technologies. These investments will help reduce dependence on oil and create long-term, sustainable economic growth in the low-carbon industries of the future, helping to foster long-term job creation. The Budget also eliminates funding for programs that provide inefficient fossil fuel subsidies that impede investment in clean energy sources and undermine efforts to deal with the threat of climate change.

Reduces Proliferation Risks and Promotes the Safety, Security, and Reliability of the Nuclear Weapons Stockpile Without Nuclear Testing. The Budget provides $2.7 billion, an increase of $550 million over the 2010 appropriation, to prevent the proliferation of nuclear weapons. This increase supports the strategy to move toward a world without nuclear weapons that the President announced in his April 2009, speech in Prague. This investment fully funds efforts to: secure nuclear material; develop technology to detect and deter nuclear testing and smuggling; and support international nonproliferation treaties, regulatory controls, and safeguards. Development work on the reliable replacement warhead has ceased. The 2011 Budget funds $8.1 billion, $750 million over the 2010 Budget, to improve the nuclear stockpile's safety, security, and effectiveness with more extensive life extension programs, upgrades to the infrastructure supporting the life extension programs, and new initiatives in naval reactors work. Funding for the stockpile and naval reactors work increases by about 10 percent over 2010 funding.

Protects the Public from Harmful Exposure to Radioactive Waste and Nuclear Materials. The Environmental Management program continues to clean up the legacy of waste and contamination at sites used to produce nuclear weapons and conduct energy research. The Administration has determined that Yucca Mountain, Nevada, is not a workable option for a nuclear waste repository and will discontinue its program to construct a repository at the mountain in 2010. The Department will carry out its responsibilities under the Nuclear Waste Policy Act within the Office of Nuclear Energy as it develops a new nuclear waste management strategy.

Department of Energy
(In millions of dollars)

	Actual 2009	Estimate	
		2010	2011
Spending			
Discretionary Budget Authority:			
National Defense:			
National Nuclear Security Administration	9,121	9,877	11,215
Other Defense Activities	1,314	847	878
Energy Resources	4,131	4,292	5,065
Science	4,773	4,895	5,121
Environmental Management	5,992	6,008	6,000
Radioactive Waste Management	288	197	—
Corporate Management	207	220	212
Power Marketing Administration	234	99	95
Offsetting receipts	−23	−27	−230
Total, Discretionary budget authority	26,037	26,406	28,354
Memorandum:			
Budget authority from American Recovery and Reinvestment Act	*36,729*	*—*	*—*
Budget authority from supplementals	*7,867*	*—*	*—*
Total, Discretionary outlays	25,154	29,667	31,609
Memorandum: Outlays from American Recovery and Reinvestment Act	*954*	*10,703*	*14,646*
Mandatory Outlays:			
Existing law	−1,206	−752	−474
Legislative proposal, Ultradeep Water, Oil, and Gas Research and Development	—	—	30
Total, Mandatory outlays	−1,206	−752	−444
Memorandum: Outlays from American Recovery and Reinvestment Act	*33*	*109*	*131*
Total, Outlays	23,948	28,915	31,165

Department of Energy—Continued
(In millions of dollars)

	Actual 2009	Estimate	
		2010	2011
Credit activity			
Direct Loan Disbursements:			
Title 17 Innovative Technology Direct Loan Financing Account	21	7,284	18,114
Advanced Technology Vehicles Manufacturing Direct Loan Financing Account...	886	5,304	11,352
Total, Direct loan disbursements	907	12,588	29,466
Guaranteed Loan Commitments:			
Title 17 Innovative Technology Loan Guarantee Program [1]	—	3,054	9,016
Total, Guaranteed loan commitments	—	3,054	9,016

[1] Commitments reflect the full face value of debt obligations, any part of which is guaranteed, supported by Title 17. These figures represent loan guarantee obligations of the Government at closing, and do not include "conditional commitments," which are legally contingent on the satisfaction of various conditions precedent.

DEPARTMENT OF HEALTH AND HUMAN SERVICES

Funding Highlights:

- Supports health insurance reform by expanding patient-centered health research to give patients and physicians the best available information on what treatments will work the best for them; supporting investments in health information technology; expanding prevention and wellness activities; and launching payment reform demonstration programs in Medicare.

- Adds $290 million for health centers to expand health care access to the medically underserved.

- Expands support for biomedical research, by providing an increase of $1 billion for the National Institutes of Health.

- Invests approximately $1.4 billion to strengthen food safety efforts and implement core principles of the President's Food Safety Working Group.

- Supports over 8,500 health care professionals in medically underserved areas through the National Health Service Corps.

- Continues a commitment to invest in the Indian health system to eliminate health disparities by increasing access to health care services among American Indians and Alaska Natives.

- Invests in our Nation's prevention and wellness activities to improve health outcomes and lower costs, through the Federal workforce, community-based and State and local efforts.

- Invests more than $3 billion for HIV/AIDS prevention and treatment activities to expand access to affordable health care and prevention services.

- Includes $25.5 billion for a six-month extension of the American Recovery and Reinvestment Act (AARA) temporary increase in the Federal Medicaid match.

- Improves preparedness by increasing funding for biodefense medical countermeasure development.

- Places a renewed emphasis on preventing, detecting, and recouping fraudulent, wasteful, and abusive payments in Medicare, Medicaid, and the Children's Health Insurance Program.

- Expands and strengthens early education and child care programs by extending the ARRA expansion of Head Start and Early Head Start, providing an increase of $1.6 billion for child care to serve 235,000 more children than could be served without the additional funds in 2011, and supporting work with the Congress to improve quality in the Child Care and Development Fund.

- Increases help for families caring for aging relatives at home.

The Department of Health and Human Services (HHS) is the principal Federal agency charged with protecting the health of all Americans and providing essential human services. This Budget includes $81.3 billion to support HHS's mission.

Builds on Health Information Technology (IT) Adoption Momentum. The Administration continues to prioritize adoption and use of health IT. The Budget includes $110 million for continuing efforts to strengthen health IT policy, coordination, and research activities. Combined with the ARRA Federal grant and incentives programs designed to assist providers with adoption and meaningful use of electronic health records, these efforts will positively affect and improve the quality of health care while protecting privacy and security of personal health information.

Increases Investment in Patient-Centered Health Research. The Budget includes $286 million in the Agency for Healthcare Research and Quality for research that compares the effectiveness of different medical options, building on the expansion of this research begun under ARRA. The dissemination of this research is expected to lead to higher quality, evidence-based medicine, arming patients and physicians with the best available information to allow them to choose the medical option that will work the best for them.

Expands Affordable High-Quality Primary and Preventive Care. The Budget includes $2.5 billion for health centers to provide affordable high quality primary and preventive care to underserved populations, including the uninsured. This will allow health centers to continue to provide care to the 2 million additional patients they served under ARRA and support approximately 25 new health center sites. In 2008, health centers provided direct health care services to 17 million people. In 2011, the Health Center program will expand its partnerships with other Federal agencies as part of the Administration's place-based initiative to revitalize neighborhoods. The Budget also includes funding to expand the integration of behavioral health into existing primary health care systems, enhancing the availability and quality of addiction care.

Funds Innovative Efforts to Improve Services for Seniors and People with Disabilities. The Budget includes new Medicare and Medicaid demonstration projects that evaluate reforms to provide higher quality care at lower costs, improve beneficiary education and understanding of benefits offered, and better align provider payments with costs and outcomes. Special emphasis will be placed on demonstrations that improve care coordination for beneficiaries with chronic conditions, that better integrate Medicare and Medicaid benefits, and that provide higher value for dollars spent. The Budget will also support the Year of Community Living Initiative to promote collaboration between HHS and the Department of Housing and Urban Development to expand access to housing and community supports to enable people with disabilities to live in the community, as opposed to in institutional settings.

Supports Biomedical Research at the National Institutes of Health (NIH). To accelerate progress in biomedical research, NIH investments will focus on priority areas including genomics, translational research, science to support health care reform, global health, and reinvigorating the biomedical research community. The Budget includes $6,036 million to support a range of bold and innovative cancer efforts, including the initiation of 30 new drug trials in 2011, and a doubling of the number of novel compounds in Phase 1–3 clinical trials by 2016. In addition, the Budget will support the completion of a comprehensive catalog of cancer mutations for the 20 most common malignancies, setting the stage for complete genomic characterization of every cancer as part of medical care within 10 years.

Supports Americans with Autism Spectrum Disorders (ASD). The Budget includes $222 million across HHS to expand research, detection, treatment, and other activities related to improving the lives of individuals and families affected by ASD. NIH will pursue comprehensive and innovative approaches to defining the genetic and environmental factors that contribute to ASD, investigate epigenomic changes in the brain, and accelerate clinical trials of novel pharmacological and behavioral interventions by 2016.

Improves Access to and the Quality of Health Care in Rural Areas. The Budget includes $79 million for an initiative to strengthen regional and local partnerships among rural health care providers, increase the number of health care providers in rural areas, and improve the performance and financial stability of rural hospitals.

Increases Number of Primary Health Care Providers. The Budget invests $169 million in the National Health Service Corps (NHSC) to place providers in medically underserved areas to improve access to needed health care services. Under NHSC, primary health professionals such as physicians, nurse practitioners, and dentists agree to serve in a medically underserved community in exchange for receiving a portion of their student loans paid off. In 2011, the requested increase will add 400 NHSC clinicians to the more than 8,100 that will be providing essential primary and preventative care services in health care facilities across the country.

Continues Efforts to Increase Access to Health Care for American Indians and Alaska Natives (AI/ANs). The Budget includes $4.4 billion for the Indian Health Service (IHS) to expand investments initiated in 2010. Increases for IHS will strengthen existing Federal, tribal, and urban programs that serve 1.9 million AI/ANs at approximately 600 facilities nationwide, and will expand access to Contract Health Services to cover health care services provided outside of the Indian health system when services are not available at IHS-funded facilities. The Budget will also fund staff and operating costs at new and expanded facilities to increase access to health care services and enhance the Indian health system. The efforts supported in the Budget to expand health services in Indian communities also include an analysis of how IHS can improve distribution of resources throughout the Indian health system.

Expands and Strengthens Prevention and Wellness Activities. The Budget bolsters core prevention activities by expanding community health activities, strengthening the public health workforce, and enhancing surveillance and health statistics to improve detection and monitoring of chronic disease and health outcomes. The Budget funds a new effort in up to 10 of the largest cities in the United States to reduce the rates of morbidity and disability due to chronic disease through effective policy and environmental change strategies. The Budget also supports a new health prevention workforce to improve capacity of State and local health departments.

Invests in Wellness Initiatives for the Federal Workplace to Improve Health and Lower Costs. The Budget invests $10 million for the Federal employee workplace wellness initiative. This initiative will implement prototype wellness programs in select locations that will be rigorously evaluated for their ability to produce a healthier workforce and lower healthcare costs. By encouraging the adoption of these programs, we can improve the productivity of our workforce, delay or avoid many of the complications of chronic disease, and slow medical cost growth.

Expands and Focuses HIV/AIDS Treatment, Care, and Prevention Activities. The Budget expands access to HIV/AIDS prevention and treatment activities consistent with the President's pledge to develop a National HIV/AIDS Strategy that will focus on reducing HIV incidence, increasing access to care and optimizing health outcomes, and reducing HIV-related health disparities. The Budget focuses HIV testing among high-risk groups, including men who have sex with men, African Americans, and Hispanics. The Budget increases resources for the Ryan White program to support the care and treatment needs for persons living with HIV/AIDS who are unable to afford health care and related support services. The Budget directs resources to reduce HIV-related health disparities by expanding HIV/AIDS medical services within populations disproportionately impacted by the epidemic. The Budget also enhances funding for collaboration and integration activities to improve overall health outcomes for those with HIV/AIDS and co-infections with tuberculosis, hepatitis, and sexually transmitted diseases.

Expands Substance Abuse Prevention and Treatment Activities. The Budget expands substance abuse treatment services at IHS facilities and federally qualified health centers, and provides $23 million for comprehensive substance abuse prevention services targeting early risk factors that can improve health outcomes for children and young adults. To assist in recovery to reduce recidivism, the Budget provides $56 million to expand the treatment capacity at drug courts and $23 million for re-entry programs. These activities are a part of over $150 million in new funding for the Departments of Health and Human Services and Justice (DOJ) to reduce the Nation's demand for drugs by strengthening efforts to detect and prevent illicit drug use in our communities, expanding early drug abuse intervention in the primary health care system, enhancing specialty addiction treatment services, and breaking the cycle of illicit drug use, crime, and incarceration.

Bolsters the Safety of our Food and Medicines. The Budget provides $2.5 billion in budget authority and $4.0 billion in total program resources for the Food and Drug Administration (FDA). The Budget enables FDA to implement the core principles recommended by the President's Food Safety Working Group: prioritizing prevention; strengthening surveillance and enforcement; and improving response and recovery. The Budget also includes increases to bring more safe, effective, and lower cost generic drugs and generic biologics to market, expand postmarket safety surveillance of medical products, and support FDA's efforts to make such safety data more comprehensive and accessible to patients, providers, and scientists in a way that also protects privacy.

Strengthens the Nation's Preparedness Against Naturally Occurring Threats and Intentional Attacks. The Budget increases support to over $400 million to enhance the Advanced Development of next generation medical countermeasures against chemical, biological, radiological and nuclear threats. The Department has invested $5.6 billion since 2005 to enhance the Nation's ability to rapidly respond to an influenza pandemic. In April 2009, the President requested resources from the Congress to enable additional efforts to respond to the 2009 H1N1 virus that had recently emerged and in June, the Congress provided $7.65 billion in the Supplemental Appropriations Act 2009. By the end of 2009, more than $3.6 billion had been spent as the Federal Government procured H1N1 vaccines, mounted a mass vaccination campaign, provided resources to the States to enhance public health response efforts, and provided critical anti-viral medications and personal protective equipment. In 2010, HHS will continue to use these resources to build the U.S.-based influenza vaccine production capacity and shift to non-egg based production technologies and invest in the development of improved diagnostics. Approximately $330 million of these resources is expected to be spent in 2011. These ongoing activities to reduce the impact of influenza pandemics will be funded from resources in the 2009 Supplemental for pandemic influenza.

Fights Waste and Abuse in Medicare, Medicaid, and the Children's Health Insurance Program (CHIP). Reducing fraud, waste, and abuse is an important part of restraining spending growth and providing quality service delivery to beneficiaries. In November 2009, the President signed an Executive Order to reduce improper payments by boosting transparency, holding agencies accountable, and creating incentives for compliance. This Budget puts forward a robust set of proposals to strengthen Medicare, Medicaid and CHIP program integrity actions, including proposals aimed at preventing fraud and abuse before they occur, detecting it as early as possible when it does occur, and vigorously enforcing all penalties and recourses available when fraud is identified. It proposes $250 million in additional resources that, among other things, will help expand the Health Care Fraud Prevention and Enforcement Action Team (HEAT) initiative, a joint effort by HHS and DOJ. As a result, the Administration will be better able to minimize inappropriate payments, close loopholes, and provide greater value for program expenditures to beneficiaries and taxpayers. Also, to improve quality and safety, the Administration will strengthen its Medicare requirements to assure that air ambulance operators comply with aviation safety standards.

Supports Young Children and Their Families. The Budget provides critical support for young children and their families by building on historic increases provided in ARRA. The Budget provides an additional $989 million for Head Start and Early Head Start to continue to serve 64,000 additional children and families funded in ARRA. The Budget also provides an additional $1.6 billion for the Child Care and Development Fund in preparation for reauthorization to expand child care opportunities, and improve health, safety, and outcomes for children. This request will allow States to provide child care subsidies to 1.6 million children, 235,000 more than could be served without the increase.

Helps Families Care for Aging Relatives. The Budget includes $103 million for the Administration on Aging's Caregiver Initiative, an effort to expand help to families and seniors so that caregivers can better manage their multiple responsibilities and seniors can live in the commu-

nity for as long as possible. Without creating new programs, this initiative provides new resources to support the network of agencies in local communities across the country that already provide critical help to seniors and caregivers.

Provides Energy Assistance to Low-Income Families. The Budget includes $3.3 billion for the Low Income Home Energy Assistance Program to help low-income families with their home heating and cooling expenses. In addition, the Administration proposes a new trigger mechanism to provide automatic increases in energy assistance whenever there is a spike in energy costs or large numbers of families in poverty. The trigger allows the program to be more responsive to volatile energy markets and to increased demand for energy assistance during times of economic hardship. Using probabilistic scoring, we expect the trigger to provide roughly $2 billion in additional assistance in 2011 and $6.5 billion over 10 years.

Help States Provide Health Care Coverage to Low-Income Individuals. The Budget includes $25.5 billion to support State Medicaid programs by temporarily increasing Federal Medicaid funding for six months through June 2011. The Federal Medical Assistance Percentage (FMAP) increase has been an effective way to help States maintain their Medicaid programs during a period of high enrollment growth and reduced State revenue, and provide immediate and ongoing State fiscal relief.

Department of Health and Human Services
(In millions of dollars)

	Actual 2009	Estimate 2010	2011
Spending			
Discretionary Budget Authority:			
Food and Drug Administration [1]	2,061	2,362	2,508
Program Level (non-add)	*2,691*	*3,284*	*4,031*
Health Resources and Services Administration	7,243	7,484	7,512
Indian Health Service	3,581	4,053	4,406

Department of Health and Human Services—Continued
(In millions of dollars)

	Actual 2009	Estimate	
		2010	2011
Centers for Disease Control and Prevention	6,357	6,467	6,342
National Institutes of Health	30,096	31,089	32,089
Substance Abuse and Mental Health Services Administration	3,335	3,432	3,541
Agency for Healthcare Research and Quality	—	—	—
Program Level (non-add)	*372*	*397*	*611*
Centers for Medicare & Medicaid Services (CMS) [2]	3,522	3,415	3,601
Discretionary Health Care Fraud and Abuse Control	198	311	561
Administration for Children and Families	17,225	17,336	17,480
Administration on Aging	1,488	1,513	1,625
General Departmental Management	395	500	544
Office of Civil Rights	40	41	44
Office of the National Coordinator for Health Information Technology	44	42	78
Program Level (non-add)	*61*	*61*	*78*
Office of Medicare Hearings and Appeals	65	71	78
Public Health and Social Services Emergency Fund	1,399	1,347	735
Office of Inspector General	45	50	52
All other	58	61	61
Subtotal, Discretionary budget authority..	77,152	79,574	81,257
Unallocated Bioshield Balances Transferred from Department of Homeland Security [3]..	—	2,424	—
Total, Discretionary budget authority	77,152	81,998	81,257
Memorandum:			
Budget authority from American Recovery and Reinvestment Act	*22,397*	*—*	*—*
Budget authority from supplementals	*9,119*	*—*	*—*
Total, Discretionary outlays [2]	74,921	82,266	82,803
Memorandum: Outlays from American Recovery and Reinvestment Act	*682*	*8,437*	*10,100*
Mandatory Outlays:			
Medicare			
Existing law [4]	424,828	450,664	489,305
Legislative proposal	—	—	-722
Medicaid [5]			
Existing law	226,885	245,118	264,498
Legislative proposal	—	15	25,280
All other			
Existing law	34,503	34,872	35,915
Legislative proposal	—	—	3,774
Total, Mandatory outlays	686,216	730,669	818,050

Department of Health and Human Services—Continued
(In millions of dollars)

	Actual 2009	Estimate	
		2010	2011
Memorandum: Outlays from American Recovery and Reinvestment Act	*32,673*	*45,674*	*21,520*
Total, Outlays	761,137	812,935	900,853

[1] FDA 2009 budget authority increased by $6 million due to timing and availability of user fees.

[2] Amounts appropriated to the Social Security Administration (SSA) from the Hospital Insurance and Supplementary Medical Insurance accounts are included in the corresponding table in the SSA chapter.

[3] In 2010, $3,033 million from the Bioshield Special Reserve Fund (SRF) was transferred from the Department of Homeland Security to the Department of Health and Human Services. Of this amount, $609 million was redirected to support Advanced Development and NIH, and $2,424 million remains as balances in the SRF. In 2011, $476 million from the SRF will be used to support the Biomedical Advanced Research and Development Authority.

[4] Includes $44 million in 2009, $36 million in 2010, and $3 million in 2011 of CMS Program Management mandatory funding. Social Security Medicare Improvements for Patients and Providers Act (MIPPA) funding is included in the corresponding table of the SSA chapter.

[5] Totals include Medicaid, CHIP, and CHIP Child Enrollment Contingency Fund outlays.

DEPARTMENT OF HOMELAND SECURITY

Funding Highlights:

- Supports aviation security by deploying up to 1,000 Advanced Imaging Technology screening machines that can identify anomalies such as firearms and explosives on passengers, and by increasing the number of international flights on which Federal Air Marshals are present.

- Protects against threats to the homeland by procuring and deploying next-generation BioWatch sensors nationwide and supporting the Comprehensive National Cybersecurity Initiative.

- Strengthens border security and immigration enforcement by supporting 20,000 Border Patrol agents, adding 300 new officers at ports of entry, completing the first segment of the virtual border fence, and by enhancing and expanding immigration verification systems.

- Supports State homeland security activities through funding provided to States and localities to protect Americans from terrorist attacks and natural disasters. Specifically, provides $4 billion in State and local programs funding for risk-informed grants and additional assistance to our Nation's first responders as well as $1.95 billion for disaster assistance.

- Continues recapitalization of key Coast Guard assets, including $538 million to construct the fifth National Security Cutter and $240 million to construct four more Fast Response Cutters.

The Department of Homeland Security (DHS) is the principal Federal agency charged with such vital missions as aviation and border security, preparedness and emergency response, maritime safety and security, and protecting our Nation's leaders. The Budget includes $44 billion to support these missions.

Safeguards Our Nation's Transportation Systems. The Budget provides $734 million to support the deployment of up to 1,000 new Advanced Imaging Technology (AIT) screening machines at airport checkpoints and new explosive detection equipment for baggage screening in 2011. AIT machines allow security officers to detect both metallic and non-metallic anomalies,

such as weapons and explosives on persons entering an airport's sterile area. Additional funding is also included for the Federal Air Marshal Service (FAMS). This funding will allow the FAMS to increase the number of international flights covered by FAMS to defend against attempted attacks on aviation. The Budget provides $54 million for the continued modernization and streamlining of transportation security vetting and credentialing, which will reduce duplicative Transportation Security Administration processes and systems. This modernization will eliminate redundancies for those applying for multiple credentials as all vetting will be performed centrally, allowing for multiple credentials to be issued with a single vetting process.

Prevents Biological, Radiological, and Nuclear Attacks. The Budget funds activities to prevent attacks to our Nation. Procurement and nationwide deployment of next-generation BioWatch sensors is funded at $89 million. These sensors will detect bio-attacks at the earliest possible instant. As part of the ongoing effort to protect against radiological or nuclear threats, the Budget funds $61 million for radiation detection equipment to enhance the Department of Homeland Security's detection capabilities at sea ports, land border crossings, and airports.

Strengthens Border Security and Immigration Verification Programs. The Budget includes funding to support 20,000 Border Patrol agents and complete the first segment of Customs and Border Protection's (CBP's) virtual border fence. The Budget also includes funding for 300 new CBP officers for passenger and cargo screening at ports of entry, as well as expansion of pre-screening operations at foreign airports and land ports of entry. The Budget provides more than $1.6 billion for Immigration and Customs Enforcement programs to expeditiously identify and remove from the United States illegal aliens who commit crimes. Included in this total is continued support for the Secure Communities program.

To enhance and expand immigration related verification programs, the Budget provides $137 million to the U.S. Citizenship and Immigration Services. Through E-Verify, U.S. employers can maintain a legal workforce by verifying the employment eligibility of their workers, while Systematic Alien Verification for Entitlements (SAVE) assists Federal, State, and local benefit-granting agencies with determining eligibility for benefits by verifying immigration status. These programs promote compliance with immigration laws and prevent individuals from obtaining benefits for which they are not eligible.

Protects Critical Information Networks. Data networks are central to the functioning of our economy and Nation. The Budget provides $364 million to support the operations of the National Cyber Security Division, which protects Federal systems as well as continuing efforts under the Comprehensive National Cybersecurity Initiative to protect our information networks from the threat of attacks or disruptions.

Promotes Citizenship and Integration. The Budget increases support for integration of new immigrants with $18 million identified to promote citizenship through education and preparation programs, replication of promising practices in integration for use by communities across the Nation, and expansion of innovative English learning tools.

Invests Significantly in Upgrading the Coast Guard Fleet. The Budget funds $538 million to construct the fifth Coast Guard National Security Cutter and $240 million to produce four new Fast Response Cutters. Funding of $45 million enables Coast Guard to move ahead with selection of a design for the Offshore Patrol Cutter. These new assets replace an aging fleet of cutters and patrol boats and provide stronger command and control platforms for more effective and efficient execution of all Coast Guard missions.

Supports First Responders, National Preparedness, and Response Capabilities. The Budget funds $4 billion in State and local programs, including Firefighter Assistance Grants, for equipping, training, exercising, and hiring first responders. Of this amount, funding of $1.1 billion for the Urban Area Security Initiative will direct resources to the metropolitan vicinities with the highest threat—based on a risk management methodology. Funding of $600 million provides essential support to the transportation sector through the Transit and Port Security Grant Programs. The Budget also supports disaster response and resilience efforts by funding the Disaster Relief Fund (DRF) at $1.95 billion. The DRF is used in the instance of a presidentially-declared disaster or emergency by the Federal Emergency Management Agency to assist State and local governments in the response, recovery, and mitigation against emergency and disaster events.

Cuts Waste and Improves Performance by Integrating and Unifying the Department. The Budget funds a number of activities to im-

prove ongoing operations at DHS, including $288 million for the consolidation of DHS into one major complex in the National Capital Region. Funding is also provided to enhance the capability and capacity of the DHS acquisition workforce.

Department of Homeland Security
(In millions of dollars)

	Actual 2009	Estimate 2010	Estimate 2011
Spending			
Discretionary Budget Authority:			
Departmental Management and Operations	963	1,131	1,618
Office of the Inspector General	123	130	130
U.S. Citizenship and Immigration Services	149	224	382
United States Secret Service	1,412	1,483	1,572
Transportation Security Administration	4,741	5,126	5,724
Federal Law Enforcement Training Center	333	282	278
Immigration and Customs Enforcement	4,992	5,437	5,524
Customs and Border Protection	9,686	10,134	9,817
U.S. Coast Guard	8,112	8,595	8,466
National Protection and Programs Directorate	3,108	−1,584	1,460
Federal Emergency Management Agency	7,001	7,108	7,294
Science and Technology	933	1,000	1,018
Domestic Nuclear Detection Office	514	376	306
Total, Gross	44,591	41,732	45,922
Less fee-funded activities	2,526	2,290	2,333
Total, Discretionary budget authority (net)	42,065	39,442	43,589
Bioshield (non-add)	*1,763*	*−3,033*	*—*
Memorandum:			
Budget authority from American Recovery and Reinvestment Act	*2,755*	*—*	*—*
Budget authority from supplementals	*500*	*3,842*	*254*
Total, Discretionary outlays	48,967	51,404	53,248
Memorandum: Outlays from American Recovery and Reinvestment Act	*107*	*1,313*	*1,077*
Mandatory Outlays:			
U.S. Citizenship and Immigration Services	2,390	2,314	2,568
Federal Emergency Management Agency	2,116	−158	−9

Department of Homeland Security—Continued
(In millions of dollars)

	Actual 2009	Estimate	
		2010	2011
Customs and Border Protection			
Existing law	1,055	1,327	1,373
Legislative proposal	—	—	5
U.S. Coast Guard	1,512	1,500	1,604
Transportation Security Administration	290	369	407
All other	−4,694	−5,154	−5,538
Total, Mandatory outlays	2,669	198	410
Total, Outlays	51,636	51,602	53,658
Credit activity			
Direct Loan Disbursements:			
Disaster Assistance	89	160	160
Total, Direct loan disbursements	89	160	160

DEPARTMENT OF HOUSING AND URBAN DEVELOPMENT

Funding Highlights:

- Provides $4.4 billion for the Community Development Fund, including full funding of Community Development Block Grant formula funds and $150 million for Catalytic Investment Competition Grants to implement economic development activities in targeted distressed communities.

- Provides a $2.1 billion increase over the 2010 Budget for rental assistance to extremely low- and low-income families through Housing Choice Vouchers and Project-Based Rental Assistance. Rental assistance helps prevent homelessness and other hardships.

- Begins a new multi-year initiative to combine the Department's multiple rental assistance programs into a single funding stream and encourage entities that administer Housing Choice Vouchers to operate on a regional basis. This initiative will more effectively preserve the public housing stock, provide assisted families greater housing mobility, and streamline Department operations.

- Strengthens communities and regions through place-based initiatives. The 2011 Budget requests an additional $250 million for Choice Neighborhoods; and includes $150 million for the Department's role in developing and supporting the Sustainable Communities initiative in partnership with the Department of Transportation and the Environmental Protection Agency.

- Provides an unprecedented $2.1 billion for the Department's Homeless Assistance Grants Program to implement the Homeless Emergency Assistance Rapid Transition to Housing (HEARTH) Act; the budget for homeless programs reflects the Administration's commitment and goal to make visible, sustained progress toward ending homelessness.

- Reforms Federal Housing Administration (FHA) mortgage insurance, increases funding for FHA information technology and risk management, and provides additional funds for combating mortgage fraud.

The Department of Housing and Urban Development (HUD) is committed to fulfilling its mission of supporting home ownership, increasing access to affordable housing free from discrimination, and supporting innovative and sustainable community development. The President's Budget provides $48.5 billion in program funding to support HUD's core programs and new initiatives to achieve these important goals while protecting taxpayer dollars and reducing costs through stronger risk management and reform of inefficient programs. This funding will be offset by estimated collections of $6.9 billion from responsible credit premiums charged for HUD mortgage insurance and other credit enhancements.

Fully Funds the Community Development Block Grant Program. The Budget provides $4.4 billion for the Community Development Fund, including $3.99 billion for the Community Development Block Grant (CDBG) formula program, and $150 million for the creation of a Catalytic Investment Competition Grants program. The new Catalytic Competition Grants program uses the authorities of CDBG, but will provide capital to bring innovative economic development projects to scale to make a measurable impact. The competitive grants will fund applicants with targeted economic investments while leveraging other federal neighborhood revitalization programs, including mainstream CDBG funding. Unlike CDBG, consortia including high capacity non-governmental entities that have developed an innovative plan may apply, along with governmental entities, and the grants will target areas experiencing significant economic distress. The program will create a well-targeted funding stream that is responsive to changes in market conditions and that enhances the economic competitiveness of distressed communities.

Increases Funding for the Housing Choice Voucher Program. The President's Budget requests $19.6 billion for the Housing Choice Voucher program to help more than two million extremely low- to low-income families with rental assistance to live in decent housing in neighborhoods of their choice. The Budget continues funding for all existing mainstream vouchers and provides flexibility to support new vouchers leased in 2009 and 2010 and $85 million in special purpose vouchers for homeless families with children, families at risk of homelessness, and persons with disabilities. The Administration remains committed to working with the Congress to focus the goals and objectives of the program, as well as address the program's costly inefficiencies, and to fully utilize available funding by alleviating the administrative burdens on the Public Housing Authorities that implement HUD voucher and other programs, and establish a funding mechanism that is transparent and predictable in order to serve more needy families.

Preserves 1.3 Million Affordable Rental Units through Project-Based Rental Assistance Program. The President's Budget pro-

vides $9.4 billion for the Project-Based Rental Assistance program to preserve approximately 1.3 million affordable rental units through increased funding for contracts with private owners of multifamily properties. This critical investment will help extremely low- to low-income households to obtain or retain decent, safe and sanitary housing.

Launches the Conversion of Public Housing to Project-based Vouchers Through the Transforming Rental Assistance Initiative. The Administration requests $350 million to fund the first phase of this multi-year initiative to regionalize the Housing Choice Voucher program and convert Public Housing to project-based vouchers. The primary goals of this initiative are to improve the physical condition and management of the public housing stock, increase the mobility of assisted families, and streamline HUD oversight of its rental assistance programs.

Combats Mortgage Fraud. The Budget provides $20 million for HUD to combat mortgage fraud and predatory lending practices. These resources will allow HUD to increase enforcement of mortgage and home purchase settlement requirements.

Provides Funding for Choice Neighborhoods. By providing $250 million in 2011, the Budget continues HUD's effort to make a range of transformative investments in high-poverty neighborhoods where public and assisted housing is concentrated. A central element of the Administration's place-based agenda, this initiative will invest in public, private and nonprofit partners that have transformative neighborhood interventions and provide the greatest returns on Federal investment.

Implements the Homeless Emergency Assistance Rapid Transition to Housing (HEARTH) Act. The President's Budget provides $2.1 billion for HUD's Homeless Assistance Programs to effectively implement the HEARTH Act. Enacted in May 2009 to fundamentally transform the Federal response to homelessness, HEARTH streamlined three current homeless programs into one, placed greater emphasis on homelessness prevention, and provided increased funds for renewal costs and permanent housing beds. The Budget will support the key priorities reflected in HEARTH, including $200 million for Emergency Solutions Grant, funding for about 10,000 new permanent housing beds, and a competitive rural program. HUD is also working in partnership with the Department of Veteran Affairs to substantially lower the number of homeless veterans.

Helps Communities Become More Sustainable and Livable. As part of the President's Partnership for Sustainable Communities, the Budget includes $150 million to help stimulate comprehensive regional and community planning efforts that integrate transportation and housing investments that result in more regional and local sustainable development patterns, reduce greenhouse gases, and increase more transit accessible housing choices for residents. HUD's Sustainable Communities Initiative also expands and better coordinates Federal efforts to create incentives for State and local governments to plan for and implement pre-disaster mitigation strategies. Coordinating hazard mitigation efforts with related sustainability goals and activities will reduce risks while protecting life, property, and the environment. Combined with the Department of Transportation's funding for strengthening the capacity of States and local governments to make smarter infrastructure investments and the Environmental Protection Agency's technical assistance, this interagency Partnership, which is one of the pillars of the Administration's place-based agenda, aims to lower the cost of living while improving the quality of life in local communities. It will do so by providing more coordinated housing and transportation options, improving environmental quality, and better leveraging Federal investments.

Enhances FHA's Risk Management and Housing Counseling. The Budget provides an additional $18 million for FHA to enhance its monitoring and management of its insurance portfolio's financial risk. In addition, the Budget includes programmatic changes to single-family mortgages insured by FHA. These changes, which include raising the minimum credit score for high-risk borrowers and restructuring of insurance premiums, will reduce risk and replenish FHA's capital reserves while allowing it to meet its mission of providing sound access to home financing for underserved populations. In addition, the Budget proposes $338 million for housing counseling, including a greater than 7 percent increase for the Neighborhood Reinvestment Corporation (NeighborWorks), which will fund vital foreclosure counseling services in communities across the Nation.

Expands Funding for High-Priority Research and Program Evaluations. The Budget provides increased funding for housing research, fully funds the American Housing Survey, and funds three new impact evaluations as part of the Government-wide evaluation initiative—a Family Self-Sufficiency Demonstration, Rent Reform Demonstration, and Choice Neighborhoods Demonstration. This increased investment in research will allow HUD to determine whether programs are achieving their intended outcomes and provide new evidence on how to efficiently and effectively provide rental assistance. The Budget also includes $25 million to support research and development (R&D) tied to the President's national goals of energy, health and sustainability. Partnering with other agencies, HUD will invest in R&D focused on the linkages between the built environment and health, hazard risk reduction and resilience, and the development of innovative building technologies and building processes.

Department of Housing and Urban Development
(In millions of dollars)

	Actual 2009	Estimate 2010	Estimate 2011
Spending			
Discretionary Budget Authority:			
Community Development Fund	3,900	4,450	4,380
Catalytic Investment Grants (non-add)	—	—	*150*
Sustainable Communities (non-add)	—	*150*	*150*
HOME Investment Partnerships Program	1,825	1,825	1,650
Homeless Assistance Grants	1,677	1,865	2,055
Housing Opportunities for Persons with AIDS	310	335	340
Tenant-based Rental Assistance	16,225	18,184	19,551
Project-based Rental Assistance	7,100	8,558	9,376
Public Housing Operating Fund	4,455	4,775	4,829
Public Housing Capital Fund	2,450	2,500	2,044
Transforming Rental Assistance	—	—	350
Choice Neighborhoods/HOPE VI	120	200	250
Native American Housing Block Grant	645	700	580
Housing for the Elderly	765	825	274
Housing for Persons with Disabilities	250	300	90
Federal Housing Administration (FHA)			
Existing Law	–874	–2,215	–1,628
Legislative proposal			–4,099
Government National Mortgage Association (GNMA)	–888	–914	–679
Salaries and Expenses	1,303	1,346	1,379
Policy Development and Research	58	48	87
All other	722	799	761
Total, Discretionary budget authority	40,043	43,581	41,590
Memorandum:			
Budget authority from American Recovery and Reinvestment Act	*13,626*	—	—
Budget authority from supplementals	*30*	—	—
Total, Discretionary outlays	44,240	46,208	46,127
Memorandum: Outlays from American Recovery and Reinvestment Act	*1,520*	*3,628*	*5,545*
Mandatory Outlays:			
FHA	15,938	12,228	1,016
Community Planning and Development	119	1,263	1,128
Housing Trust Fund (non-add)	—	—	*20*
All other	–798	–807	–732
Total, Mandatory outlays	15,259	12,684	1,412
Total, Outlays	59,499	58,892	47,539

Department of Housing and Urban Development—Continued
(In millions of dollars)

	Actual 2009	Estimate	
		2010	2011
Credit activity			
Direct Loan Disbursements:			
FHA	—	50	50
GNMA	10	27	25
Green Retrofit Program for Multifamily Housing	—	143	—
Total, Direct loan disbursements	10	220	75
Guaranteed Loan Commitments:			
FHA	355,723	340,080	265,705
GNMA	418,938	380,942	283,042
All other	608	1,126	1,220
Total, Guaranteed loan commitments	775,269	722,148	549,967

DEPARTMENT OF THE INTERIOR

Funding Highlights:

- Promotes renewable energy development on Federal lands and waters with the goal of permitting at least 9,000 megawatts of energy capacity on Department of the Interior lands by the end of 2011.

- Stays on track to fully fund Land and Water Conservation Fund programs by 2014 by providing nearly $620 million to acquire new lands for national parks, forests and refuges, protect endangered species habitat, and promote outdoor recreation.

- Helps Federal land managers address the impact of climate change by expanding the Department's science capability to develop vital decision support tools.

- Improves the return to taxpayers from U.S. mineral production through royalty reforms and industry fees.

- Strengthens Native American communities with funds to enhance the management capacity of tribal governments and improve coordination between Federal agencies on law enforcement.

- Prepares responsibly for wildfires with full funding for suppression and a contingency reserve fund.

- Promotes water conservation and science while balancing competing water resource needs.

The Department of the Interior (DOI) is committed to fulfilling its mission to protect and manage the Nation's natural resources and cultural heritage; provide scientific and other information about those resources; and honor its trust responsibilities or special commitments to American Indians, Alaska Natives, and affiliated Island Communities. The President's 2011 Budget provides $12 billion to DOI to achieve these goals, while reforming inefficient programs and generating mandatory savings of about $2.7 billion over 10 years.

Invests in a Clean Energy Future. DOI plays a key role in supporting the President's plan to create a clean energy future that holds the promise of an improved environment, enhanced energy security, and green jobs in new industries. DOI already manages public lands and offshore resources that provide about one-third of the domestic supply of fossil fuel resources. The Department is now expanding on that role to become a leader in promoting clean, renewable energy on Federal lands. The 2011 Budget adds $14 million—on top of $50 million in 2010 increases—to build agency capacity to review and permit renewable energy projects on Federal lands. This includes conducting the environmental evaluations and technical studies needed to spur development of renewable energy projects, assess available alternative resources, and mitigate the impacts of development. DOI has set a goal to permit at least 9,000 megawatts of new solar, wind, and geothermal electricity generation capacity on DOI-managed lands by the end of 2011.

Conserves Landscapes and Ecosystems. The Administration continues its commitment to acquire and conserve landscapes and ecosystems that lack adequate protection with increased funding from the Land and Water Conservation Fund (LWCF). The Budget provides an increase of $106 million, or 31 percent, for LWCF programs in DOI that protect Federal lands for wildlife and public enjoyment and provide State grants for park and recreational improvements. Total LWCF funding for the Departments of Agriculture and the Interior is nearly $620 million, keeping the Administration on track to fully fund LWCF programs at $900 million by 2014. In addition, the Budget proposes to reauthorize and expand DOI's authority under the Federal Land Transaction Facilitation Act, so that the proceeds from the sale of low-conservation value lands may be used to acquire additional high-priority conservation lands.

Establishes Climate Science Centers. Managing ecosystems and wildlife habitat that are facing the impact of climate change requires reliable data on changes, supporting science, and tools to bring these together to inform land management decisions. DOI is establishing a framework, which includes Climate Science Centers that will focus on the impact of climate change on a broad array of Departmental resources. The Budget includes an increase of $14 million for these Centers to provide land managers with vital decision support tools based on the latest science.

Provides a Better Return to Taxpayers from Mineral Development. The public received about $10 billion in 2009 from fees, royalties, and other Federal payments related to oil,

gas, coal, and other mineral development. Yet a number of recent studies by the Government Accountability Office and DOI's Inspector General have found that this return could be improved through more rigorous oversight and policy changes, such as charging appropriate fees and reforming how royalties are set. The Budget proposes a number of actions to ensure that Federal taxpayers receive a fair return from the development of U.S. mineral resources:

- Terminating payments to coal-producing States and Tribes that no longer need funds to clean up abandoned coal mines.

- Extending the practice of having States with mineral revenue payments help to defray the Federal costs in managing the mineral leases that generate the revenue.

- Charging user fees to oil companies for processing oil and gas drilling permits and inspecting operations on Federal lands and waters.

- Establishing fees for new non-producing oil and gas leases (both onshore and offshore) to encourage more timely production.

- Making administrative changes to Federal oil and gas royalties, such as adjusting royalty rates and terminating the royalty-in-kind program.

Empowers Tribal Nations. The Administration supports tribal self-determination and will assist tribal governments in enhancing their management capacity. The Budget provides increased funding to better compensate Tribes for the work they perform in managing Federal programs under self-determination contracts and self-governance compacts. In addition, the Budget includes proposals to foster better coordination between the Departments of the Interior and Justice on Indian law enforcement issues.

Prepares Responsibly for Wildfires. The Budget continues the long-standing practice of fully funding the 10-year average cost of wildland fire suppression operations. To reduce the need for emergency appropriations, the Budget for DOI includes an additional $75 million funding reserve to be used only as a contingency when regular suppression funding is exhausted. The Budget also targets hazardous fuels reduction funding for activities in the wildland-urban interface where they are most effective. Priority is given to projects in communities that have met "Firewise" standards, identified acres to be treated, and invested in local solutions to protect against wildland fire.

Invests in Water Resources Infrastructure and Science. The Budget continues to focus resources on the Department's Water Conservation initiative, which assists local communities in increasing water availability by encouraging voluntary water banks, reuse of treated wastewater, and other market-based conservation measures. The initiative also includes the Bureau of Reclamation's water reuse and recycling (Title XVI) program and invests an additional $9 million in a multi-year, nationwide study of water availability and use by the U.S. Geological Survey. Moreover, in coordination with other Federal agencies and the State of California, the Department is also participating in activities and dedicating resources to foster continued progress in the restoration of a number of sensitive ecosystems, including the California Bay-Delta. The Department will work with Federal interagency working groups to develop performance measures and tools to identify those restoration activities that yield the highest returns to taxpayers.

Department of the Interior
(In millions of dollars)

	Actual 2009	Estimate 2010	Estimate 2011
Spending			
Discretionary Budget Authority:			
Bureau of Land Management	1,062	1,143	1,151
Minerals Management Service	163	181	190
Office of Surface Mining	164	163	146
Bureau of Reclamation/CUPCA	1,124	1,129	1,108
U.S. Geological Survey	1,044	1,112	1,133
Fish and Wildlife Service	1,443	1,647	1,642
National Park Service	2,558	2,791	2,759
Bureau of Indian Affairs	2,379	2,619	2,566
Office of the Special Trustee	182	186	160
All other	1,133	1,183	1,250
Wildland Fire (non-add)	*859*	*856*	*934*
Subtotal, Gross discretionary budget authority	11,252	12,154	12,105
Mandatory Savings Proposals	—	—	−70
Total, Discretionary budget authority	11,252	12,154	12,035
Memorandum:			
Budget authority from American Recovery and Reinvestment Act	*3,005*	*—*	*—*
Budget authority from supplementals	*50*	*—*	*—*
Total, Discretionary outlays	11,298	12,387	12,439

Department of the Interior—Continued
(In millions of dollars)

	Actual 2009	Estimate	
		2010	2011
Memorandum: Outlays from American Recovery and Reinvestment Act	*168*	*1,255*	*1,128*
Mandatory Outlays:			
Cobell Settlement			
Legislative proposal, Payments from the Judgment Fund	—	−2,000	—
Legislative proposal, Payments for Trust Land Purchasing	—	100	400
All other			
Existing law	485	420	334
Legislative proposals	—	—	−96
Total, Mandatory outlays	485	−1,480	638
Total, Outlays	11,783	10,907	13,077

Credit activity

Guaranteed Loan Commitments:			
Indian Guaranteed Loan Program	78	134	132
Total, Guaranteed loan commitments	78	134	132

DEPARTMENT OF JUSTICE

Funding Highlights:

- Continues to strengthen and expand local law enforcement agencies by providing $600 million as part of the President's multi-year commitment to fund the hiring of 50,000 additional police officers nationwide.

- Steps up the effort to combat financial fraud and protect public investments in our Nation's financial stability.

- Expands targeted, place-based efforts to combat violent crime.

- Strengthens efforts to combat violence against women by providing $538 million, an increase of 29 percent.

- Reinvigorates Federal Civil Rights Enforcement.

- Promotes public safety and economic opportunity by providing re-entry programming for prisoners who need support to successfully reintegrate into their communities.

- Strengthens the Department's capacity to target violent criminal activity and makes sure the Nation's borders are secure.

- Addresses the national security and intelligence challenges confronting the FBI and other Department of Justice components.

- Increases efforts to target and combat violent drug trafficking cartels and organized criminal enterprise operations.

- Expands law enforcement, prosecutorial and grant assistance, and improves their coordination in Indian Country.

The President's Budget for the Department of Justice (DOJ) is $29.2 billion. The Budget addresses key priorities in national security and crime-fighting programs in the FBI and other DOJ components; addresses needs in Indian Country, and combats financial fraud. The Budget also puts more police officers on the beat by funding the Community Oriented Policing Services (COPS) hiring program; provides other vital support for innovative State and local law enforcement efforts; and secures the Nation's borders.

Increases Funding to Support the Hiring of Additional Police Officers Across the Country. The Budget includes $600 million, an increase of $302 million, to support the hiring or retention of police officers in communities across the country. Supporting the hiring of police officers will help States and communities prevent the growth of crime in our communities.

Combats Financial Fraud. To combat financial and other sophisticated crime problems, DOJ has developed a strategy of using intelligence-based and prosecutor-led task forces to leverage the resources and expertise of the complete law enforcement spectrum. For example, the Department has established an interagency task force to combat financial crime. The Attorney General and the Secretary of the Department of Health and Human Services have also established a Health Care Fraud Prevention and Enforcement Teams (HEAT) task force initiative to combat medical fraud. The task forces establish and coordinate investigative and enforcement priorities across multiple agencies. The Budget supports these efforts by providing resources for additional FBI agents and DOJ attorneys to investigate and prosecute major white collar crime, as well as mortgage and healthcare fraud cases.

Expands Targeted, Place-Based Efforts to Curb Violent Crime. The Budget provides $112 million for place-based, evidence-supported, initiatives to combat violence in local communities, including $25 million for the Community-Based Violence Prevention Initiatives that aim to reduce gun and other violence among youth gangs in cities and towns across the country, and $37 million for the Attorney General's Children Exposed to Violence Initiative, which targets the youth most affected by violence and most susceptible to propagating it as they grow up. A new initiative, the Byrne Criminal Justice Innovation Program, for which the Budget requests $40 million, is a central component of the Administration's interagency initiative on Neighborhood Revitalization.

Strengthens Efforts to Combat Violence Against Women. The Budget includes $538 million, an increase of $120 million, to support women victims of violence, including domestic abuse and sexual assault victims. The numbers are staggering: last year, over a half million non-fatal violent victimizations were committed against women by an intimate partner. In 2007, 64 per-

cent of female homicide victims were murdered by a family member or intimate partner. Many other women were harmed by people they did not know.

Reinvigorates Federal Civil Rights Enforcement. To strengthen civil rights enforcement against racial, ethnic, sexual orientation, religious, and gender discrimination, the Budget includes an 11 percent increase in funding for DOJ's Civil Rights Division. This investment will help the Division handle implementation of a historic new hate crimes law.

Combats Drug-trafficking and Organized Criminal Enterprises. The Budget includes an increase of $37 million for a comprehensive approach to combating drugs and crime through enhancing the Organized Crime Drug Enforcement Task Forces (OCDETF) and provides an additional $54 million to expand the Drug Enforcement Administration's El Paso Intelligence Center (EPIC). The OCDETF task forces utilize the full capabilities of DOJ, including both agents and attorneys, to target major drug-trafficking and criminal organizations. EPIC enables Federal, State and local law enforcement partners to share real-time intelligence and unique capabilities of participating members to target, disrupt, and dismantle major drug trafficking cartels and criminal enterprise operations. The initiative also enhances the Department's ability to combat gunrunners along the U.S. Southwest Border. Additionally, the Budget includes additional funding for enforcement along the Nation's borders, combining the efforts of law enforcement and prosecutorial units to investigate arrest, detain, and prosecute criminal illegal aliens, as well as those who enter or stay in the country without proper documentation.

Counters the Threat of Terrorism and Strengthens National Security. The Budget includes $145 million in enhancements for the FBI's national security programs, and $100 million, including $8 million in program enhancements, for the National Security Division to protect the American people from terrorist acts. Funding supports counterterrorism, counter-intelligence, cyber-security and other threats against our National Security. The Budget also provides $73 million for the transfer, prosecution, and incarceration of Guantanamo Bay detainees. The Administration further anticipates working with the Congress to identify additional funding and other resources that may be needed in 2010 to address extraordinary Federal, State, and local security requirements associated with terrorism trials that may begin in 2010 and continue into 2011.

Supports Detention and Incarceration Programs and Expands Prisoner Re-entry Programs. The Budget provides $6.8 billion for the Bureau of Prisons to activate new prisons and increase correctional staff, and $1.5 billion for the Office of the Detention Trustee so that sentenced criminals and detainees are housed in facilities that are safe, humane, cost-efficient, and appropriately secure. The Budget also provides $330 million for the State Criminal Alien Assistance Program to assist States and localities in the identification, status determination and conduct of removal proceedings of incarcerated illegal aliens. The Budget also provides $144 million for prisoner re-entry programs, including $100 million for the Office of Justice Programs to administer grant programs authorized by the Second Chance Act and $30 million for residential substance abuse treatment programs in State and local prisons and jails. These programs reduce recidivism by providing counseling, job training, drug treatment, and other transitional assistance so that former prisoners can reintegrate into the job market and community life.

Enhances Capacity to Address Needs in Indian Country. The Budget includes $19 million to support 45 additional FBI agents for Indian country, and $256 million in grants and technical assistance to increase public safety efforts in tribal areas. The funding for additional FBI agents will be provided on a reimbursable basis through the Department of the Interior. The Departments of Justice and the Interior will coordinate the deployment of Federal public safety resources to best address the public safety needs in Indian Country.

Department of Justice
(In millions of dollars)

	Actual 2009	Estimate 2010	Estimate 2011
Spending			
Discretionary Budget Authority:			
Federal Bureau of Investigation	7,340	7,736	8,165
Drug Enforcement Administration	2,045	2,028	2,130
Federal Prison System	6,172	6,188	6,804
United States Marshals Service	956	1,145	1,207
Bureau of Alcohol, Tobacco, Firearms, and Explosives	1,054	1,119	1,163
Detention Trustee	1,289	1,439	1,534
United States Attorneys	1,837	1,934	2,041
General Legal Activities	806	875	976
National Security Division	84	88	100
Office of Justice Programs, Office of Community Oriented Policing Services, Office on Violence Against Women	2,915	3,540	3,364

Department of Justice—Continued
(In millions of dollars)

	Actual 2009	Estimate	
		2010	2011
Organized Crime and Drug Enforcement Task Force	515	528	579
All other	940	925	1,127
Subtotal, Discretionary budget authority	25,953	27,545	29,190
Less Crime Victims' Fund cancellation	—	—	-4,552
Less Assets Forfeiture Fund cancellation	—	—	-495
Total, Discretionary budget authority	25,953	27,545	24,143
Memorandum:			
Budget authority from American Recovery and Reinvestment Act	*4,012*	*—*	*—*
Budget authority from supplementals	*245*	*—*	*—*
FBI Overseas Contingency Operations	*—*	*101*	*—*
Total, Discretionary outlays	24,509	26,709	26,075
Memorandum: Outlays from American Recovery and Reinvestment Act	*1,160*	*1,843*	*664*
Mandatory Outlays:			
Existing law	2,060	1,868	5,232
Legislative proposal	—	—	—
Total, Mandatory outlays	2,060	1,868	5,232
Memorandum: Outlays from American Recovery and Reinvestment Act	*—*	*—*	*—*
Total, Outlays	26,569	28,577	31,307

DEPARTMENT OF LABOR

Funding Highlights:

- Supports reform of the Workforce Investment Act (WIA), which authorizes $10 billion for job training and employment services.

- Creates a Workforce Innovation Partnership with the Department of Education and establishes two innovation funds that will support and test promising approaches to job training as well as encourage States and localities to work across programmatic silos to improve services.

- Starts a joint Labor-Treasury initiative to stop the inappropriate misclassification of employees as independent contractors.

- Rebuilds worker protection programs to strengthen enforcement of labor standards.

- Expands families' access to paid leave by creating a new fund to help States launch paid leave programs.

- Boosts funding for unemployment insurance integrity efforts and proposes legislative changes that would reduce improper payments by over $4 billion and employer tax evasion by $300 million over 10 years.

- Initiates a multi-agency legislative proposal to establishes automatic workplace pensions and expand access to the saver's credit, and proposes regulatory reforms to give all workers access to retirement savings opportunities, provide Americans with incentives to save throughout their working careers, and protect pension plans.

The President's Budget provides $14 billion for the Department of Labor (DOL) to prepare workers for good jobs that will allow them to support their families; guarantee fair, safe and healthy workplaces and secure retirements for America's workers; and fulfill its other core responsibilities.

Reforming the Job Training System. Whether they want to find a job, build basic or occupational skills, earn a postsecondary certificate, credential, or degree, or get guidance on charting a career path, all Americans deserve ac-

cess to high-quality job training throughout their careers. That is why the Budget calls for reform of the Workforce Investment Act (WIA), which supports almost 3,000 One-Stop Career Centers nationwide and a range of other services. With $6 billion for WIA at DOL—and an additional $4 billion in the Department of Education—the Budget calls for reforms to improve WIA by:

- **Creating a Workforce Innovation Partnership to Streamline Service Delivery and Invest in What Works.** Over 30 Federal programs provide job training and related services. Yet today, workers and young people looking for effective training must navigate a maze of programs with little information about how well these programs work. Leveraging funding from the WIA formula programs, the 2011 Budget sets aside $261 million to establish two innovation funds that will support and test promising approaches to training, breaking down program silos, building evidence about effective practices, and investing in what works. With a $101 million increase in the Youth funding stream, the Budget redirects 15 percent of total Youth funding to a Youth Innovation Fund to pilot innovative models for delivering summer and year-round work experiences and comprehensive services to disconnected youth. The Workforce Innovation Fund pulls 5 percent from the Adult and Dislocated Worker streams to support and test "learn and earn" strategies like apprenticeships and on-the-job training; promote regional and sectoral collaborations; and support other innovations. In addition, DOL will work closely with the Department of Education to administer the innovation grants, and use them as a mechanism for encouraging States and localities to work across programs to improve service delivery and participant outcomes.

- **Meeting the Needs of Regional Economies and Employers.** Labor markets are typically regional, yet the workforce system is designed around State and local boundaries. The system also does not do a good enough job matching training with employer demand. Through new innovation funds and WIA reauthorization, the Administration will facilitate regional collaboration and close linkages with employers so that training leads to good jobs.

- **Establishing a Transparent Accountability System that Encourages Success.** The current accountability system dissuades States and localities from serving the populations that most need their assistance, like low-skilled adults, individuals with disabilities, and others needing more specialized and intensive services. The Budget supports efforts to overhaul performance measures and incentives to discourage "cream-skimming," more accurately capture the value added by different services, and encourage better outcomes for individuals at every level of the workforce system. Performance data should be widely available to policymakers, program managers, and the participants themselves, so they can make informed choices about training.

- **Focusing on High-Growth Sectors and Workers Often Left Behind.** The Budget makes strategic investments in competitive programs to target high-growth sectors and serve populations often left behind, including $85 million for green job training and $40 million for transitional jobs programs. The Budget also supports an initiative to reform and improve Job Corps, by setting high standards for Job Corps centers and taking quick and decisive action to address problems.

Protecting Benefits for Employees by Ensuring Proper Classification. When employees are misclassified as independent contractors, they are deprived of benefits and protections to which they are legally entitled. For example, independent contractors do not receive overtime and are ineligible to receive unemployment benefits. Misclassification also has a budgetary impact, reducing receipts in Treasury and the Social Security, Medicare and Unemployment Insurance Trust Funds. As part of the 2011 Budget, the Departments of Labor and Treasury are pursuing a joint proposal that eliminates incentives in law for employers to misclassify their employees; enhances the ability of both agencies to penalize employers who misclassify; and restores protections to employees who have been denied them because of their improper classification. This proposal would increase Treasury receipts by more than $7 billion over 10 years. The 2011 Budget for DOL includes an additional $25 million to target misclassification with 100 additional enforcement personnel and competitive grants to boost States' incentives and capacity to address this problem.

Rebuilding Worker Protection Programs. The Budget includes a $67 million (4 percent) increase for the Department's worker protection agencies to ensure they have the resources to meet their responsibilities to protect the health, safety, wages and working conditions, and retirement security of the nation's workforce. The 2011 Budget builds on the 2010 Budget policy of returning worker protection programs to the 2001 staffing levels, after years of decline. In addition, the Budget provides additional resources for the regulatory and enforcement activities of these agencies.

Helping States Provide Paid Family Leave to Workers. Too many families must make the painful choice between the care of their families and a paycheck they desperately need. The Family and Medical Leave Act allows workers to take job-protected time off unpaid, but millions of families cannot afford to use unpaid leave. A handful of States have enacted policies to offer paid family leave, but more States should have the chance. The Budget establishes a $50 million State Paid Leave Fund within DOL that will provide competitive grants to help States that choose to launch paid-leave programs cover their start-up costs. The Budget also provides resources to allow DOL to explore ways to improve the collection of data related to intersection of work and family responsibilities.

Strengthening Access to, and Accuracy of, Unemployment Benefits. Working with the Congress, the Administration has already extended and expanded unemployment insurance (UI) benefits to historic levels and offered powerful incentives for States to make permanent changes to modernize their UI programs. In response to these incentives, 26 States have changed their laws so that up to 20 weeks of additional benefits are available to workers who have exhausted their regular and Emergency Unemployment Compensation benefits; and 32 States now offer benefits to recent entrants to the workforce who lose their jobs. States have also granted benefits to part-time workers, those who must leave their jobs because of domestic violence or other compel-

ling family reasons, and those seeking to retool for another career.

At the same time, the Administration believes UI benefits should go to the right workers in the right amounts. When States have to finance high levels of UI improper payments, employers face higher taxes and workers may see cuts in their benefit levels. Despite the efforts of States to reduce improper payments, over $11.4 billion in UI benefits were erroneously paid in 2009— an overpayment rate of almost 10 percent. The Administration will tackle this problem by boosting funding for UI integrity efforts and proposing legislative changes that together would reduce improper payments by over $4 billion and employer tax evasion by $300 million over 10 years.

Improving Retirement Security. After a lifetime of employment, American workers deserve to know that their efforts have resulted in a secure retirement. The Administration is committed to giving Americans more and better choices to save for retirement while also strengthening the existing private pension system. The Budget proposes a multi-agency effort to expand and improve employment-based retirement security by:

- **Establishing Automatic Workplace Pensions.** Currently, 78 million working Americans—roughly half the workforce— lack employer-based retirement plans. The 2011 Budget proposes a system of automatic workplace pensions that will expand access to tens of millions of workers who currently lack pensions. Under the proposal, employers who do not currently offer a retirement plan will be required to enroll their employees in a direct-deposit IRA account that is compatible with existing direct-deposit payroll systems. Employees may opt-out if they choose. The smallest firms would be exempt.

- **Doubling the Small Employer Pension Plan Startup Credit.** Under current law, small employers are eligible for a tax credit equal to 50 percent (up to a maximum of $500 a year for three years) of the start-up expenses of establishing or administering a new retirement plan. To encourage small employers to offer pensions to their workers in connection with the automatic IRA proposal, the Budget will increase the maximum credit from $500 a year to $1,000 per year.

- **Reforming and Expanding the Saver's Credit.** The Budget proposes to expand retirement savings incentives for working families by modifying the existing Saver's Credit to provide a 50 percent match on the retirement savings of families that earn less than $85,000 (up to $1,000 of savings would be matched). The credit would be fully refundable to create savings incentives fair to all workers. Studies indicate that automatic enrollment combined with a savings match significantly increases the savings participation rate for low and middle income workers. This proposal is expected to increase significantly both the number of Americans who save for retirement and the overall amount of amount of retirement wealth they accumulate.

- **Improving the Defined-Contribution Savings System.** A majority of American workers rely on 401(k)-style plans to finance their retirements. The Budget proposes a number of initiatives to improve the transparency and adequacy of 401(k) retirement savings. Specifically, DOL will undertake regulatory efforts to reduce barriers to annuitization of 401(k) plan assets; increase the transparency of pension fees; improve transparency of target date and other default retirement investments; and reduce conflicts of interest between pension advisers and fiduciaries.

- **Expanding Opportunities for Automatic Enrollment in 401(K) and Other Retirement Savings Plans.** Automatic enrollment typically boosts participation in 401(k) retirement plans from about 70 percent to more than 90 percent, and it is particularly effective in increasing the participation of low-income and minority workers. But while nearly half of larger companies with 401(k) plans have adopted automatic enrollment, fewer medium-sized or small businesses have done so. The Administration will streamline the process for 401(k) plans to adopt automatic enrollment; make it easier to increase saving over time; and allow automatic enrollment in SIMPLE-IRAs.

Department of Labor
(In millions of dollars)

	Actual 2009	Estimate	
		2010	2011
Spending			
Discretionary Budget Authority:			
Training and Employment Service	3,626	3,829	3,925
Unemployment Insurance Administration	3,511	3,990	3,581
Employment Service/One-Stop Career Centers	793	788	788
Office of Job Corps	1,684	1,708	1,707
Community Service Employment for Older Americans	572	825	600
Bureau of Labor Statistics	597	611	645
Occupational Safety and Health Administration	513	559	573
Mine Safety and Health Administration	347	357	361
Wage and Hour Division [1]	193	224	244
Office of Federal Contract Compliance Programs	82	103	113

Department of Labor—Continued
(In millions of dollars)

	Actual 2009	Estimate	
		2010	2011
Office of Labor-Management Standards	45	41	45
Office of Workers' Compensation Programs	103	108	127
Employee Benefits Security Administration	143	155	162
Veterans Employment and Training	239	256	262
Departmental Management:	314	356	429
Bureau of International Labor Affairs (non-add)	*86*	*93*	*115*
Solicitor of Labor (non-add)	*101*	*117*	*123*
Foreign Labor Certification	68	68	66
Office of Disability Employment Policy	27	39	39
State Paid Leave Fund	—	—	50
All other	36	241	251
Total, Discretionary budget authority	12,893	14,266	13,967
Memorandum: Budget authority from American Recovery and Reinvestment Act	*4,805*	*—*	*—*
Total, Discretionary outlays	12,125	14,674	13,936
Memorandum: Outlays from American Recovery and Reinvestment Act	*882*	*2,941*	*565*
Mandatory Outlays:			
Unemployment Insurance Benefits			
Existing law	93,783	126,787	82,385
Legislative proposal	—	31,000	17,912
Trade Adjustment Assistance			
Existing law	416	810	1,497
Legislative proposal	—	—	145
Pension Benefit Guaranty Corporation	194	-86	-1,073
Black Lung Benefits Program	3,060	524	512
Federal Employees' Compensation Act [2]			
Existing law	1,246	184	180
Legislative proposal	—	—	-10
Energy Employees Occupational Illness Compensation Program Act	1,168	1,080	960
All other	-2,146	-2,534	271
Total, Mandatory outlays	97,721	157,765	102,779
Memorandum: Outlays from American Recovery and Reinvestment Act	*27,434*	*33,896*	*1,533*
Total, Outlays	109,846	172,439	116,715

[1] In the 2011 Budget, funding previously requested for the component agencies and offices under the heading "Employment Standards Administration Salaries and Expenses" is requested separately for the Office of Workers' Compensation Programs, Wage and Hour Division, Office of Federal Contract Compliance Programs, and Office of Labor-Management Standards.

[2] 2009 outlays are lower due to delayed reimbursements from the Postal Service.

DEPARTMENT OF STATE AND OTHER INTERNATIONAL PROGRAMS

Funding Highlights:

- Increases funding for the President's Global Health Initiative, including increased efforts to reduce mortality of mothers and children under five, avoid unintended pregnancies, and work towards the elimination of some neglected tropical diseases. As part of this effort, the Budget also expands support for the President's Emergency Plan for AIDS Relief to prevent new HIV infections while providing care and treatment to millions of people, and for the President's Malaria Initiative to dramatically reduce the prevalence of this disease.

- Increases funding for the President's Global Hunger and Food Security Initiative to help poor countries improve the nutritional and income status of millions of people living in extreme poverty and suffering from hunger by 2015.

- Increases aid to Afghanistan and Pakistan to revitalize economic development and confront the resurgence of the Taliban.

- Supports continued progress toward a sovereign, stable, and self-reliant Iraq and prepares the Department of State to assume responsibility for security, logistics, and police training programs as part of the military-to-civilian transition in Iraq.

- Helps developing nations adapt to climate change and pursue low-carbon development.

- Recognizes that diplomacy and development activities are instrumental in promoting U.S. National Security interests and provides critical funding necessary to support greater civilian capacity to meet expanded roles.

- Maintains path to achieve goal of 11,000 Peace Corps volunteers by 2016.

- Supports President Obama's vision of Global Engagement through activities to expand economic opportunity, foster scientific and technological innovation, and strengthen people-to-people connections.

- Promotes sustainable economic growth to help reduce global poverty with support for new Millennium Challenge Corporation compacts.

- Supports the poorest populations globally through U.S. contributions to the Multilateral Development Banks.

The Department of State, the U.S. Agency for International Development (USAID), and other international programs advance the interests of the United States through engagement, partnership, and the promotion of universal values. Through the power of example and the empowerment of people, using diplomatic and development tools, the Administration is working to forge the global consensus required to defeat the threats, manage the challenges, and seize the opportunities of the 21st century.

Increases Funding for the President's Global Health Initiative. The Administration will build on its commitment to save millions of lives through increased investments in global health activities. The Budget includes increased funding to combat the HIV/AIDS crisis by: focusing on increasing treatment and prevention; ramping up maternal and child health programming to reduce mortality of mothers and children under five and decrease the prevalence of malnutrition; expanding investments in family planning activities, malaria, tuberculosis, and neglected tropical diseases; and strengthening local health systems to enhance capacity and long-run sustainability of each health program. Alongside our multilateral partners, the United States will continue to provide global leadership in fulfilling our shared responsibility and our common promise to improve the health of the world's poorest populations.

Promotes U.S. Strategy in Afghanistan and Pakistan. The 2011 Budget increases U.S. resources in support of the President's strategy to disrupt, dismantle, and defeat al Qaeda in Afghanistan and Pakistan. The Budget increases assistance to both countries, providing additional funding for governance, reconstruction, and other development activities that will counter extremists. For Pakistan, the Budget also increases security assistance and funds a new signature energy project. The Budget expands the number of civilian personnel in Afghanistan and Pakistan in an effort to build government capacity, increase diplomatic engagement, manage expanded assistance programs, and reduce the potential for fraud and misuse of American funding.

Supports Strategic Realignments in Iraq. The 2011 Budget aligns U.S. assistance efforts in Iraq with the U.S.-Iraq Strategic Framework Agreement and provides support for continued progress toward a sovereign, stable, and self-reliant Iraq. The Budget provides the Department of State with the resources to prepare to assume responsibility for key programs that have been funded and led by the Department of Defense, including police capacity building, and provides security and logistic support for U.S. civilians deployed around the country. The Budget also continues to provide support for Iraqis who have been displaced from their homes.

Fights Hunger and Expands Food Security Efforts. The 2011 Budget increases funding for agriculture development and nutrition programs as part of a multi-year plan to lift a significant number of people out of poverty and reduce under-five malnutrition for millions of children by 2015. The Budget provides assistance through bilateral assistance and a new multi-donor facility administered by the World Bank to poor countries that make policy and financial commitments to address their internal food security needs. Additional assistance will help targeted countries increase agricultural productivity, improve agricultural research and development, and expand markets and trade while monitoring and evaluating program performance. The Budget also maintains strong support for food aid and other humanitarian assistance.

Helps Developing Nations to Adapt to Climate Change and Pursue Low-Carbon Development. To reduce greenhouse gas emissions worldwide, the United States will spur the development and dissemination of clean energy technologies and increase the sequestration of carbon stored in soils, plants, and trees. The United States will take prompt, substantial action to help vulnerable countries adapt and build resilience to the effects of climate change. The top priority is to support the development of low-carbon development strategies that contain measureable, reportable, and verifiable actions, laying the groundwork for meaningful reductions in national emissions trajectories.

Maintains Path to Increase Peace Corps Volunteers. The 2011 Budget funds the second year of the President's initiative to significantly increase the number of Peace Corps volunteers, and puts the Peace Corps on track to grow by 50 percent so that it reaches 11,000 volunteers by 2016.

Aligns Resources with Global Engagement Priorities. The 2011 Budget supports President Obama's vision of global engagement that is based on mutual respect, the pursuit of sustainable partnerships in areas of mutual interest, and a commitment to listening to and working with local stakeholders, with an emphasis on women and youth. The Budget supports activities designed to expand economic opportunity including job creation and employment-focused education efforts; foster scientific and technological innovation; and strengthen people-to-people connections through exchange programs.

Combats Trafficking in Persons Worldwide. The 2011 Budget supports the Administration's efforts to combat trafficking in persons and assist in the coordination of anti-trafficking efforts both worldwide and domestically. It will allow the United States to lead in advancing public awareness and advocacy in concert with non-governmental organizations, international organizations, Congress and the media; with our programs focusing on the "3P" paradigm of prosecuting traffickers, protecting victims, and preventing trafficking in persons.

Supports the Poorest Populations Globally. The Multilateral Development Banks (MDBs) provide concessional financing to meet the needs of the poorest populations globally, including in fragile and post-conflict countries and in countries that have disproportionally felt the effects of the global financial crisis. The MDBs play a particularly important role in regions of high need like Sub-Saharan Africa, while working throughout the developing world to help countries achieve sustained economic growth and poverty reduction. U.S. contributions to the MDBs leverage other donor resources and increase the U.S.'s influence, credibility, and effectiveness globally. The Budget also provides funding for new Millennium Challenge Corporation compacts in eligible countries, such as Indonesia and Zambia, to reduce poverty and stimulate economic growth.

Realigns Non-Military Contingency and Stabilization Activities of the Department of Defense and the Department of State. The Budget proposes a Complex Crises Fund within the Department of State that would replace current authorities of the Department of Defense to provide non-military reconstruction, security, and stabilization assistance funding. The account would provide a source of flexible contingency funding to meet unforeseen reconstruction and stabilization needs.

Department of State and Other International Programs
(In millions of dollars)

	Actual 2009	Estimate	
		2010[1]	2011
Spending			
Discretionary Budget Authority:			
Administration of Foreign Affairs	9,974	13,320	12,377
International Organizations and Peacekeeping	3,993	3,808	3,778
Economic Support Fund	7,122	8,164	7,812
Global Health and Child Survival	7,289	7,829	8,513

Department of State and Other International Programs—Continued
(In millions of dollars)

	Actual 2009	Estimate	
		2010[1]	2011
International Narcotics and Law Enforcement (includes ACP)	1,844	2,448	2,136
Migration and Refugee Assistance	1,675	1,693	1,605
Non-proliferation, Anti-terrorism, Demining Programs	632	754	758
Foreign Military Financing	5,007	5,480	5,473
Pakistan Counterinsurgency Capability Fund	700	—	1,200
Assistance for Europe, Eurasia, and Central Asia	918	742	716
Development Assistance	2,004	2,495	2,946
USAID Operating Expenses	1,059	1,389	1,476
Broadcasting Board of Governors	725	746	769
Millennium Challenge Corporation	875	1,105	1,280
Export-Import Bank	−177	3	−9
Overseas Private Investment Corporation	−173	−172	−189
Peace Corps	340	400	446
Multilateral Development Banks	1,493	2,044	2,957
Other State and International Programs	3,595	2,924	2,726
Food for Peace, USDA P.L. 480 Title II (non-add)	*2,321*	*1,690*	*1,690*
Total, Discretionary budget authority (including supplementals)	48,895	55,172	56,770
Memorandum:			
Budget authority from American Recovery and Reinvestment Act	*600*	*—*	*—*
Budget authority from enacted supplementals	*11,946*	*1,841*	*—*
Budget authority from requested supplementals	*—*	*4,461*	*—*
Total, Discretionary outlays	41,044	49,906	54,662
Memorandum: Outlays from American Recovery and Reinvestment Act	*29*	*356*	*135*
Total, Mandatory outlays	−3,941	1,087	−853
Total, Outlays	37,103	50,993	53,809
Credit activity			
Direct Loan Disbursements:			
Export-Import Bank	1,481	50	25
All other programs	360	7,435	5,909
Total, Direct loan disbursements	1,841	7,485	5,934
Guaranteed Loan Commitments:			
Export-Import Bank	14,599	13,500	14,425
All other programs	692	2,226	2,394
Total, Guaranteed loan commitments	15,291	15,726	16,819

[1] The 2010 Estimate includes $1.8 billion of the 2010 President's Request that was forward funded in the 2009 supplemental.

DEPARTMENT OF TRANSPORTATION

Funding Highlights:

- Provides $4 billion for a new National Infrastructure Innovation and Finance Fund, which will invest in high-value projects of regional or national significance.

- Establishes a new $30 million Federal transit safety program to address critical needs.

- Invests in modernizing the air traffic control system by increasing funding for NextGen by more than 30 percent.

- Commits to developing long-run solutions for surface transportation finance and for improving program performance.

- Helps communities to become more livable and sustainable by allocating $527 million for the Department's investments as part of the President's multi-agency Partnership for Sustainable Communities.

- Sustains large-scale, multi-year support for high-speed rail, with $1 billion to fund promising and transformative projects.

The Department of Transportation (DOT) is focused on its core mission of promoting safety and increasing mobility, and supporting the development of infrastructure that will underpin job creation for years to come. For 2011, DOT has several major initiatives in these areas, in addition to plans to deliver transportation funds based on greater use of analysis and consideration of program performance.

Creates a National Infrastructure Innovation and Finance Fund. The Budget includes $4 billion to create a National Infrastructure Innovation and Finance Fund to invest in projects of regional or national significance. This marks an important departure from the Federal Government's traditional way of spending on infrastructure through grants to specific States and

localities. Established as a new operational unit within DOT, the Fund will directly provide resources for projects through grants, loans, or a blend of both, and will effectively leverage non-Federal resources, including private capital. The Fund will allocate resources based on demonstrable merit and analytical measures of performance. The Fund will provide planning, feasibility, and analytical capacity to help sponsors identify projects from around the country and then carefully select the most worthwhile.

Establishes a New Federal Transit Safety Program. Unlike other modes of transportation, closed system rail transit services (generally, metro area subways and light rail systems) are not overseen by Federal safety regulators, but rather are subject to review by a patchwork of State safety organizations. Recent deadly accidents in Washington D.C., Boston, and San Francisco underscore the need for common nationwide safety standards and for Federal enforcement of these standards. The Budget includes $30 million for a new transit safety oversight program within the Federal Transit Administration (FTA). This will enable FTA to hire new staff and to implement a comprehensive safety oversight strategy, as proposed in legislation.

Invests in Modernizing the Air Traffic Control System. The Budget provides $1.14 billion, more than a 30 percent increase from 2010 for the Next Generation Air Transportation System. NextGen is the Federal Aviation Administration's long-term effort to improve the efficiency, safety, and capacity of the aviation system. The 2011 Budget supports the transformation from a national ground-based radar surveillance system to a more accurate satellite-based surveillance system; the development of more efficient routes through the airspace; and the improvement of aviation weather information.

Commits to Developing Long-Run Solutions for Surface Transportation Finance and for Improving Program Performance. Surface transportation programs are at a crossroads. The current framework for financing and allocating surface transportation investments is not financially sustainable, nor does it effectively allocate resources to meet our critical national needs. The Administration recommends extending the current authorization through March 2011, during which time it will work with the Congress to reform surface transportation programs and put the system on a viable financing path. Careful consideration is needed to design a Federal surface transportation program that leads to higher performing investments, increases people's transportation options, promotes a sustainable environment, and makes our economy more productive. Further, the Federal program must generate the best investments to reduce congestion and improve safety. To do so, the Administration seeks to integrate economic analysis and performance measurement in transportation

planning to ensure that taxpayer dollars are better targeted and spent.

Helps Communities to Become More Livable and Sustainable. As part of the President's Partnership for Sustainable Communities initiative, the Budget includes $527 million in DOT to help State and local governments invest smarter in transportation infrastructure and leverage that investment to advance sustainable development. The Federal Government will help stimulate comprehensive regional and community planning efforts that integrate transportation, housing, and other critical investments. This approach aims to reduce greenhouse gases, improve mobility and transportation access to economic opportunity, and improve housing choices. Combined with $150 million in Department of Housing and Urban Development planning grants, and $10 million in Environmental Protection Agency technical assistance, DOT will dedicate $527 million, focused on capacity building and transportation projects, to this multi-agency effort. Because improving local quality of life is a universal challenge, this place-based interagency initiative will help communities across the Nation make better coordinated, higher-performing infrastructure investments.

Sustains Multi-Year Support for High-Speed Rail. Building on the historic $8 billion down payment provided through the American Recovery and Reinvestment Act, the President's Budget includes $1 billion for high-speed rail. The 2011 request supports the President's five-year, $5 billion pledge in the 2010 Budget. High-speed rail promises to give the traveling public a practical alternative to flying or driving, particularly where there is congestion in the skies and on the roads. With trains efficiently connecting city and business centers, travelers would enjoy a new level of convenience not available in most parts of the country today. The Administration is dedicated to working with States and project sponsors to identify high-speed rail projects that will provide the greatest transportation, social, and environmental benefits, while maximizing the return on taxpayer dollars.

Department of Transportation
(In millions of dollars)

	Actual 2009	Estimate 2010	2011
Spending			
Discretionary Budgetary Resources:			
Federal Aviation Administration	11,959	12,477	12,953
Obligation Limitation	3,515	3,515	3,515
Federal Highway Administration	176	936	−263
Obligation Limitation	39,715	41,107	41,363
Federal Motor Carrier Safety Administration Obligation Limitation	541	550	570
National Highway Traffic Safety Administration	127	143	136
Obligation Limitation	729	730	743
Federal Railroad Administration	1,798	4,360	2,831
Federal Transit Administration	1,969	2,388	2,167
Obligation Limitation	9,247	8,343	8,632
Federal Maritime Administration	333	363	352
St. Lawrence Seaway Development Corporation	32	32	32
Pipeline and Hazardous Materials Safety Administration	144	164	174
Research and Innovative Technology Administration	13	13	17
National Infrastructure Innovation and Finance Fund:			
Legislative proposal	—	—	4,000
Office of the Secretary	207	890	352
All other	21	18	14
Total, Discretionary budgetary resources [1]	70,526	76,029	77,588
Memorandum:			
Budget authority from American Recovery and Reinvestment Act	*48,120*	*—*	*—*
Budget authority from supplementals	*3,013*	*—*	*—*
Total, Discretionary outlays	68,778	73,393	74,376
Memorandum: Outlays from American Recovery and Reinvestment Act	*3,652*	*16,363*	*11,359*
Mandatory Outlays:			
Federal Aviation Administration	−162	−159	−178
Federal Highway Administration	793	1,094	900
Federal Railroad Administration	10	15	−3
Federal Maritime Administration	265	254	176
Pipeline and Hazardous Materials Safety Administration	16	37	35
Office of the Secretary	38	53	50
All other	−384	−106	−50
Total, Mandatory outlays	576	1,188	930
Total, Outlays	69,354	74,581	75,306

Department of Transportation—Continued
(In millions of dollars)

	Actual 2009	Estimate	
		2010	2011
Credit activity			
Direct Loan Disbursements:			
Transportation Infrastructure Financing and Innovation Program	317	1,159	1,107
Railroad Rehabilitation and Improvement Program	96	600	600
National Infrastructure Innovation and Finance Fund	—	—	250
Total, Direct loan disbursements	413	1,759	1,957
Guaranteed Loan Commitments:			
Transportation Infrastructure Financing and Innovation Program	—	40	80
Railroad Rehabilitation and Improvement Program	—	100	100
Minority Business Resource Centers	3	18	18
Maritime Guaranteed Loans	269	350	450
Total, Guaranteed loan commitments	272	508	648

¹ Includes discretionary budget authority and obligation limitations.

DEPARTMENT OF THE TREASURY

Funding Highlights:

- Includes resources to implement the Administration's proposal to reform financial regulation including a new agency to protect consumers, and increases the security and convenience of Federal payment and collection transactions.

- Manages responsibly Troubled Asset Relief Program (TARP) investments to protect taxpayer interests while winding down extraordinary market interventions.

- Provides $250 million to expand job-creating investments and access to credit in disadvantaged communities through the Community Development Financial Institutions Fund.

- Invests over $8 billion in the Internal Revenue Service's enforcement and modernization programs, while continuing to drive innovation and responsiveness in taxpayer services. The Budget supports significant new revenue-generating initiatives that will target critical areas of non-compliance, and enhances a multi-year modernization strategy that will deliver a vastly improved IRS within the next five years.

- Supports the capacity of the Department to respond to future economic challenges by expanding Treasury's finance and tax policy resources. This increased analytical capability will also fund the Administration's plan to strengthen oversight of financial institutions and markets so that the system is safer for consumers and investors.

The Department of the Treasury is a leader in the President's efforts to promote the economic prosperity and financial security of the United States. Treasury operations are critical to the core functions of government, including collecting over $2.3 trillion in revenue and disbursing over $2.3 trillion in payments, managing Federal finances, and protecting the financial system from threats. Treasury also plays a key role in modernizing the American financial regulatory framework and ensuring effective, transparent administration of programs designed to strengthen the economy.

Supports the Administration's Reform of Financial Regulation and Consumer Protection. In June 2009, the Administration proposed comprehensive financial reform legislation designed to create a robust financial regulatory system that could help prevent future economic crises. The proposal includes changes to improve the safety and soundness of the financial sector, especially large and interconnected firms, and creates a new Government entity responsible for monitoring financial businesses and practices that impact consumers directly.

Redirects TARP to Small Businesses and Homeowners. The Budget continues to support activities authorized under the Emergency Economic Stability Act of 2008 and the Housing and Economic Recovery Act of 2008 that help stabilize the financial system and restart markets critical to financing American households and businesses, through new and existing investment agreements with financial institutions including banks, servicers, insurance companies, and the Government-Sponsored Enterprises Fannie Mae and Freddie Mac. New TARP agreements will be directed toward assisting homeowners threatened with foreclosure and small businesses needing access to affordable credit. The Budget emphasizes effective, transparent, and accountable management of the TARP. Over the past year, financial markets have rebounded faster than expected, and as a result the Budget reflects a significantly lower cost and volume of TARP asset purchases than previously estimated.

Supports Lending in Low-Income Communities. The Budget supports the availability of affordable financing in low-income communities by providing targeted support to Community Development Financial Institutions throughout the Nation. The $250 million in financial support will help these local financial institutions offer affordable loans to small businesses, consumers, nonprofit developers, and home buyers in communities that lack access to affordable credit. These resources will also be coordinated with resources in other agencies to support the Administration's place-based initiatives. New initiatives will expand financing for access to healthy foods and access to financial services in underserved communities. Supporting the Department's efforts to improve protections for consumers of complicated financial products, Treasury will continue its work to improve financial literacy, especially among youth and young adult populations. Treasury along with its partners, will work to improve access to financial services for America's unbanked and underbanked, building upon findings from its multi-year community financial access pilot, which concludes in 2010.

Improves Services to Taxpayers. The Administration will improve the quality of IRS services to taxpayers, providing for a better tax filing experience. The Budget provides additional resources for high-quality phone service so that taxpayers' questions are answered quickly and correctly. A top priority of the IRS is to promptly and correctly answer a taxpayer's question the first time asked, through the most efficient and taxpayer-friendly means. The IRS will also work to improve interactions between taxpayers and tax preparation service providers through a new targeted strategy, and will further enhance electronic filing capabilities through increased availability of electronic forms and improved information technology infrastructure.

Streamlines Internal Processes to Deliver Tax Fairness while Targeting Waste and Fraud. The Budget supports the IRS' continued progress in reducing the tax gap through fair, robust, and equal application of the tax laws—including new revenue-generating enforcement initiatives that will increase recovery of tax debts by nearly $2 billion a year once the initiatives are fully mature in 2013. This set of initiatives will be balanced with an increased focus on IRS modernization, for which the Budget makes a significant commitment through nearly $200 million in targeted investments in the IRS' new core taxpayer database and processing platform. Once complete, this modernized system will improve both the taxpayer experience through, for example, enhanced service capabilities such as more individualized self-service offerings, as well as the IRS' operational effectiveness, creating a more responsive, nimble organization. The Budget also includes a set of innovative legislative proposals to improve the fairness, effectiveness and efficiency of tax administration, which will also narrow the tax gap.

Achieves New Savings Through Commonsense Reforms. The Budget will increase collections of delinquent debt owed to the Federal Government, as well as child support payments through States, expand the use of electronic payment and collection transactions, and propose other cross-cutting initiatives that are expected to yield approximately $2 billion in savings over the next 10 years. The Budget eliminates nearly $250 million in Federal subsidies to insurance companies for terrorism insurance. These subsidies are no longer necessary given the robust private market for such insurance, and domestic terrorism insurance policies are now sufficiently available and affordable to meet demand. According to industry data, property and casualty insurers' surpluses—the balances available to pay claims associated with covered terrorist attacks—are currently estimated at over $490 billion.

Strengthens the Analytic Capacity of Departmental Offices. The Budget funds additional staff with expertise in finance and tax policy. This investment will allow the Department to identify more effectively and address emerging economic challenges and improve policy-making capacity. Some of the new positions will support implementation of Financial Regulation Reform initiatives, including the launch of the Office of National Insurance and the Financial Services Oversight Council, which will improve supervision and regulation of financial institutions and markets.

Department of the Treasury
(In millions of dollars)

	Actual 2009	Estimate 2010	Estimate 2011
Spending [1]			
Discretionary Budget Authority:			
Internal Revenue Service	11,522	12,147	12,633
Financial Management Service	240	244	235
Departmental Offices	279	305	346
Department-wide Systems and Capital Investments Programs	27	10	22
Bureau of the Public Debt	179	182	176
Department and IRS Inspectors General	172	182	185
Special Inspector General for TARP	—	23	50
Alcohol and Tobacco Tax and Trade Bureau	99	103	—
Financial Crimes Enforcement Network	91	111	100
Community Development Financial Institutions Fund	107	247	250
All other	−92	—	−62
Total, Discretionary budget authority	12,624	13,554	13,935
Memorandum:			
Budget authority from American Recovery and Reinvestment Act	*318*	*—*	*—*
Total, Discretionary outlays	12,224	13,278	13,738
Memorandum: Outlays from American Recovery and Reinvestment Act	*139*	*149*	*16*
Mandatory Outlays:			
Payment where tax credit exceeds liability for tax (multiple programs)	78,604	71,821	59,438
GSE MBS and HFA Purchases	−4,500	−9,879	—

Department of the Treasury—Continued
(In millions of dollars)

	Actual 2009	Estimate	
		2010	2011
GSE Preferred Stock Purchase Agreements and Dividends	91,264	56,746	5,435
Troubled Asset Relief Program (TARP)	151,151	41,427	10,734
TARP Downward Reestimate of Subsidies	—	−114,531	—
Office of Financial Stability	90	443	309
Special Inspector General for TARP	12	37	11
Internal Revenue Collections for Puerto Rico	473	356	348
Legislative Proposal	—	66	91
Terrorism Insurance Program	2	104	236
Legislative proposal	—	—	−26
All other	−2,633	5,239	3,163
Total, Mandatory outlays	314,463	51,763	79,674
Memorandum: Outlays from American Recovery and Reinvestment Act ...	*2,433*	*49,156*	*44,181*
Total, Outlays	326,687	65,041	93,412

Credit activity
Direct Loan Disbursements:

GSE MBS and HFA Purchases	190,574	48,676	—
Troubled Asset Relief Program	363,825	85,713	5,168
Total, Direct loan disbursements	554,399	134,389	5,168
Guaranteed Loan Commitments:			
Troubled Assets Relief Program	301,000	—	—
Total, Guaranteed loan commitments	301,000	—	—

[1] Excludes International Programs.

DEPARTMENT OF VETERANS AFFAIRS

Funding Highlights:

- Builds on the historic past increase in funding for the Department of Veterans Affairs (VA), for a 20 percent total increase since 2009.

- Secures timely, sufficient, and predictable funding for health care services through 2012 with advance appropriations for VA Medical Care.

- Increases access to medical care services by focusing on the unique needs of women veterans and continuing the enrollment of over 500,000 previously ineligible veterans into VA health care by 2013.

- Supports timely and high-quality delivery of health care and benefits through 21st Century technology, including the Virtual Lifetime Electronic Record and benefits processing systems.

- Funds the Administration's commitment to dramatically reduce veteran homelessness.

- Continues the emphasis on specialized care for veterans with psychological and cognitive health needs, especially due to post-traumatic stress and traumatic brain injury.

- Provides greater benefits to veterans who are medically retired from service.

- Dramatically expands access to national cemeteries for eligible veterans.

Veterans earn an array of benefits and services through their dedicated service to America. The President's Budget makes it easier for veterans to access the benefits and services they have earned, by investing in 21st Century technology and in improved services for veterans with specialized needs.

Builds on the Historic Past Increase in Funding for VA. The Budget provides $57 billion in funding for a 20 percent total increase since 2009. This significant increase contributes to the President's pledge to increase funding for the VA, providing a foundation to transform the Department and better serve veterans and their families today.

Provides Advance Appropriations for VA Medical Care. The 2011 Budget requests $50.6 billion in advance appropriations for the VA medical care program so that care for the Nation's veterans is not hindered by budget delays. This funding will enable the Department to have timely and predictable funding from year to year, ultimately making it easier for veterans to rely on accessible VA care.

Focuses on the Unique Needs of Women Veterans. The 2011 President's Budget responds to the growing number of women veterans by providing for their unique needs, from an appropriate environment of care to specialized medical and counseling services.

117

Continues to Increase Enrollment of Previously Ineligible Veterans into VA Health Care. The President's Budget continues enrolling more than 500,000 moderate-income veterans into the VA health care system by 2013 while maintaining high-quality and timely care for the lower-income and disabled veterans who currently rely on VA.

Supports Timely and High-Quality Delivery of Health Care and Benefits through 21st Century Technology. VA and the Department of Defense (DOD) are jointly implementing the Virtual Lifetime Electronic Record, which will enable VA to maintain a complete health record for each veteran and to deliver care and benefits to veterans with efficiency and accuracy. The President's Budget also invests over $200 million in automated processing to directly improve the accuracy and timeliness of veterans benefits, particularly disability compensation and the new Post-9/11 GI Bill benefit.

Works to Dramatically Reduce Veteran Homelessness. With an investment of almost $800 million, the President's Budget expands VA's services for homeless veterans and those at risk of becoming homeless through the expansion of collaborative partnerships with local governments, non-profit organizations, and the Departments of Housing and Urban Development, Justice, and Labor.

Continues the Emphasis on Specialized Care for Veterans with Psychological and Cognitive Health Needs. The President's Budget strengthens VA's ability to provide veterans the best possible care for Post-Traumatic Stress, Traumatic Brain Injury, and other mental health conditions by investing $5.2 billion in specialized care. These conditions will continue to be urgent issues for the VA for many years to come. The Budget increases collaboration between joint DOD and VA programs that target psychological health; increases research to develop new evidence-based approaches; and increases outreach to veterans.

Provides Greater Benefits to Veterans who are Medically Retired from Service. For the first time, highly-disabled veterans who are medically retired from service will be eligible for concurrent receipt of disability benefits from VA in addition to DOD retirement benefits. All medically retired servicemembers will be eligible for concurrent receipt of VA and DOD benefits by 2015.

Dramatically Expands Access to National Cemeteries for Eligible Veterans. VA will reduce the population threshold used to determine where new national veterans cemeteries should be built from 170,000 to 80,000 veterans living within 75 miles of a potential location. The lower threshold will provide a nearby national cemetery burial option to at least 500,000 additional veterans and will result in 94 percent of all veterans having a veterans cemetery burial option within a reasonable distance of their homes.

Department of Veterans Affairs

(In millions of dollars)

	Actual 2009	Estimate 2010	Estimate 2011
Spending			
Discretionary Budget Authority:			
Medical Care	40,183	44,512	48,183
Medical Collections (non-add)	*2,767*	*3,026*	*3,355*
Total Medical Care including collections (non-add)	*42,950*	*47,538*	*51,538*
Medical Care and Prosthetics Research	510	581	590
Information Technology	2,748	3,307	3,307
Construction	1,882	2,043	1,750
Veterans Benefits Administration	1,461	1,689	2,149
General Administration	336	398	463
Housing and Other Credit	158	166	165
National Cemetery Administration	230	250	251
Office of Inspector General	88	109	109
Total, Discretionary budget authority	47,596	53,055	56,967
Memorandum:			
Budget authority from American Recovery and Reinvestment Act	*1,408*	—	—
Budget authority from supplementals	*198*	—	—
Total, Discretionary outlays	46,580	51,516	55,224
Memorandum: Outlays from American Recovery and Reinvestment Act	*86*	*590*	*465*
Mandatory Outlays:			
Disability Compensation and Pensions:			
Existing law	44,270	47,901	57,109
Supplemental	—	13,377	—
Legislative proposal	—	531	44
Education Benefits	3,155	8,444	9,704
Vocational Rehabilitation and Employment	720	787	830
Housing (credit)	329	828	19
Insurance	48	49	63
All other	−188	549	764
Total, Mandatory outlays	48,334	72,466	68,533
Memorandum: Outlays from American Recovery and Reinvestment Act	*465*	—	—
Total, Outlays	94,914	123,982	123,757
Credit activity			
Direct Loan Disbursements:			
Vendee and Acquired Loans	79	965	1,102

Department of Veterans Affairs—Continued

(In millions of dollars)

	Actual 2009	Estimate	
		2010	2011
All other programs	22	15	12
Total, Direct loan disbursements	101	980	1,114
Guaranteed Loan Commitments:			
Veterans Home Loans...	67,849	58,286	53,570

CORPS OF ENGINEERS—CIVIL WORKS

Funding Highlights:

- Helps build infrastructure to support economic growth and restore aquatic ecosystems by allocating $1.7 billion to fund construction for projects that provide the highest economic and environmental return to the Nation while achieving public safety objectives.

- Emphasizes the safe and reliable operation and maintenance of key inland and coastal waterways and other infrastructure.

- Focuses resources on the restoration of significant aquatic ecosystems, such as the Everglades, the California Bay-Delta, and the Louisiana coastal wetlands.

- Begins to chart a new direction for the Corps to meet 21st Century water resources challenges, including reforming the procedures for planning future projects and eliminating funding for ongoing projects and activities that are ineffective or duplicative.

The Army Corps of Engineers civil works program (Corps) develops, manages, and protects the Nation's water resources through its studies of potential projects; its construction, operation and maintenance of projects; and its regulatory program. The Corps, working with other Federal agencies, also helps communities respond to and recover from floods and other natural disasters. The Corps conducts much of its work in partnership with State and local governments and other non-Federal entities.

Funds High-Return Construction Projects. The Budget for the construction program supports high-return investments for ongoing work in the three main mission areas of the Corps: commercial navigation; flood and storm damage reduction; and aquatic ecosystem restoration. The Budget also gives priority for funding to dam safety work, projects that reduce sig-

nificant risks to human safety, and projects that will complete construction during 2011.

Supports Capital Investment on the Inland Waterways. The Budget proposes to replace the current excise tax on diesel fuel for the inland waterways with a new funding mechanism that raises the revenue needed to meet the authorized non-Federal cost-share of inland waterways capital investments in a way that is more efficient and more equitable than the fuel tax. It will also preserve the landmark cost-sharing reform established by the Congress in 1986, while supporting inland waterways construction, expansion, replacement, and rehabilitation work.

Advances Aquatic Ecosystem Restoration. The Budget supports ongoing, high-performing ecosystem restoration efforts, including continued progress toward restoring the Florida

Everglades, the California Bay-Delta, and the Louisiana coast. Based on sound science, these and other aquatic ecosystem efforts supported in the Budget focus on those activities that cost effectively provide high-quality, reliable, and sustainable long-term solutions that restore the environmental integrity and sustainability of the affected ecosystems. The Corps will work with Federal interagency working groups led by the White House Council on Environmental Quality to develop performance measures and tools to identify those restoration activities with the highest returns to taxpayers.

Emphasizes the Operation and Maintenance of Existing Infrastructure. The Budget focuses resources on furthering the operational reliability, safety, and availability of the key features of the existing Corps infrastructure. The Budget funds high-priority maintenance work that will improve the overall performance of the Corps aging infrastructure, including work on the Ohio, Upper Mississippi, and Illinois Waterway, and development of models to help the Corps understand the impact of climate change on its projects and how to adapt to those changes.

Supports a New Direction for the Corps. The Budget supports Corps activities to plan and implement water resources projects that advance sustainable economic development and preserve and restore ecosystems. It also supports the Administration's effort to revise the over 25-year old procedures for planning future Federal water resources projects and supports improving the management of existing projects to incorporate current water resources planning concepts and analytical methods. In addition, the Administration intends to develop a set of broad principles to chart the future course of the Corps and to help guide authorization of Corps studies, projects, and programs in the next Water Resources Development Act.

Eliminates Funding for Ineffective or Duplicative Programs. The Budget eliminates funding for dozens of projects that have a low economic or environmental return or that are duplicative of programs in other agencies, including cutting $129 million for water and wastewater infrastructure projects that are better addressed through other Federal programs.

Corps of Engineers—Civil Works
(In millions of dollars)

	Actual 2009	Estimate 2010	2011
Spending			
Discretionary Budget Authority:			
Construction	2,080	2,029	1,690
Operation and Maintenance	2,202	2,400	2,361
Mississippi River and Tributaries	384	340	240
Flood Control and Coastal Emergencies	—	—	30
Investigations	168	162	104
Regulatory Program	183	190	193
Expenses	179	185	185
Office of the Assistant Secretary of the Army (Civil Works)	5	5	6
Formerly Utilized Sites Remedial Action Program	140	134	130
Subtotal, Discretionary budget authority	5,341	5,446	4,939
Cancellation of Unobligated Balances, Mississippi River and Tributaries ...	—	—	−58
Total, Discretionary budget authority	5,341	5,446	4,881
Memorandum:			
Budget authority from American Recovery and Reinvestment Act	*4,600*	*—*	*—*
Budget authority from supplementals	*6,558*	*—*	*—*
Total, Discretionary outlays	6,777	7,566	5,951
Memorandum: Outlays from American Recovery and Reinvestment Act	*346*	*2,965*	*976*
Mandatory Outlays:			
Existing law	−261	38	35
Total, Mandatory outlays	−261	38	35
Total, Outlays	6,516	7,604	5,986

ENVIRONMENTAL PROTECTION AGENCY

Funding Highlights:

- Provides $3.3 billion total for the Clean Water and Drinking Water State Revolving Funds. This will allow States and Tribes to initiate approximately 800 clean water and 500 drinking water projects nationally, continuing a major Federal commitment to water infrastructure investment.

- Provides new funding to support the Administration's commitment to mitigate climate change.

- Continues support for collaborative, interagency ecosystem restoration efforts in the Great Lakes, Chesapeake Bay and Mississippi River Basin.

- Provides grants for States and Tribes to administer delegated environmental programs at $1.3 billion, the highest level ever.

- Funds the Agency's operating budget at $3.8 billion to support regulatory, research, and enforcement activities.

- Supports economic growth and job creation in hard hit regions by bolstering Brownfields cleanup.

The Environmental Protection Agency (EPA) is committed to protecting human health and the environment. To achieve this mission, EPA collaborates with States and Tribes to implement air, water, waste, and chemical programs. The Budget requests $10 billion for EPA, a substantially higher annual amount than requested under any previous Administration. This total expands the Administration's 2010 increase to the Agency's core operating budget, which provides funds for program implementation, priority research, enhanced regulation, and comprehensive enforcement activities. EPA's budget also provides more funding for State and tribal program implementation grants than any previous budget.

Invests in Clean Water Infrastructure. The Budget requests $3.3 billion for the Clean Water and Drinking Water State Revolving Funds (SRFs). The Federal SRF funding provides grants to States for low-interest loans to communities through a combination of Federal capitalization, State matches, State leveraging, interest, and loan repayments. Since loan interest and principal payments are returned to the program, the SRFs continue to generate funding for new loans even without continued Federal funding. The Federal contribution to water and waste water infrastructure has been substantially incorporated into SRFs. These Funds, combined, now produce approximately $5 billion in repayments each year. As the Funds have grown, the need for Federal capitalization will decline over the next decade. Some ongoing contribution will be maintained so the neediest communities are adequately served.

For 2011, EPA proposes a new approach to helping small drinking water systems, as well as reforms to improve the long-term financial, managerial, and environmental sustainability of the SRFs. As part of that strategy, Federal dollars provided through the SRFs will act as a catalyst for efficient system-wide planning, improvements in technical, financial and managerial capacity, and the design, construction and on-going management of sustainable water infrastructure.

Supports Efforts to Mitigate Climate Change. The President has called on the Congress to enact forward-looking energy legislation that would spur U.S. development of advanced, clean energy technologies to reduce our dependence on oil, strengthen our energy and national security, create new jobs, and restore America's position as a global leader in efforts to mitigate climate change and address its worst consequences. The Administration supports a comprehensive market-based climate change policy to reduce greenhouse gas emissions in the United States more than 80 percent below 2005 levels by 2050. The President also supports a near-term target in the range of a 17-percent reduction by 2020. The Budget includes $21 million, an increase of $4 million from 2010 enacted levels, to implement the Mandatory Greenhouse Gas Reporting Rule and ensure the availability of high quality emissions data that will serve as the basis for effective climate policy.

In order for EPA and States to quickly and effectively address climate change, the Budget requests $43 million in new funding for regulatory initiatives to control greenhouse gas emissions under existing Clean Air Act authorities. Requested funds include $25 million to aid States in permitting activities for greenhouse gas (GHG) emissions under the New Source Review, and Title V operating permits programs. The Budget also requests $7 million to develop New Source Performance Standards to control GHG emissions from a few categories of major stationary sources. The Budget requests an increase of $6 million to support regulatory programs to reduce GHG emissions from mobile sources. These initiatives will help the United States meet its target for emissions reductions.

Advances Restoration of Great Lakes and Other Imperiled Waters. The 2011 Budget supports ecosystem restoration efforts, including $300 million for the Great Lakes, the largest freshwater system in the world. This EPA-led interagency effort to restore the Great Lakes focuses on priority environmental issues such as contaminated sediments and toxics, nonpoint source pollution, habitat degradation and loss, and invasive species.

The Budget also provides $17 million in new funding for the Mississippi River Basin and increases support for the Chesapeake Bay by $13 million. In the Mississippi River Basin, EPA will work with the Department of Agriculture to target nonpoint source reduction practices on agricultural land to reduce nutrient loadings. Funding for the Chesapeake Bay supports the President's May 2009 Chesapeake Bay Protection and Restoration Executive Order and will enable EPA to conduct robust regulatory, permitting, modeling, and reporting efforts. EPA and Federal partners will continue to coordinate with States, Tribes, municipalities, and industry to restore the integrity of imperiled waters of the United States.

Assists States and Tribes Clean Air and Water Efforts. For grants that support eligible States and Tribes that implement environmental programs, the Budget requests $1.3 billion, a 14-percent increase from 2010 enacted and the highest level ever. In addition to the $25 million provided for States to conduct GHG permitting activities, the Budget recognizes State fiscal constraints and provides substantial increases for select State and tribal programs, including a $45 million increase for State water pollution control grants and a $58 million increase for air quality management grants. The Budget includes $30 million for a new tribal multimedia grant program targeted at Tribes and tribal consortia that can implement environmental program requirements on tribal lands.

Promotes Economic Growth with Increased Funding for Brownfields Cleanup. Brownfields are lightly contaminated sites—many in economically hard-hit regions—that pollution may keep from being used productively.

To stimulate economic growth and job creation in economically distressed areas, the Budget provides a substantial increase for the Brownfields program to integrate area-wide planning and environmental remediation activities.

Environmental Protection Agency
(In millions of dollars)

	Actual 2009	Estimate 2010	Estimate 2011
Spending			
Discretionary Budget Authority:			
Operating Budget [1]	3,281	3,940	3,843
State and Tribal Assistance Grants	1,082	1,116	1,276
Clean Water State Revolving Fund	689	2,100	2,000
Drinking Water State Revolving Fund	829	1,387	1,287
Brownfields Assessment and Cleanup	97	100	138
Clean Diesel Grants	75	80	60
Targeted Water Infrastructure	192	195	20
Requested (non-add)	*39*	*30*	*20*
Unrequested (non-add)	*153*	*165*	*—*
Superfund	1,285	1,307	1,293
Leaking Underground Storage Tanks	113	113	113
Cancellation of unobligated balances	−10	−40	−10
Total, Discretionary budget authority	7,633	10,298	10,020
Memorandum: Budget authority from American Recovery and Reinvestment Act	*7,220*	*—*	*—*
Total, Discretionary outlays	7,885	8,591	9,351
Memorandum: Outlays from American Recovery and Reinvestment Act	*302*	*2,841*	*2,005*
Mandatory Outlays:			
Agency-wide			
Existing law	−117	−131	−129
Legislative proposals, Pesticide and PMN user fees	—	—	−50
Total, Mandatory outlays	−117	−131	−179
Total, Outlays	7,768	8,460	9,172

[1] Includes funding for Great Lakes Initiative.

NATIONAL AERONAUTICS AND SPACE ADMINISTRATION

Funding Highlights:

- Adds $6 billion to NASA's budget over five years and draws upon American ingenuity to enable us to embark on an ambitious 21st Century program of human space exploration.

- Initiates flagship exploration technology development and demonstration programs of "game-changing" technologies that will increase the reach and reduce the costs of future human space exploration as well as other NASA, government, and commercial space activities.

- Embraces the commercial space industry and the thousands of new jobs that it can create by contracting with American companies to provide astronaut transportation to the Space Station—thus reducing the risk of relying exclusively on foreign crew transport capabilities.

- Ends NASA's Constellation program, which was planning to use an approach similar to the Apollo program to return astronauts back to the Moon 50 years after that program's triumphs. An independent panel found that Constellation was years behind schedule and would require large budget increases to land even a handful of astronauts back on the Moon before 2030. Instead, we are launching a bold new effort that invests in American ingenuity for developing more capable and innovative technologies for future space exploration.

- Extends the International Space Station and enhances its utilization, bringing nations together in a common pursuit of knowledge and excellence in space.

- Enhances the Nation's global climate change research and monitoring system, including re-flight of a satellite that will help identify global carbon sources and sinks.

- Provides for a robust program of robotic solar system exploration and new astronomical observatories, including a probe that will fly through the Sun's atmosphere and an expanded effort to detect potentially hazardous asteroids.

- Revitalizes and realigns NASA to put in place the right workforce and facilities to function as an efficient 21st Century research and development agency.

The mission of the National Aeronautics and Space Administration (NASA) is to drive advances in science, technology, and exploration to enhance knowledge, education, innovation, economic vitality, stewardship of the Earth, and solutions to national and global challenges. The President's Budget will allow NASA to improve our knowledge of the Earth, explore space with humans and robots, foster strong partnerships with other nations, and educate and inspire the next generation of scientists and engineers.

Lays the Foundation for a Bold New Course for Human Space Flight. NASA's Constellation program—based largely on existing technologies—was begun to realize a vision of returning astronauts back to the Moon by 2020. However, the program was over budget, behind schedule, and lacking in innovation due to a failure to invest in critical new technologies. Using a broad range of criteria, an independent review panel determined that even if fully funded, NASA's program to repeat many of the achievements of the Apollo era, 50 years later, was the least attractive approach to space exploration as compared to potential alternatives. Furthermore, NASA's attempts to pursue its Moon goals had drawn funding away from other NASA programs, including robotic space exploration, science, and Earth observations. The President's Budget cancels Constellation and replaces it with a bold new approach that invests in the building blocks of a more capable approach to space exploration that includes:

- Research and development to support future heavy-lift rocket systems that will increase the capability of future exploration architectures with significantly lower operations costs than current systems—potentially taking us farther and faster into space.

- A vigorous new technology development and test program that aims to increase the capabilities and reduce the cost of future exploration activities. NASA, working with industry, will build, fly, and test in orbit key technologies such as automated, autonomous rendezvous and docking, closed-loop life support systems, in-orbit propellant transfer, and advanced in-space propulsion so that our future human and robotic exploration missions are both highly capable and affordable.

- A steady stream of precursor robotic exploration missions to scout locations and demonstrate technologies to increase the safety and capability of future human missions and provide scientific dividends.

Develops and Deploys Technologies to Reduce Future Space Mission Costs, Expand Opportunities, and Grow the American Economy. NASA will embark on a new agency-wide technology development and test program aimed at increasing the capabilities and reducing the cost of future NASA, other government, and commercial space activities. NASA will increase its support for transformative research that can enable a broad range of NASA missions. This program, which will involve work at NASA, in private industry, and at all levels of academia, will also generate spin-off technologies and potentially entire new industries.

Supports Extension and Enhanced Utilization of the Space Station. The International Space Station is poised to reach its full complement of international crew and laboratories in 2010. The President's Budget provides funds to extend operations of the Space Station past its previously planned retirement date of 2016. Working with partners around the world, NASA will maximize return on this investment by deploying new research facilities to conduct scientific research and test technologies in space and by making Space Station research capabilities available to educators and new researchers. New capabilities could include a centrifuge to support research into human physiology, inflatable space habitats, and a program to continuously upgrade Space Station capabilities.

Supports Promising Commercial Space Transportation. Commercial launch vehicles have for years carried all U.S. military and commercial—and most NASA—satellites to orbit. The Budget funds NASA to contract with industry to provide astronaut transportation to the International Space Station as soon as possible, reducing the risk of relying solely on foreign crew transports for years to come. A strengthened U.S. commercial space launch industry will bring needed competition, act as a catalyst for the development of other new businesses capitalizing on affordable access to space, help create thousands of new jobs, and help reduce the cost of human access to space.

Commits Funds to Safely and Prudently Fly the Remaining Space Shuttle Flights. The President's Budget promotes a safe and orderly retirement of the Space Shuttle program by providing funding for the Shuttle to fly its final five missions, even if their schedule slips into 2011.

Improves Our Understanding of Global Climate Change. NASA's Earth science program conducts first-of-a-kind demonstration flights of sensors in air and space in an effort to foster scientific understanding of the Earth system and to improve the ability to forecast climate change and natural disasters. The Budget accelerates the development of new satellites the National Research Council recommended as Earth science priorities. The Budget also supports several research satellites currently in development, a campaign to monitor changes in polar ice sheets, and enhancements to climate models. In addition, the Budget provides funds for NASA to develop and fly a replacement for the Orbiting Carbon Observatory, a mission designed to identify global carbon sources and sinks that was lost when its launch vehicle failed in 2009.

Increases Scientific Understanding of the Solar System and Universe. NASA's space probes, rovers, and telescopes have revolutionized humanity's scientific understanding of the cosmos. The Budget supports space science research grants and dozens of operating missions and telescopes currently studying the planets and stars as well as many more in development—including a telescope to succeed the Hubble Space Telescope, missions to study the Moon, and two Mars exploration missions. The Budget also funds early work on a mission that will make the closest-ever approach to the Sun, flying through its outer atmosphere in an attempt to understand how it is heated and how it ejects the stream of charged particles known as the solar wind. In addition, the Budget increases funding to detect asteroids that could potentially pose a hazard to the Earth.

Increases Support for Green Aviation and a More Efficient Air Transportation System. The President's Budget increases support for NASA's green aviation initiative by focusing on both innovative fundamental research and systems-level applications to reduce fuel needs, noise, and emissions of aircraft. These improvements to future air transportation will promote both the economic and environmental health of this country.

Revitalizes and Realigns NASA. The Budget supports the revitalization of NASA to put in place the right workforce and facilities to function as an efficient 21st Century research and development agency. A major focus of this effort will be to create the 21st Century launch facilities and infrastructure needed at Kennedy Space Center, transforming the facility to more effectively support future NASA, commercial, and other government launches.

Inspires More Young People to Engage in Science, Technology, Engineering, and Mathematics. The Budget supports NASA programs that are designed to meet the goals of the President's "Educate to Innovate" campaign in Science, Technology, Engineering and Mathematics education. NASA's Summer of Innovation, for example, will work with thousands of middle school teachers and students to engage students in stimulating, evidence-based math and science-based education programs.

National Aeronautics and Space Administration
(In millions of dollars)

	Actual 2009	Estimate 2010	Estimate 2011
Spending			
Discretionary Budget Authority:			
Science	4,503	4,469	5,006
Exploration	3,505	3,746	4,263
Aeronautics and Space Research and Technology	500	501	1,152
Space Operations	5,765	6,147	4,888
Education	169	183	146
Cross Agency Support	3,306	3,194	3,111
Construction and Environmental Compliance and Restoration	—	448	397
Inspector General	34	36	37
Total, Discretionary budget authority	17,782	18,724	19,000
Memorandum:			
Budget authority from American Recovery and Reinvestment Act	*1,002*	*—*	*—*
Total, Discretionary outlays	19,138	18,347	17,694
Memorandum: Outlays from American Recovery and Reinvestment Act	*37*	*790*	*183*
Mandatory Outlays:			
All Other General Funds and Proprietary Receipts	–6	–15	–15
Undistributed Intragovernmental Payments and Receivables	–2	—	—
Science, Space, and Technology Education Trust Fund	1	1	1
Total, Mandatory outlays	–7	–14	–14
Total, Outlays	19,131	18,333	17,680

NATIONAL SCIENCE FOUNDATION

Funding Highlights:

- Provides $7.4 billion for the National Science Foundation, an 8 percent increase over the 2010 enacted level, as part of the President's Plan for Science and Innovation.

- Drives the creation of the industries and jobs of the future by doubling funding for multidisciplinary research targeted at next-generation information and biological technologies.

- Provides $19 million in graduate and undergraduate fellowships and scholarships for a joint initiative with the Department of Energy to inspire tens of thousands of American students to pursue careers in science, engineering, and entrepreneurship related to clean energy.

- Creates a new $766 million, cross-agency sustainability research effort focused on renewable energy technologies and complex environmental- and climate-system processes.

- Increases funding by 14 percent for a new consolidated program aimed at building the science and technology workforce by recruiting and retaining undergraduate students from under-represented groups.

The National Science Foundation (NSF) is the key Federal agency responsible for supporting the full breadth of non-biomedical science and technology research at the Nation's universities and colleges. This basic research and the agency's high-tech workforce development programs help drive future economic growth and the creation of high-wage jobs for American workers. The Budget fully funds the President's Plan for Science and Innovation by providing NSF with $552 million over the 2010 enacted level, and maintains the Administration's commitment to doubling funding for key basic research agencies.

Lays the Groundwork for the Industries and Jobs of the Future. The Budget doubles funding to $90 million for basic research aimed at creating a future bio-economy by enhancing our ability to design biological systems, and

starting the next revolution in computing by designing new materials. The Budget also supports advanced manufacturing technologies by funding research on nano-manufacturing and cyber-physical systems such as automated traffic control and zero-net energy buildings.

Inspires Students to Pursue Clean Energy Careers. In partnership with the Department of Energy, NSF will dedicate at least 5 percent of its undergraduate and graduate fellowship, scholarship, and traineeship programs, roughly $19 million in 2011, to students pursuing clean energy careers.

Increases Sustainability Research. The Budget provides $766 million, an increase of $105 million over comparable 2010 levels, for a new effort at NSF that represents a fundamental shift in how the agency defines and supports multidisciplinary energy and climate research. This new cross-agency effort is an integrated approach to increasing U.S. energy independence, enhancing environmental stewardship, reducing energy and carbon intensity, and generating sustained economic growth.

Broadens Reach and Increases Funding to Promote Study of Science and Technology. The Budget proposes to launch a comprehensive science and technology workforce program to engage undergraduates at Historically Black, Tribal, and Hispanic-serving colleges and universities by realigning and building on existing programs. Funding for these activities would increase by over 14 percent to $103 million.

National Science Foundation
(In millions of dollars)

	Actual 2009	Estimate 2010	Estimate 2011
Spending			
Discretionary Budget Authority:			
Research and Related Activities	5,183	5,564	6,019
Education and Human Resources	845	873	892
Major Research Equipment and Facilities Construction	152	117	165
Agency Operations and Award Management	294	300	329
Inspector General	4	5	5
National Science Board	12	14	14
Total, Discretionary budget authority	6,490	6,873	7,424
Memorandum:			
Budget authority from American Recovery and Reinvestment Act	*3,002*	—	—
Total, Discretionary outlays	5,834	6,149	6,653
Memorandum: Outlays from American Recovery and Reinvestment Act	*27*	*1,463*	*859*
Mandatory Outlays:			
H-B Fee Programs	96	165	137
All other	1	42	-2
Total, Mandatory outlays	97	207	135
Total, Outlays	5,931	6,356	6,788

SMALL BUSINESS ADMINISTRATION

Funding Highlights:

- Supports $28 billion in loan guarantees to help small businesses access the credit they need to grow and create jobs.

- Provides competitive technical assistance grants to better support business development and regional economic growth.

- Provides long-term disaster recovery loans for homeowners, renters, and businesses of all sizes.

- Strengthens lender and procurement program oversight to protect taxpayer dollars.

- Upgrades the Agency's information technology systems and human capital resources to increase SBA's impact on businesses and communities.

The 2011 Budget provides $994 million for the Small Business Administration (SBA), a $170 million, or 21 percent, increase over the 2010 enacted level. This reflects the Administration's strong support of small businesses, which play a vital role in the Nation's economy.

Provides Small Business Access to Credit. The Budget provides $165 million in subsidy costs to support $17.5 billion in 7(a) loan guarantees that will help small businesses operate and expand. This includes an estimated $16 billion in term loans and $1.5 billion in revolving lines of credit; the latter are expected to support $39 billion in total economic activity through draws and repayments over the life of the guarantee. The Budget also supports $7.5 billion in guaranteed lending for commercial real estate development and heavy machinery purchases; $3 billion in Small Business Investment Company debentures to support new businesses and new jobs

through early-stage and mezzanine small business financing; and $25 million in direct Microloans, for intermediaries to provide small loans to emerging entrepreneurs and other promising but "un-bankable" borrowers.

The Budget also includes the following legislative proposals, to improve small business access to credit. It proposes to increase the maximum 7(a) loan size from $2 million to $5 million; to increase the maximum Certified Development Company (or "504") loan size from $2 million to $5 million for regular projects and from $4 million to $5.5 million for manufacturing projects; and to increase the maximum Microloan size to $50,000. The Budget also proposes to increase the maximum outstanding loan amount to Microloan intermediaries in their first year of participation from $750,000 to $1 million, and from $3.5 million to $5 million in the subsequent years.

Supports Business Growth and Cluster Development. The Budget includes $14 million for competitive technical assistance grants to expand SBA's Emerging Leaders (formerly Emerging 200) initiative and to enhance small business participation in regional economic clusters. The Emerging Leaders initiative ($3 million) provides intensive technical assistance to companies that have high growth potential and are located in distressed economic areas, such as inner cities and Native American communities, and connects them to regional business networks to accelerate growth. SBA will also support enhanced small business participation in regional economic clusters ($11 million) by awarding competitive grants to facilitate greater coordination of resources (business counseling, training, mentor-protégé partnerships).

Funds Long-Term Disaster Recovery. The Budget supports $1.1 billion in direct loans, the normalized 10-year average, for homeowners and businesses whose property is damaged by natural disasters. The Budget requests $203 million in new budget authority for disaster-loan administrative expenses, an increase of $126 million from the 2010 enacted level.

Strengthens Oversight to Protect Taxpayer Dollars. Due to the economic downturn and higher defaults on prior loans, SBA's guaranteed loan programs are recording a $4.5 billion increase in losses and subsidy costs on its outstanding loan portfolio, particularly on those made between 2005 and 2007. This reestimate increases the deficit in 2010. In addition, project-ed defaults and economic conditions have doubled the estimated cost of new 7(a) loan guarantees for 2011 compared to 2010. The Budget provides funding for these increased costs in 2011, as noted above. However, to strengthen the program's long-term economic foundation, the Administration will submit a legislative package to provide SBA the flexibility to adjust fees in the program to enable it to be self-sustaining over time. These changes in the program's fee structure would become effective for loans originated in 2012.

The Budget also provides additional resources to improve program management through enhanced lender oversight and credit risk mitigation activities, to promote prudent use of taxpayer dollars in SBA's programs. In addition, an increase of $4 million is requested to improve SBA's oversight of Government contracting programs ($2 million), including the HUBzone program, and to strengthen performance assessment and management of the Small Business Innovation Research program ($2 million), which provides small business opportunities through set-asides of over $2 billion annually in Federal research and development funding.

Strengthens Core Agency Capabilities. The Budget provides the resources needed to modernize SBA information technology systems, including migrating additional loan programs to a modern loan management and accounting system. The Budget also contains funds to continue SBA personnel training initiatives, to allow the agency to continue to make progress on improving its human capital and customer relationships.

Small Business Administration
(In millions of dollars)

	Actual 2009	Estimate	
		2010	2011
Spending			
Discretionary Budget Authority:			
Salaries and Expenses	390	433	446
Business Loans:			
Loan Subsidy	2	83	169
Loan Administration	138	153	157
Subtotal, Business Loans	140	236	326
Disaster Loans:			
Loan Subsidy	—	2	—
Loan Administration	—	77	203
Subtotal, Disaster Loans	—	79	203
Office of the Inspector General	17	16	18
Surety Bond Revolving Fund	2	1	1
Unrequested Projects	66	59	—
Subtotal, Gross Discretionary budget authority	615	824	994
Negative subsidy receipts	—	−2	−1
Total, Net Discretionary budget authority	615	822	993
Memorandum:			
Budget authority from American Recovery and Reinvestment Act	*730*	*—*	*—*
Budget authority from supplementals	*—*	*125*	*—*
Total, Discretionary outlays	924	916	1,233
Memorandum: Outlays from American Recovery and Reinvestment Act	*119*	*380*	*160*
Mandatory Outlays:			
Business Loan Subsidy Reestimates	1,051	4,475	N/A
Disaster Loan Subsidy Reestimates	159	211	N/A
Liquidating Credit Accounts	−7	−4	−5
Total, Mandatory outlays	1,203	4,682	−5
Total, Outlays	2,127	5,598	1,228
Credit activity			
Direct Loan Disbursements:			
Direct Disaster Loans	727	738	738
Direct Business Loans	24	400	450
Total, Direct loan disbursements	751	1,138	1,188

Small Business Administration—Continued
(In millions of dollars)

	Actual 2009	Estimate	
		2010	2011
Guaranteed Loan Commitments:			
Guaranteed Business Loans	12,116	22,803	23,900
Guaranteed Disaster Loans	—	75	—
Total, Guaranteed loan commitments	12,116	22,878	23,900

SOCIAL SECURITY ADMINISTRATION

Funding Highlights:

- Provides $12.5 billion for the Social Security Administration, an 8 percent increase, targeted at reducing backlogs and improving service for the American public.

- Expands program integrity efforts to make sure payments are made to the right person and in the right amount.

- Restructures Federal Wage Reporting.

The President believes that all Americans should be able to retire with dignity. He is committed to protecting Social Security and working in a bipartisan manner to preserve its original purpose as a reliable source of income for American seniors. The Social Security Administration (SSA) administers the Old Age, Survivors, and Disability Insurance program and the Supplemental Security Income (SSI) program. In 2009, more than 51 million retired or disabled workers, survivors, and their families received over $659 billion in benefit payments. Nearly 8 million Americans received SSI benefits totaling $49 billion.

Protects Social Security. The President recognizes that Social Security is indispensable to workers, people with disabilities, seniors, and survivors and is probably the most important and most successful program that our country has ever established. Based on current forecasts, Social Security can pay full benefits until 2037. The President is committed to making sure that Social Security is solvent and viable for the American people, now and in the future. He is strongly opposed to privatizing Social Security

and looks forward to working in a bipartisan way to preserve it for future generations.

Provides an 8 Percent Funding Increase to Provide Services Faster and Reduce Backlogs. This year, SSA will process almost 5 million retirement, survivor, and Medicare claims; 3.3 million disability claims; and over 326,000 Supplemental Security Income (SSI) aged claims. The Budget proposes $12.5 billion for SSA, an increase of $930 million, or (8 percent), above the 2010 enacted level of $11.6 billion. This amount includes resources to increase staffing in 2011 and will allow SSA to provide services faster with a focus on key service delivery areas, such as processing initial retirement and disability claims, and disability appeals. At the end of 2010, the initial disability claims backlog is expected to reach record highs with over one million people waiting for a decision. This is unacceptable. The 2011 Budget funds SSA to lower the backlog below one million by processing over three million claims. The Budget also allows SSA to continue to reduce the appeals hearing backlog. By hearing approximately 799,000 cases in 2011, the backlog will fall to 657,000 hearings pending. In addition, the Budget also includes resources to enable SSA to more effectively and efficiently verify hundreds of millions of Social Security Numbers and issue about 19 million Social Security cards.

Increases Significantly Program Integrity Efforts. SSA's program integrity efforts are part of a strong framework for making sure the Government is spending tax dollars efficiently and that benefits are paid only to those beneficiaries who are eligible and are paid in correct amounts. The President's 2011 Budget provides $796 million for SSA program integrity, including an over 9 percent increase in the level of medical Continuing Disability Reviews over the prior year. Continuing Disability Reviews make sure

that Disability Insurance and SSI recipients continue to the meet the medical criteria for those programs.

Restructures the Federal Wage Reporting Process. The President's 2011 Budget proposes to restructure the Federal wage reporting process by reverting to quarterly wage reporting. Currently, wages are reported to the Federal Government once a year. Increasing the timeliness of wage reporting would enhance tax administration, improve program integrity for a range of programs, and facilitate implementation of automatic workplace pensions. The Administration will work with the States so that the overall reporting burden on employers is not increased.

Social Security Administration
(In millions of dollars)

	Actual 2009	Estimate	
		2010	2011
Spending			
Discretionary Budget Authority:			
Limitation on Administrative Expenses (LAE) Base [1,2]	10,285	11,281	12,195
Office of Inspector General	100	103	106
Research and Development	28	42	36
Total, Discretionary budget authority	10,413	11,426	12,338
Memorandum:			
Budget authority from American Recovery and Reinvestment Act	*1,092*	—	—
Total, Discretionary outlays	10,163	11,124	12,142
Memorandum: Outlays from American Recovery and Reinvestment Act	*165*	*389*	*31*
Mandatory Outlays:			
Old-age, Survivors, and Disability Insurance	664,732	702,582	729,523
Supplemental Security Income	44,906	47,478	52,761
Special Benefits for Certain World War II Veterans	9	9	8
Offseting collections	–24,452	–28,006	–30,285
Legislative proposals	—	12,543	569
All other	20,838	24,440	26,889
Total, Mandatory outlays	706,033	759,046	779,465

Social Security Administration—Continued
(In millions of dollars)

	Actual 2009	Estimate	
		2010	2011
Memorandum: Outlays from American Recovery and Reinvestment Act ...	*13,079*	*300*	*45*
Total, Outlays	716,173	770,379	791,681

[1] The LAE account includes funding from the Hospital Insurance and Supplementary Medical Insurance trust funds for services that support the Medicare program, including implementation of Medicare Reform.

[2] This amount reflects offsetting collections from SSI State Supplemental Fees.

CORPORATION FOR NATIONAL AND COMMUNITY SERVICE

Funding Highlights:

- Expands AmeriCorps, the national service program, to a record-level 105,000 members from 85,000 members, providing more opportunities for all Americans to serve their communities.

- Fosters the replication of innovative, proven and transformative evidence-based programs through the Social Innovation Fund.

- Strengthens the Corporation's management and information technology infrastructure to meet the President's vision and support the growth and excellence in its programs.

The President believes that service is central to addressing our Nation's greatest challenges. The Corporation for National and Community Service (CNCS) provides an on-ramp for Americans of all ages to serve their community and country in sustained and effective ways throughout their lives, from tutoring at-risk youth to responding to natural disasters to building the capacity of community organizations. The President also believes that many of the best solutions to America's challenges can be found outside of Washington, in communities across the country. That is why the President's Budget proposes $1.416 billion for CNCS, an increase of $266 million from 2010, providing more Americans the opportunity to serve and fostering community innovation.

Expands National Service. In April 2009, the President signed the Edward M. Kennedy Serve America Act, which authorized an unprecedented expansion of the AmeriCorps program to 250,000 members by 2017. This Budget keeps the program on that trajectory by funding over 105,000 members in 2011, an increase of 20,000 from 2010. The increase for

AmeriCorps includes additional funds for the National Civilian Community Corps program, a full-time, team-based, residential program with a focus on disaster relief.

Invests in Innovative Non-Profits. Innovators often come up with great ideas for addressing critical national challenges, but too often they lack the capital to develop, evaluate, and replicate successful approaches. The Budget invests $60 million in the Social Innovation Fund to test promising new approaches to major challenges, leverage private and foundation capital to meet these needs, and grow evidence-based programs.

Strengthens the Management Capacity of the Corporation. The success of the Corporation's programs and growth requires an investment in its management, so the Budget provides resources to strengthen the Corporation's capacity to meet the President's vision and manage its growing portfolio. In addition to staffing, the Budget supports targeted enhancements to the agency's information technology (IT) infrastructure. These IT improvements are critical to the effective performance of nearly every aspect of the Corporation's business. The Budget likewise invests in the Corporation's capacity to measure its performance, evaluate its programs, and make data-driven decisions.

Corporation for National and Community Service
(In millions of dollars)

	Actual 2009	Estimate 2010	2011
Spending			
Discretionary Budget Authority:			
Operating Expenses	812	1,054	1,298
AmeriCorps (non-add)	*526*	*698*	*914*
Learn and Serve America (non-add)	*37*	*40*	*40*
Senior Corps (non-add)	*214*	*221*	*221*
Social Innovation Fund (non-add)	*—*	*50*	*60*
Salaries and Expenses	72	88	109
Office of the Inspector General	7	8	9
Total, Discretionary budget authority	891	1,150	1,416
Memorandum:			
Budget authority from American Recovery and Reinvestment Act	*201*	*—*	*—*
Total, Discretionary outlays	860	732	945
Memorandum: Outlays from American Recovery and Reinvestment Act	*56*	*50*	*26*
Mandatory Outlays:			
Interest, National Service Trust	—	30	22
Total, Mandatory outlays	—	30	22
Total, Outlays	859	762	967

SUMMARY TABLES

Table S–1. Budget Totals
(In billions of dollars)

	2009	2010	2011	2012	2013	2014	2015	2016	2017	2018	2019	2020	Totals 2011-2015	Totals 2011-2020
Budget (Without Fiscal Commission)														
Budget Totals in Billions of Dollars:														
Receipts	2,105	2,165	2,567	2,926	3,188	3,455	3,634	3,887	4,094	4,299	4,507	4,710	15,771	37,268
Outlays	3,518	3,721	3,834	3,755	3,915	4,161	4,386	4,665	4,872	5,084	5,415	5,713	20,051	45,800
Deficit	1,413	1,556	1,267	828	727	706	752	778	778	785	908	1,003	4,280	8,532
Debt held by the public	7,545	9,298	10,498	11,472	12,326	13,139	13,988	14,833	15,686	16,535	17,502	18,573		
Debt net of financial assets	6,647	8,164	9,418	10,246	10,972	11,677	12,428	13,205	13,983	14,767	15,675	16,677		
Gross domestic product (GDP)	14,237	14,624	15,299	16,203	17,182	18,193	19,190	20,163	21,136	22,087	23,065	24,067		
Budget Totals as a Percent of GDP:														
Receipts	14.8%	14.8%	16.8%	18.1%	18.6%	19.0%	18.9%	19.3%	19.4%	19.5%	19.5%	19.6%	18.3%	18.9%
Outlays	24.7%	25.4%	25.1%	23.2%	22.8%	22.9%	22.9%	23.1%	23.1%	23.0%	23.5%	23.7%	23.3%	23.3%
Deficit	9.9%	10.6%	8.3%	5.1%	4.2%	3.9%	3.9%	3.9%	3.7%	3.6%	3.9%	4.2%	5.1%	4.5%
Debt held by the public	53.0%	63.6%	68.6%	70.8%	71.7%	72.2%	72.9%	73.6%	74.2%	74.9%	75.9%	77.2%		
Debt net of financial assets	46.7%	55.8%	61.6%	63.2%	63.9%	64.2%	64.8%	65.5%	66.2%	66.9%	68.0%	69.3%		

FISCAL COMMISSION

The Administration supports the creation of a Fiscal Commission. The Fiscal Commission is charged with identifying policies to improve the fiscal situation in the medium term and to achieve fiscal sustainability over the long run. Specifically, the Commission is charged with balancing the budget excluding interest payments on the debt by 2015. The result is projected to stabilize the debt-to-GDP ratio at an acceptable level once the economy recovers. The magnitude and timing of the policy measures necessary to achieve this goal are subject to considerable uncertainty and will depend on the evolution of the economy. In addition, the Commission will examine policies to meaningfully improve the long-run fiscal outlook, including changes to address the growth of entitlement spending and the gap between the projected revenues and expenditures of the Federal Government.

Table S–2. Effect of Budget Proposals on Projected Deficits

(Deficit increases (+) or decreases (−) in billions of dollars)

	2010	2011	2012	2013	2014	2015	2016	2017	2018	2019	2020	Totals 2011–2015	Totals 2011–2020
Projected deficits in the baseline projection of current policy[1]	1,430	1,145	934	940	934	983	1,013	1,042	1,077	1,227	1,346	4,936	10,640
Percent of GDP	9.8%	7.5%	5.8%	5.5%	5.1%	5.1%	5.0%	4.9%	4.9%	5.3%	5.6%	5.8%	5.5%
Temporary recovery measures:													
Tax cuts	29	53	20	−7	−5	−4	−3	−2	−2	−1	−1	57	47
Mandatory proposals	45	44	1	*	.....	.....	.....	.....	.....	.....	.....	46	46
Allowance for other jobs initiatives	24	50	16	6	4	.....	.....	.....	.....	.....	.....	76	76
Total, temporary recovery measures	98	147	37	−1	−1	−4	−3	−2	−2	−1	−1	179	169
Allowance for health reform[2]	6	−23	−34	−39	−28	−3	12	2	−6	−12	−20	−127	−150
Allowance for climate policy[3]													
Tax cuts for families and businesses[4, 5]	12	29	31	23	24	25	27	28	30	32	35	133	284
Other revenue changes and loophole closers[4, 6]	−1	−36	−66	−74	−77	−78	−79	−81	−83	−86	−90	−331	−749
Proposed changes in mandatory programs and user fees[7]	2	−2	4	2	4	−2	−4	−6	−7	−7	−6	6	−24
Proposed changes in appropriated ("discretionary") programs:													
Overseas contingency operations (OCO)	9	37	−41	−75	−83	−87	−91	−93	−95	−98	−101	−250	−728
Security (except OCO)	2	12	18	23	26	30	32	34	35	36	37	109	284
Non-security	*	−10	−15	−24	−27	−29	−29	−30	−31	−30	−25	−105	−249
Subtotal, appropriated programs	11	39	−38	−76	−84	−86	−88	−89	−91	−92	−88	−245	−693
Subtotal, policy proposals	**127**	**154**	**−67**	**−164**	**−161**	**−147**	**−135**	**−148**	**−158**	**−166**	**−170**	**−386**	**−1,164**
Upper-income tax provisions dedicated to deficit reduction	−1	−34	−41	−50	−60	−68	−74	−80	−85	−91	−97	−252	−678
Credit and other indirect interest effects	−*	−2	−2	−*	1	2	2	2	3	3	3	−1	13
Debt service	*	2	5	1	−8	−18	−28	−39	−51	−64	−79	−17	−279
Total reduction in projected deficits	**125**	**121**	**−105**	**−213**	**−228**	**−231**	**−235**	**−264**	**−292**	**−319**	**−343**	**−656**	**−2,108**
Resulting deficits in 2011 Budget	1,556	1,267	828	727	706	752	778	778	785	908	1,003	4,280	8,532
Percent of GDP	10.6%	8.3%	5.1%	4.2%	3.9%	3.9%	3.9%	3.7%	3.6%	3.9%	4.2%	5.1%	4.5%

Table S–2. Effect of Budget Proposals on Projected Deficits—Continued

(Deficit increases (+) or decreases (–) in billions of dollars)

	2010	2011	2012	2013	2014	2015	2016	2017	2018	2019	2020	Totals 2011–2015	Totals 2011–2020
Memorandum, proposed changes in appropriated ("discretionary") budgetary resources:													
Overseas contingency operations	33	28	–84	–86	–88	–90	–93	–95	–98	–101	–103	–320	–810
Security (except OCO)	8	16	27	30	33	37	38	39	39	40	41	144	341
Non-security	......	–14	–19	–31	–29	–27	–32	–34	–34	–32	–25	–120	–278
Total, appropriated funding	41	30	–75	–86	–85	–80	–87	–91	–93	–93	–87	–296	–747
Memorandum, deficit reduction exclusive of OCO proposals and related debt service	117	84	–65	–136	–140	–135	–131	–153	–173	–192	–208	–391	–1,249

Note: Figures displayed in the table do not reflect the impact of any recommendations from the Fiscal Commission.

* $500 million or less.

[1] See tables S–3 and S–7 for information on the baseline projection of current policy.

[2] Allowance for pending health reform legislation. See Table S–8 for further detail.

[3] A comprehensive market-based climate change policy will be deficit neutral because proceeds from emissions allowances will be used to compensate vulnerable families, communities, and businesses during the transition to a clean energy economy. Receipts will also be reserved for investments to reduce greenhouse gas emissions, including support of clean energy technologies, and in adapting to the impacts of climate change, both domestically and in developing countries.

[4] Includes refundable tax credits.

[5] Includes the effects of continuing certain expiring provisions through calendar year 2011.

[6] Includes limiting itemized deductions, trade initiatives, and other tax initiatives on Table S–8.

[7] Includes PAYGO impact of changes in mandatory programs included in appropriations language.

Table S–3. Baseline Projection of Current Policy by Category[1]
(In billions of dollars)

	2009	2010	2011	2012	2013	2014	2015	2016	2017	2018	2019	2020	Totals 2011–2015	Totals 2011–2020
Outlays:														
Appropriated ("discretionary") programs:														
Security	782	844	846	850	863	882	903	921	944	968	993	1,019	4,344	9,187
Non-security	437	553	530	490	480	484	493	504	516	528	541	554	2,477	5,120
Subtotal, appropriated programs	1,219	1,397	1,376	1,340	1,343	1,367	1,396	1,425	1,460	1,496	1,534	1,573	6,821	14,307
Mandatory programs:														
Social Security	678	703	730	762	801	846	894	947	1,004	1,067	1,133	1,204	4,033	9,388
Medicare	425	451	492	502	557	625	654	727	760	795	886	957	2,830	6,955
Medicaid	251	275	271	274	293	313	337	363	390	420	453	488	1,488	3,602
Troubled Asset Relief Program (TARP)[2]	151	–73	11	10	7	6	3	1	*	*	.....	.....	37	39
Other mandatory programs	607	701	596	532	532	526	525	542	543	542	588	606	2,710	5,532
Subtotal, mandatory programs	2,112	2,057	2,100	2,079	2,191	2,316	2,413	2,579	2,698	2,823	3,060	3,256	11,098	25,515
Net interest	187	188	250	340	434	516	586	652	716	779	844	912	2,126	6,029
Disaster costs[3]	.....	1	3	4	4	4	5	5	5	5	5	5	21	46
Total outlays	3,518	3,643	3,728	3,762	3,973	4,203	4,400	4,661	4,879	5,103	5,443	5,746	20,066	45,897
Receipts:														
Individual income taxes	915	951	1,126	1,271	1,387	1,507	1,625	1,739	1,853	1,966	2,078	2,186	6,917	16,739
Corporation income taxes	138	176	293	333	361	415	383	422	437	449	461	478	1,785	4,031
Social insurance and retirement receipts:														
Social Security payroll taxes	654	635	674	720	764	810	854	908	949	994	1,038	1,077	3,823	8,788
Medicare payroll taxes	191	180	192	208	222	236	250	266	278	292	305	317	1,108	2,566
Unemployment insurance	38	51	60	66	71	75	77	77	76	74	74	75	349	725
Other retirement	8	9	8	9	9	9	9	9	9	9	9	10	43	89
Excise taxes	62	74	80	83	84	86	87	88	89	89	90	91	419	867
Estate and gift taxes	23	17	24	21	22	24	25	27	29	32	34	36	116	274
Customs duties	22	24	29	33	36	38	40	43	45	48	50	53	175	413
Deposits of earnings, Federal Reserve System	34	77	79	67	59	52	48	50	52	55	57	59	305	578
Other miscellaneous receipts	18	18	18	18	18	18	19	19	19	19	20	20	91	188
Total receipts	2,105	2,213	2,583	2,829	3,033	3,269	3,417	3,648	3,838	4,026	4,215	4,400	15,130	35,257
Deficit	1,413	1,430	1,145	934	940	934	983	1,013	1,042	1,077	1,227	1,346	4,936	10,640
On-budget deficit	1,550	1,508	1,241	1,054	1,074	1,080	1,139	1,183	1,209	1,243	1,385	1,486	5,589	12,094
Off-budget surplus (–)	–137	–78	–96	–120	–135	–147	–156	–170	–168	–166	–157	–140	–653	–1,454

Table S–3.   Baseline Projection of Current Policy by Category [1]–Continued
(In billions of dollars)

	2009	2010	2011	2012	2013	2014	2015	2016	2017	2018	2019	2020	Totals	
													2011–2015	2011–2020
Memorandum, funding ("budgetary resources") for appropriated programs:														
Security	824	814	834	854	874	895	917	939	963	988	1,013	1,040	4,374	9,318
Non-security	689	447	456	465	477	488	499	511	523	536	549	563	2,385	5,067
Total, appropriated funding	1,513	1,260	1,290	1,319	1,351	1,383	1,416	1,450	1,486	1,524	1,562	1,602	6,760	14,385

* $500 million or less.

[1] See Table S–7 for information on adjustments to the Budget Enforcement Act (BEA) baseline.

[2] Outlays for TARP in 2011 and subsequent years result from obligations for the Home Affordable Modification Program, and other estimated TARP obligations incurred through October 3, 2010.

[3] These amounts represent a placeholder for major disasters requiring Federal assistance for relief and reconstruction. Such assistance might be provided in the form of discretionary or mandatory outlays or tax relief. These amounts are included as outlays for convenience.

Table S–4. Proposed Budget by Category
(In billions of dollars)

	2009	2010	2011	2012	2013	2014	2015	2016	2017	2018	2019	2020	Totals 2011–2015	Totals 2011–2020
Outlays:														
Appropriated ("discretionary") programs:														
Security	782	855	895	827	811	825	845	862	885	907	931	955	4,203	8,743
Non-security	437	553	520	475	456	457	465	475	486	497	511	529	2,373	4,871
Subtotal, appropriated programs	1,219	1,408	1,415	1,301	1,267	1,283	1,310	1,337	1,371	1,405	1,442	1,484	6,576	13,614
Mandatory programs:														
Social Security	678	715	730	762	801	845	893	945	1,002	1,064	1,130	1,201	4,030	9,373
Medicare	425	451	491	501	556	623	652	724	757	791	881	953	2,822	6,927
Medicaid	251	275	297	274	292	313	336	362	389	419	451	487	1,512	3,619
Troubled Asset Relief Program (TARP)[1]	151	–73	11	10	7	6	3	1	*	*	.....	.....	37	39
Allowance for jobs initiatives	.....	12	25	8	3	2	.....	.....	.....	.....	.....	.....	38	38
Allowance for health reform[2]	.....	6	–7	–17	2	30	72	101	100	100	104	106	80	590
Other mandatory programs	607	737	619	570	547	546	544	563	567	568	616	637	2,826	5,775
Subtotal, mandatory programs	2,112	2,123	2,165	2,107	2,208	2,364	2,500	2,696	2,815	2,942	3,182	3,384	11,344	26,363
Net interest	187	188	251	343	436	510	571	627	681	733	786	840	2,110	5,777
Disaster costs[3]	.....	1	3	4	4	4	5	5	5	5	5	5	21	46
Total outlays	3,518	3,721	3,834	3,755	3,915	4,161	4,386	4,665	4,872	5,084	5,415	5,713	20,051	45,800
Receipts:														
Individual income taxes	915	936	1,121	1,326	1,468	1,604	1,733	1,856	1,980	2,102	2,223	2,338	7,253	17,752
Corporation income taxes	138	157	297	366	393	445	411	449	463	473	486	502	1,913	4,285
Social insurance and retirement receipts:														
Social Security payroll taxes	654	635	674	720	766	809	856	911	954	1,000	1,044	1,084	3,825	8,819
Medicare payroll taxes	191	180	192	208	223	237	251	267	280	293	307	318	1,112	2,578
Unemployment insurance	38	51	60	67	73	77	79	79	78	77	76	77	357	743
Other retirement	8	9	8	9	9	9	9	9	9	9	9	10	43	89
Excise taxes	62	73	74	81	85	87	88	89	90	90	91	92	415	867
Estate and gift taxes	23	17	25	23	24	26	28	30	32	35	37	40	124	298
Customs duties	22	24	27	32	35	37	39	42	44	47	49	52	170	404
Deposits of earnings, Federal Reserve System	34	77	79	67	59	52	48	50	52	55	57	59	305	578
Allowance for jobs initiatives	.....	–12	–25	–8	–3	–2	.....	.....	.....	.....	.....	.....	–38	–38
Allowance for health reform[2]	.....	.....	16	18	39	58	74	86	93	101	110	119	204	712
Other miscellaneous receipts	18	18	17	17	17	18	18	18	18	19	19	19	87	180
Total receipts	2,105	2,165	2,567	2,926	3,188	3,455	3,634	3,887	4,094	4,299	4,507	4,710	15,771	37,268
Deficit	1,413	1,556	1,267	828	727	706	752	778	778	785	908	1,003	4,280	8,532

Table S–4. Proposed Budget by Category—Continued
(In billions of dollars)

	2009	2010	2011	2012	2013	2014	2015	2016	2017	2018	2019	2020	Totals 2011–2015	Totals 2011–2020
On-budget deficit	1,550	1,634	1,363	949	863	852	910	952	952	959	1,075	1,153	4,937	10,028
Off-budget surplus (–)	–137	–78	–96	–120	–136	–146	–158	–175	–174	–174	–167	–151	–656	–1,496
Primary deficit	1,226	1,368	1,016	486	291	196	181	151	97	52	123	163	2,170	2,755
Net interest	187	188	251	343	436	510	571	627	681	733	786	840	2,110	5,777
Memorandum, funding ("budgetary resources") for appropriated programs:														
Security	824	855	879	798	819	840	864	885	906	929	953	978	4,198	8,849
Non-security	689	447	441	446	446	459	472	479	489	502	517	538	2,265	4,789
Total, appropriated funding	1,513	1,302	1,320	1,244	1,265	1,299	1,336	1,363	1,395	1,431	1,470	1,515	6,464	13,638

Note: Figures displayed in the table do not reflect the impact of any recommendations from the Fiscal Commission.

* $500 million or less.

[1] Outlays for TARP in 2011 and subsequent years result from obligations for the Home Affordable Modification Programs, and other estimated TARP obligations incurred through October 3, 2010.

[2] Reflects on-budget effects only. See Table S–8 for further detail.

[3] These amounts represent a placeholder for major disasters requiring Federal assistance for relief and reconstruction. Such assistance might be provided in the form of discretionary or mandatory outlays or tax relief. These amounts are included as outlays for convenience.

Policy Outlays by Category

Policy Revenues by Source

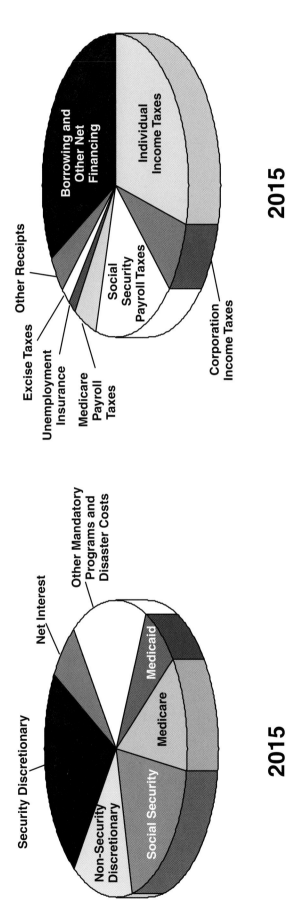

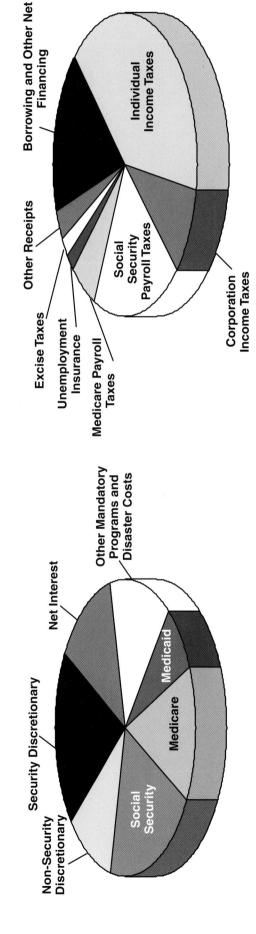

Table S-5. Proposed Budget by Category as a Percent of GDP
(As a percent of GDP)

	2009	2010	2011	2012	2013	2014	2015	2016	2017	2018	2019	2020	Averages 2011–2015	Averages 2011–2020
Outlays:														
Appropriated ("discretionary") programs:														
Security	5.5	5.8	5.8	5.1	4.7	4.5	4.4	4.3	4.2	4.1	4.0	4.0	4.9	4.5
Non-security	3.1	3.8	3.4	2.9	2.7	2.5	2.4	2.4	2.3	2.3	2.2	2.2	2.8	2.5
Subtotal, appropriated programs	8.6	9.6	9.2	8.0	7.4	7.1	6.8	6.6	6.5	6.4	6.3	6.2	7.7	7.0
Mandatory programs:														
Social Security	4.8	4.9	4.8	4.7	4.7	4.6	4.7	4.7	4.7	4.8	4.9	5.0	4.7	4.8
Medicare	3.0	3.1	3.2	3.1	3.2	3.4	3.4	3.6	3.6	3.6	3.8	4.0	3.3	3.5
Medicaid	1.8	1.9	1.9	1.7	1.7	1.7	1.8	1.8	1.8	1.9	2.0	2.0	1.8	1.8
Troubled Asset Relief Program (TARP)[1]	1.1	-0.5	0.1	0.1	*	*	*	*	*	*	.....	.....	*	*
Allowance for jobs initatives	.....	0.1	0.2	*	*	*	.....	.....	.....	.....	.....	.....	*	*
Allowance for health reform[2]	*	*	–*	-0.1	*	0.2	0.4	0.5	0.5	0.5	0.4	0.4	0.1	0.3
Other mandatory programs	4.3	5.0	4.0	3.5	3.2	3.0	2.8	2.8	2.7	2.6	2.7	2.6	3.3	3.0
Subtotal, mandatory programs	14.8	14.5	14.2	13.0	12.9	13.0	13.0	13.4	13.3	13.3	13.8	14.1	13.2	13.4
Net interest	1.3	1.3	1.6	2.1	2.5	2.8	3.0	3.1	3.2	3.3	3.4	3.5	2.4	2.9
Disaster costs[3]	.....	*	*	*	*	*	*	*	*	*	*	*	*	*
Total outlays	24.7	25.4	25.1	23.2	22.8	22.9	22.9	23.1	23.1	23.0	23.5	23.7	23.3	23.3
Receipts:														
Individual income taxes	6.4	6.4	7.3	8.2	8.5	8.8	9.0	9.2	9.4	9.5	9.6	9.7	8.4	8.9
Corporation income taxes	1.0	1.1	1.9	2.3	2.3	2.4	2.1	2.2	2.2	2.1	2.1	2.1	2.2	2.2
Social insurance and retirement receipts:														
Social Security payroll taxes	4.6	4.3	4.4	4.4	4.5	4.4	4.5	4.5	4.5	4.5	4.5	4.5	4.4	4.5
Medicare payroll taxes	1.3	1.2	1.3	1.3	1.3	1.3	1.3	1.3	1.3	1.3	1.3	1.3	1.3	1.3
Unemployment insurance	0.3	0.4	0.4	0.4	0.4	0.4	0.4	0.4	0.4	0.3	0.3	0.3	0.4	0.4
Other retirement	0.1	0.1	0.1	0.1	*	*	*	*	*	*	*	*	0.1	*
Excise taxes	0.4	0.5	0.5	0.5	0.5	0.5	0.5	0.4	0.4	0.4	0.4	0.4	0.5	0.4
Estate and gift taxes	0.2	0.1	0.2	0.1	0.1	0.1	0.1	0.1	0.2	0.2	0.2	0.2	0.1	0.2
Customs duties	0.2	0.2	0.2	0.2	0.2	0.2	0.2	0.2	0.2	0.2	0.2	0.2	0.2	0.2
Deposits of earnings, Federal Reserve System	0.2	0.5	0.5	0.4	0.3	0.3	0.2	0.2	0.2	0.2	0.2	0.2	0.4	0.3
Allowance for jobs initatives	.....	-0.1	-0.2	–*	–*	–*	.....	.....	.....	.....	.....	.....	–*	–*
Allowance for health reform	.....	.....	0.1	0.1	0.2	0.3	0.4	0.4	0.4	0.5	0.5	0.5	0.2	0.3
Other miscellaneous receipts	0.1	0.1	0.1	0.1	0.1	0.1	0.1	0.1	0.1	0.1	0.1	0.1	0.1	0.1
Total receipts	14.8	14.8	16.8	18.1	18.6	19.0	18.9	19.3	19.4	19.5	19.5	19.6	18.3	18.9
Deficit	**9.9**	**10.6**	**8.3**	**5.1**	**4.2**	**3.9**	**3.9**	**3.9**	**3.7**	**3.6**	**3.9**	**4.2**	**5.1**	**4.5**

Table S–5. Proposed Budget by Category as a Percent of GDP—Continued

(As a percent of GDP)

	2009	2010	2011	2012	2013	2014	2015	2016	2017	2018	2019	2020	Averages 2011–2015	Averages 2011–2020
On-budget deficit	10.9	11.2	8.9	5.9	5.0	4.7	4.7	4.7	4.5	4.3	4.7	4.8	5.8	5.2
Off-budget surplus (–)	–1.0	–0.5	–0.6	–0.7	–0.8	–0.8	–0.8	–0.9	–0.8	–0.8	–0.7	–0.6	–0.8	–0.8
Primary deficit	8.6	9.4	6.6	3.0	1.7	1.1	0.9	0.7	0.5	0.2	0.5	0.7	2.7	1.6
Net interest	1.3	1.3	1.6	2.1	2.5	2.8	3.0	3.1	3.2	3.3	3.4	3.5	2.4	2.9
Memorandum, funding ("budgetary resources") for appropriated programs:														
Security	5.8	5.8	5.7	4.9	4.8	4.6	4.5	4.4	4.3	4.2	4.1	4.1	4.9	4.6
Non-security	4.8	3.1	2.9	2.8	2.6	2.5	2.5	2.4	2.3	2.3	2.2	2.2	2.6	2.5
Subtotal, appropriated programs	10.6	8.9	8.6	7.7	7.4	7.1	7.0	6.8	6.6	6.5	6.4	6.3	7.6	7.0

Note: Figures displayed in the table do not reflect the impact of any recommendations from the Fiscal Commission.

* 0.05 percent of GDP or less.

[1] Outlays for TARP in 2011 and subsequent years result from obligations for the Home Affordable Modification Program, and other estimated TARP obligations incurred through October 3, 2010.

[2] Reflects on-budget effects only. See Table S–8 for further detail.

[3] These amounts represent a placeholder for major disasters requiring Federal assistance for relief and reconstruction. Such assistance might be provided in the form of discretionary or mandatory outlays or tax relief. These amounts are included as outlays for convenience.

Table S-6. Proposed Budget by Category Adjusted for Inflation and Population Growth

(In billions of dollars, based on 2011 prices and population)

	2011	2012	2013	2014	2015	2016	2017	2018	2019	2020
Outlays:										
Appropriated ("discretionary") programs:										
Security	895	804	766	756	752	745	741	738	734	731
Non-security	520	461	430	419	413	410	407	404	403	405
Subtotal, appropriated programs	1,415	1,265	1,196	1,175	1,165	1,155	1,149	1,142	1,137	1,137
Mandatory programs:										
Social Security	730	740	756	774	794	816	840	865	891	920
Medicare	491	487	524	570	580	625	634	643	695	730
Medicaid	297	266	276	287	299	313	326	340	356	373
Troubled Asset Relief Program (TARP)[1]	11	10	7	6	3	1	*	*	.....	.....
Allowance for jobs initiatives	25	8	3	2	.....	.....	.....	.....	.....	.....
Allowance for health reform[2]	–7	–17	1	27	65	87	83	82	82	82
Other mandatory programs	619	554	517	500	484	486	475	461	486	488
Subtotal, mandatory programs	2,165	2,048	2,084	2,166	2,225	2,329	2,358	2,391	2,510	2,592
Net interest	251	333	411	467	508	542	571	596	620	643
Disaster costs[3]	3	4	4	4	4	4	4	4	4	4
Total outlays	3,834	3,650	3,695	3,813	3,902	4,030	4,082	4,133	4,271	4,376
Receipts:										
Individual income taxes	1,121	1,289	1,386	1,470	1,542	1,604	1,659	1,709	1,753	1,791
Corporation income taxes	297	356	371	408	366	388	388	384	383	385
Social insurance and retirement receipts:										
Social Security payroll taxes	674	700	723	741	762	787	800	813	823	830
Medicare payroll taxes	192	203	210	217	224	231	235	239	242	244
Unemployment insurance	60	66	69	71	70	68	65	62	60	59
Other retirement	8	8	8	8	8	8	7	7	7	7
Excise taxes	74	79	80	79	78	77	75	74	72	70
Estate and gift taxes	25	22	22	23	25	26	27	28	29	31
Customs duties	27	31	33	34	35	36	37	38	39	40
Deposits of earnings, Federal Reserve System	79	65	56	48	42	43	44	44	45	45
Allowance for jobs initiatives	–25	–8	–3	–2	.....	.....	.....	.....	.....	.....
Allowance for health reform[2]	16	17	37	53	66	74	78	82	86	91
Other miscellaneous receipts	17	17	16	16	16	16	15	15	15	15
Total receipts	2,567	2,845	3,009	3,167	3,233	3,358	3,431	3,495	3,554	3,607
Deficit	1,267	805	686	647	669	672	652	638	716	768

Table S–6. Proposed Budget by Category Adjusted for Inflation and Population Growth—Continued

(In billions of dollars, based on 2011 prices and population)

	2011	2012	2013	2014	2015	2016	2017	2018	2019	2020
On-budget deficit	1,363	922	815	781	810	823	798	779	848	883
Off-budget surplus (−)	−96	−117	−128	−134	−141	−151	−146	−141	−131	−115
Primary deficit	1,016	472	275	179	161	130	81	42	97	125
Net interest	251	333	411	467	508	542	571	596	620	643
Memorandum, funding ("budgetary resources") for appropriated programs:										
Security	879	775	773	769	769	764	760	755	751	749
Non-security	441	434	421	421	420	414	410	408	408	412
Subtotal, appropriated programs	1,320	1,209	1,194	1,190	1,189	1,178	1,169	1,163	1,159	1,160

Note: Figures displayed in the table do not reflect the impact of any recommendations from the Fiscal Commission.

* $500 million or less.

[1] Outlays for TARP in 2011 and subsequent years result from obligations for the Home Affordable Modification Program, and other estimated TARP obligations incurred through October 3, 2010.

[2] Reflects on-budget effects only. See Table S–8 for further detail.

[3] These amounts represent a placeholder for major disasters requiring Federal assistance for relief and reconstruction. Such assistance might be provided in the form of discretionary or mandatory outlays or tax relief. These amounts are included as outlays for convenience.

Table S–7. Bridge From Budget Enforcement Act Baseline to Baseline Projection of Current Policy

(Deficit increases (+) or decreases (–) in billions of dollars)

	2009	2010	2011	2012	2013	2014	2015	2016	2017	2018	2019	2020	Totals 2011–2015	Totals 2011–2020
BEA baseline deficit	1,413	1,404	912	613	561	495	492	469	445	421	507	557	3,073	5,472
Adjustments to reflect current policies:														
Index to inflation the 2009 parameters of the AMT	.....	13	64	32	38	45	53	62	72	84	97	110	233	659
Continue the 2001 and 2003 tax cuts[1]	.....	5	135	237	266	295	318	335	352	369	386	403	1,251	3,097
Prevent reduction in Medicare physician payments	.....	7	22	27	32	34	35	38	40	43	48	53	150	371
Correct baseline growth rates for pay increases	.....	.....	–2	–3	–3	–3	–3	–3	–3	–4	–4	–4	–14	–32
Subtotal	.....	25	219	294	333	371	403	432	461	492	527	562	1,620	4,095
Adjustment to reflect costs of possible emergencies[2]	.....	1	3	4	4	4	5	5	5	5	5	5	21	46
Adjustments to Pell Grants:														
Reflect cost of funding existing maximum grant award	.....	.....	9	12	12	12	12	12	12	12	12	13	56	118
Remove Pell Grants from appropriated category	–19	–27	–27	–29	–30	–30	–31	–31	–32	–32	–32	–33	–147	–307
Add Pell Grants to mandatory category	19	27	27	29	30	30	31	31	32	32	32	33	147	307
Subtotal	.....	.....	9	12	12	12	12	12	12	12	12	13	56	118
Total program adjustments	.....	26	231	310	349	387	420	449	478	510	545	580	1,697	4,259
Debt service on adjustments	.....	*	2	11	31	51	71	94	118	146	175	209	167	909
Total adjustments	.....	26	233	321	379	438	491	543	597	655	720	789	1,863	5,167
Baseline projection of current policy deficit	1,413	1,430	1,145	934	940	934	983	1,013	1,042	1,077	1,227	1,346	4,936	10,640

*$500 million or less.

[1] In continuing the 2001 and 2003 tax cuts, the estate tax is maintained at its 2009 parameters.

[2] These amounts represent a placeholder for major disasters requiring Federal assistance for relief and reconstruction. Such assistance might be provided in the form of discretionary or mandatory outlays or tax relief. These amounts are included as outlays for convenience.

S–8. Mandatory and Receipt Proposals
(Deficit increases (+) or decreases (–) in millions of dollars)

	2010	2011	2012	2013	2014	2015	2016	2017	2018	2019	2020	Totals 2011–2015	Totals 2011–2020
Temporary Recovery Measures (emergency, exempt from PAYGO):													
Tax Cuts:													
Extend making work pay tax credit in 2011[1]	....	30,132	31,075	....	....	....	....	....	....	....	....	61,207	61,207
Extend COBRA health insurance premium assistance[1]	3,188	5,237	228	....	....	....	....	....	....	....	....	5,465	5,465
Provide additional tax credits for investment in qualified property used in a qualified advanced energy manufacturing project	....	284	731	1,145	1,114	539	122	–72	–114	–62	–26	3,813	3,661
Extend temporary increase in expensing for small businesses	706	440	–434	–268	–186	–135	–76	–43	–24	–15	–12	–583	–753
Extend temporary bonus depreciation for certain property	22,445	15,216	–11,912	–7,478	–5,149	–3,912	–2,580	–1,685	–1,063	–792	–744	–13,235	–20,099
Extend option for grants to States in lieu of housing tax credits[1]	2,435	1,798	–91	–269	–429	–511	–538	–538	–538	–538	–538	498	–2,192
Total, tax cuts	28,774	53,107	19,597	–6,870	–4,650	–4,019	–3,072	–2,338	–1,739	–1,407	–1,320	57,165	47,289
Mandatory Initiatives:													
Provide 6-month extension of FMAP relief to states:													
Medicaid impact	....	25,500	....	....	....	....	....	....	....	....	....	25,500	25,500
Foster care impact	....	214	19	4	....	....	....	....	....	....	....	237	237
Extend EUC/EB unemployment insurance benefits	31,000	18,000	....	....	....	....	....	....	....	....	....	18,000	18,000
Enhance TANF emergency fund	508	1,357	1,363	273	....	....	....	....	....	....	....	2,993	2,993
Extend ARRA suspension of SNAP time limits	....	25	25	....	....	....	....	....	....	....	....	25	25
Provide $250 Economic Recovery Payments[2]	13,585	681	95	....	....	....	....	....	....	....	....	776	776
Interaction with the making work pay tax credit	–348	–1,986	–2	....	....	....	....	....	....	....	....	–1,988	–1,988
Total, mandatory initiatives	44,745	43,791	1,475	277	....	....	....	....	....	....	....	45,543	45,543
Allowance for other jobs initiatives[2]	24,000	50,000	16,000	6,000	4,000	....	....	....	....	....	....	76,000	76,000
Health insurance reform (allowance)[2,3]	5,500	–23,000	–34,500	–39,000	–27,500	–3,000	12,000	2,000	–5,500	–12,000	–19,500	–127,000	–150,000
Climate policy (deficit-neutral reserve)[4]	....	....	....	....	....	....	....	....	....	....	....	....	....

S-8. Mandatory and Receipt Proposals—Continued
(Deficit increases (+) or decreases (-) in millions of dollars)

	2010	2011	2012	2013	2014	2015	2016	2017	2018	2019	2020	Totals 2011-2015	Totals 2011-2020
Other Tax Provisions:[5]													
Tax Cuts for Families and Individuals:[6]													
Expand earned income tax credit[1]	.....	85	1,674	1,645	1,636	1,628	1,639	1,663	1,692	1,730	1,766	6,668	15,158
Expand the child and dependent care tax credit	.....	377	1,345	1,359	1,368	1,373	1,377	1,374	1,365	1,354	1,349	5,822	12,641
Provide for automatic enrollment in IRAs and double the tax credit for small employer plan startup costs[1]	.....	.....	506	825	876	982	1,113	1,261	1,423	1,604	1,801	3,189	10,391
Expand saver's credit[1]	.....	323	2,683	2,996	3,029	3,109	3,195	3,323	3,490	3,716	3,910	12,140	29,774
Extend American opportunity tax credit[1]	.....	951	6,875	7,444	7,815	8,400	8,841	8,632	8,738	8,870	8,907	31,485	75,473
Total, tax cuts for families and individuals	.....	1,736	13,083	14,269	14,724	15,492	16,165	16,253	16,708	17,274	17,733	59,304	143,437
Tax Cuts for Businesses:													
Eliminate capital gains taxation on small businesses	.....	.....	.....	.....	55	280	731	1,217	1,591	1,933	2,248	335	8,055
Make research and experimentation tax credit permanent	3,044	5,346	5,969	6,622	7,286	7,945	8,597	9,244	9,887	10,530	11,182	33,168	82,608
Remove cell phones from listed property	69	277	226	238	248	266	281	296	314	332	348	1,255	2,826
Total, tax cuts for businesses	3,113	5,623	6,195	6,860	7,589	8,491	9,609	10,757	11,792	12,795	13,778	34,758	93,489
Continue certain expiring provisions through calendar year 2011[1]	8,867	21,539	11,926	2,205	1,581	1,422	1,309	1,013	1,138	1,435	3,109	38,673	46,677
Other Revenue Changes and Loophole Closers:													
Reform treatment of financial institutions and products:													
Impose a financial crisis responsibility fee	.....	-8,000	-8,000	-9,000	-9,000	-9,000	-9,000	-9,000	-9,000	-10,000	-10,000	-43,000	-90,000
Require accrual of income on forward sale of corporate stock	-1	-5	-12	-19	-26	-33	-36	-38	-40	-42	-44	-95	-295
Require ordinary treatment of income from day-to-day dealer activities for certain dealers of equity options and commodities	-49	-169	-214	-226	-240	-254	-270	-286	-303	-321	-341	-1,103	-2,624
Modify the definition of "control" for purposes of section 249	-2	-15	-30	-32	-34	-36	-38	-41	-43	-46	-48	-147	-363
Subtotal, reform treatment of financial institutions and products	-52	-8,189	-8,256	-9,277	-9,300	-9,323	-9,344	-9,365	-9,386	-10,409	-10,433	-44,345	-93,282
Reinstate Superfund taxes	.....	-1,203	-1,608	-1,729	-1,837	-1,921	-1,995	-2,068	-2,129	-2,196	-2,239	-8,298	-18,925
Repeal LIFO method of accounting for inventories	.....	.....	-2,667	-6,007	-7,070	-7,120	-7,162	-7,224	-7,207	-7,278	-7,350	-22,864	-59,085
Repeal gain limitation for dividends received in reorganization exchanges	.....	-46	-77	-78	-78	-81	-83	-85	-86	-86	-88	-360	-788

S–8. Mandatory and Receipt Proposals—Continued

(Deficit increases (+) or decreases (–) in millions of dollars)

	2010	2011	2012	2013	2014	2015	2016	2017	2018	2019	2020	Totals 2011–2015	Totals 2011–2020
Reform U.S. international tax system:													
Defer deduction of interest expense related to deferred income	....	–2,024	–3,357	–3,343	–3,350	–3,434	–3,520	–3,572	–1,803	–613	–626	–15,508	–25,642
Reform foreign tax credit: Determine the foreign tax credit on a pooling basis	....	–1,928	–3,198	–3,184	–3,191	–3,271	–3,353	–3,403	–3,439	–3,462	–3,532	–14,772	–31,961
Reform foreign tax credit: Prevent splitting of foreign income and foreign taxes	....	–1,226	–2,223	–2,494	–2,707	–2,875	–3,006	–3,106	–3,186	–3,253	–3,327	–11,525	–27,403
Tax currently excess returns associated with transfers of intangibles offshore	....	–635	–1,580	–1,573	–1,577	–1,616	–1,657	–1,681	–1,699	–1,711	–1,745	–6,981	–15,474
Limit shifting of income through intangible property transfers	....	–12	–32	–54	–78	–104	–131	–159	–189	–220	–254	–280	–1,233
Disallow the deduction for excess nontaxed reinsurance premiums paid to affiliates	....	–22	–53	–54	–54	–50	–50	–54	–58	–60	–64	–233	–519
Limit earnings stripping by expatriated entities	....	–211	–352	–353	–356	–368	–379	–385	–390	–393	–402	–1,640	–3,589
Repeal 80/20 company rules	....	–83	–111	–111	–112	–116	–120	–122	–123	–124	–127	–533	–1,149
Prevent the use of equity swaps to avoid dividend withholding taxes	–219	–275	–135	–91	–94	–96	–97	–102	–109	–115	–123	–691	–1,237
Modify tax rules for dual capacity taxpayers	....	–381	–676	–734	–788	–846	–907	–972	–1,044	–1,121	–1,080	–3,425	–8,549
Combat under-reporting of income on accounts and entities in offshore jurisdictions	–27	–72	–161	–716	–919	–447	–381	–549	–686	–740	–762	–2,315	–5,433
Subtotal, reform U.S. international tax system	–246	–6,869	–11,878	–12,707	–13,226	–13,223	–13,601	–14,105	–12,726	–11,812	–12,042	–57,903	–122,189
Eliminate fossil fuel tax preferences:													
Oil and gas company preferences:													
Repeal enhanced oil recovery credit[7]	....	....	....	....	....	....	....	....	....	....	....	....	....
Repeal credit for oil and gas produced from marginal wells[7]	....	....	....	....	....	....	....	....	....	....	....	....	....
Repeal expensing of intangible drilling costs	....	–1,202	–1,582	–1,089	–914	–848	–694	–482	–374	–344	–310	–5,635	–7,839
Repeal deduction for tertiary injectants	....	–5	–9	–9	–8	–7	–6	–6	–5	–6	–6	–38	–67
Repeal exception to passive loss limitations for working interests in oil and natural gas properties	....	–20	–24	–19	–18	–17	–17	–17	–16	–16	–16	–98	–180
Repeal percentage depletion for oil and natural gas wells	....	–522	–895	–933	–969	–1,009	–1,052	–1,095	–1,141	–1,184	–1,226	–4,328	–10,026

S–8. Mandatory and Receipt Proposals—Continued
(Deficit increases (+) or decreases (−) in millions of dollars)

	2010	2011	2012	2013	2014	2015	2016	2017	2018	2019	2020	Totals 2011–2015	Totals 2011–2020
Repeal domestic manufacturing tax deduction for oil and natural gas companies	......	–851	–1,470	–1,559	–1,650	–1,742	–1,831	–1,920	–2,007	–2,096	–2,188	–7,272	–17,314
Increase geological and geophysical amortization period for independent producers to seven years	......	–44	–160	–246	–231	–177	–122	–67	–28	–17	–18	–858	–1,110
Subtotal, oil and gas company preferences	......	–2,644	–4,140	–3,855	–3,790	–3,800	–3,722	–3,587	–3,571	–3,663	–3,764	–18,229	–36,536
Coal tax preferences:													
Repeal expensing of exploration and development costs	......	–32	–55	–49	–45	–45	–44	–40	–37	–34	–32	–226	–413
Repeal percentage depletion for hard mineral fossil fuels	......	–57	–98	–102	–106	–109	–111	–115	–119	–122	–123	–472	–1,062
Repeal capital gains treatment for royalties	–10	–18	–25	–48	–67	–78	–87	–95	–103	–111	–119	–236	–751
Repeal domestic manufacturing deduction for hard mineral fossil fuels	......	–3	–5	–5	–5	–6	–6	–6	–7	–7	–7	–24	–57
Subtotal, coal tax preferences	–10	–110	–183	–204	–223	–238	–248	–256	–266	–274	–281	–958	–2,283
Subtotal, eliminate fossil fuel tax preferences	–10	–2,754	–4,323	–4,059	–4,013	–4,038	–3,970	–3,843	–3,837	–3,937	–4,045	–19,187	–38,819
Tax carried interest as ordinary income	......	–1,452	–3,289	–3,914	–3,741	–3,176	–2,534	–1,975	–1,530	–1,355	–1,011	–15,572	–23,977
Modify cellulosic biofuel producer credit	–784	–6,569	–8,058	–4,901	–2,659	–1,491	–309	......	......	......	......	–23,678	–23,987
Eliminate advanced earned income tax credit[1]	......	–120	–72	–70	–69	–68	–69	–69	–72	–74	–77	–399	–760
Deny deduction for punitive damages	......	......	–22	–32	–33	–34	–35	–36	–38	–38	–39	–121	–307
Repeal lower-of-cost-or-market inventory accounting method	......	......	–286	–1,423	–2,045	–1,402	–1,127	–283	–296	–309	–323	–5,156	–7,494
Make unemployment insurance surtax permanent	......	......	–1,458	–1,501	–1,539	–1,571	–1,596	–1,616	–1,631	–1,642	–1,642	–6,069	–14,196
Reduce the tax gap and make reforms:													
Expand information reporting:													
Require information reporting on payments to corporations	......	–84	–612	–777	–924	–983	–1,040	–1,095	–1,152	–1,212	–1,275	–3,380	–9,154
Require information reporting for rental property expense payments	......	–179	–267	–281	–296	–312	–327	–342	–357	–372	–387	–1,335	–3,120
Require information reporting for private separate accounts of life insurance companies	......	–1	–2	–3	–4	–4	–6	–7	–8	–10	–13	–14	–58
Require a certified Taxpayer Identification Number for contractors	......	–17	–44	–63	–72	–76	–79	–83	–86	–90	–94	–272	–704
Require increased information reporting for certain government payments	......	–25	–70	–58	–28	–30	–32	–34	–35	–37	–39	–211	–388
Increase information return penalties	......	–20	–34	–35	–35	–36	–42	–43	–43	–44	–44	–160	–376
Subtotal, expand information reporting	......	–326	–1,029	–1,217	–1,359	–1,441	–1,526	–1,604	–1,681	–1,765	–1,852	–5,372	–13,800

S–8. Mandatory and Receipt Proposals—Continued

(Deficit increases (+) or decreases (-) in millions of dollars)

	2010	2011	2012	2013	2014	2015	2016	2017	2018	2019	2020	Totals 2011–2015	Totals 2011–2020
Improve compliance by businesses:													
Require electronic filing by certain large organizations	....	....	....	....	....	....	....	....	....	....	....	....	....
Implement standards clarifying when employee leasing companies can be held liable for their clients' Federal employment taxes	....	–4	–6	–6	–7	–7	–7	–8	–8	–9	–9	–30	–71
Strengthen rules pertaining to classification of employees as independent contractors	....	–11	–214	–543	–688	–766	–848	–933	–1,020	–1,112	–1,208	–2,222	–7,343
Subtotal, improve compliance by businesses	....	–15	–220	–549	–695	–773	–855	–941	–1,028	–1,121	–1,217	–2,252	–7,414
Strengthen tax administration:													
Codify "economic substance doctrine" ...	....	–23	–77	–157	–272	–366	–476	–593	–682	–758	–838	–895	–4,242
Allow assessment of criminal restitution as tax	....	....	–3	–4	–4	–4	–4	–4	–4	–4	–4	–15	–35
Revise offer-in-compromise application rules	–1	–3	–3	–3	–3	–3	–3	–3	–3	–3	–4	–15	–31
Expand IRS access to information in the National Directory of New Hires for tax administration purposes	....	....	....	....	....	....	....	....	....	....	....	....	....
Make repeated willful failure to file a tax return a felony	....	....	....	....	–1	–1	–1	–1	–2	–2	–2	–2	–10
Facilitate tax compliance with local jurisdictions	....	....	....	....	....	–1	–1	–1	–1	–1	–1	–1	–6
Extend statute of limitations where State adjustment affects Federal tax liability	....	–3	–4	–4	–4	–4	–5	–5	–5	–5	–6	–19	–45
Improve investigative disclosure statute ...	....	....	....	....	–1	–1	–1	–1	–2	–2	–2	–2	–10
Subtotal, strengthen tax administration	–1	–29	–87	–168	–285	–380	–491	–608	–699	–775	–857	–949	–4,379
Expand penalties:													
Clarify the bad check penalty applies to electronic checks and other payment forms	....	–1	–2	–2	–2	–3	–3	–3	–3	–4	–4	–10	–27
Impose a penalty on failure to comply with electronic filing requirements ...	....	....	....	....	....	–1	–1	–1	–2	–2	–2	–1	–9
Subtotal, expand penalties	....	–1	–2	–2	–2	–4	–4	–4	–5	–6	–6	–11	–36
Modify estate and gift tax valuation discounts and make other reforms:													
Require consistent valuation for transfer and income tax purposes	–40	–135	–171	–182	–192	–204	–216	–229	–243	–258	–273	–884	–2,103
Modify rules on valuation discounts	....	–666	–1,413	–1,531	–1,671	–1,818	–1,972	–2,135	–2,305	–2,484	–2,672	–7,099	–18,667

S–8. Mandatory and Receipt Proposals—Continued
(Deficit increases (+) or decreases (–) in millions of dollars)

	2010	2011	2012	2013	2014	2015	2016	2017	2018	2019	2020	Totals 2011–2015	Totals 2011–2020
Require a minimum term for grantor retained annuity trusts (GRATs)	....	–15	–46	–93	–160	–231	–308	–389	–477	–570	–670	–545	–2,959
Subtotal, modify estate and gift tax valuation discounts and make other reforms	–40	–816	–1,630	–1,806	–2,023	–2,253	–2,496	–2,753	–3,025	–3,312	–3,615	–8,528	–23,729
Subtotal, reduce the tax gap and make reforms	–41	–1,187	–2,968	–3,742	–4,364	–4,851	–5,372	–5,910	–6,438	–6,979	–7,547	–17,112	–49,358
Reform treatment of insurance institutions and products:													
Modify rules that apply to sales of life insurance contracts		–22	–71	–84	–101	–117	–136	–156	–179	–204	–233	–395	–1,303
Modify dividends-received deduction for life insurance company separate accounts		–149	–379	–407	–432	–441	–468	–492	–511	–512	–515	–1,808	–4,306
Expand pro rata interest expense disallowance for corporate-owned life insurance		–20	–87	–183	–276	–437	–659	–910	–1,293	–1,731	–2,188	–1,003	–7,784
Permit partial annuitization of a nonqualified annuity contract		–5	–21	–39	–59	–81	–105	–132	–160	–192	–226	–205	–1,020
Subtotal, reform treatment of life insurance and products		–196	–558	–713	–868	–1,076	–1,368	–1,690	–2,143	–2,639	–3,162	–3,411	–14,413
Total, other revenue changes and loophole closers	–1,133	–28,585	–45,520	–50,153	–50,842	–49,375	–48,565	–48,269	–47,519	–48,754	–49,998	–224,475	–467,580
Upper-Income Tax Provisions:													
Upper-income tax provisions devoted to deficit reduction:													
Expand the 28-percent rate and reinstate the 36-percent and 39.6-percent rates for those taxpayers with income over $250,000 (married) and $200,000 (single):													
PAYGO	....	698	1,075	1,211	1,349	1,479	1,617	1,757	1,899	2,035	2,175	5,812	15,295
Non-PAYGO	....	–15,207	–27,292	–30,506	–33,905	–37,155	–40,426	–43,717	–47,034	–50,434	–54,058	–144,065	–379,734
Reinstate the personal exemption phaseout and limitation on itemized deductions for those taxpayers with income over $250,000 (married) and $200,000 (single) (non-PAYGO)	....	–6,840	–14,925	–17,119	–18,991	–20,808	–22,571	–24,324	–26,054	–27,687	–29,170	–78,683	–208,489
Impose 20-percent tax rate on capital gains and dividends for those taxpayers with income over $250,000 (married) and $200,000 (single) (non-PAYGO)	–1,344	–12,165	263	–3,315	–8,230	–11,372	–12,370	–13,288	–14,162	–14,973	–15,752	–34,819	–105,364
Subtotal, upper-income provisions devoted to deficit reduction	–1,344	–33,514	–40,879	–49,729	–59,777	–67,856	–73,750	–79,572	–85,351	–91,059	–96,805	–251,755	–678,292

S–8. Mandatory and Receipt Proposals—Continued

(Deficit increases (+) or decreases (-) in millions of dollars)

	2010	2011	2012	2013	2014	2015	2016	2017	2018	2019	2020	Totals 2011–2015	Totals 2011–2020
Limit the tax rate at which itemized deductions reduce tax liability to 28 percent	.....	-7,896	-21,582	-24,500	-27,019	-29,351	-31,570	-33,938	-36,268	-38,426	-40,625	-110,348	-291,175
Total, upper-income tax provisions	-1,344	-41,410	-62,461	-74,229	-86,796	-97,207	-105,320	-113,510	-121,619	-129,485	-137,430	-362,103	-969,467
Trade Initiatives:													
Promote trade	.....	145	430	552	606	647	680	705	729	753	777	2,380	6,024
Other Initiatives:													
Extend and modify the New Markets tax credit		113	229	345	430	480	511	510	441	279	103	1,597	3,441
Reform and extend build America bonds[1]		-8	3	3	3	4	4	4	4	4	3	5	24
Total, other initiatives	.....	105	232	348	433	484	515	514	445	283	106	1,602	3,465
Mandatory Initiatives and Savings:[8]													
Agriculture:													
Enact Animal Plant and Health Inspection Service (APHIS) fees	.....	-20	-27	-27	-28	-29	-30	-31	-32	-33	-34	-131	-291
Enact Food Safety and Inspection Service (FSIS) performance fee	.....	-11	-13	-13	-13	-14	-14	-14	-14	-15	-15	-64	-136
Enact Grain Inspection, Packers, and Stockyards Administration (GIPSA) fees	.....	-29	-30	-31	-31	-31	-32	-32	-32	-33	-34	-152	-315
Enact Natural Resources Conservation Service (NRCS) fee	.....	-19	-19	-19	-19	-19	-19	-19	-19	-19	-19	-95	-190
Eliminate Commodity Storage payments	.....	-2	.....	.....	.....	.....	.....	.....	.....	.....	.....	-2	-2
Reduce commodity payments to wealthy farmers	.....	-1	-172	-201	-241	-245	-258	-262	-277	-297	-309	-860	-2,263
Reauthorize Child Nutrition programs	.....	860	1,000	1,000	1,000	1,000	1,000	1,000	1,000	1,000	1,000	4,860	9,860
Reform Market Access Program	.....	-8	-38	-40	-40	-40	-40	-40	-40	-40	-40	-166	-366
Total, Agriculture	.....	770	701	669	628	622	607	602	586	563	549	3,390	6,297
Commerce:													
Eliminate grants to manufacturers of worsted wool	.....	-5	-5	-5	-5	-5	.....	.....	.....	.....	.....	-25	-25
Corps of Engineers:													
Support capital investment in the inland waterways (receipt effect)[2]	.....	.....	-196	-163	-187	-129	-100	-72	-70	-68	-68	-675	-1,053
Defense:													
Implement concurrent receipt policy:													
Effect on military retirement	.....	217	346	435	511	531	541	550	560	570	581	2,040	4,842
Accrual payments to the Military Retirement Fund (non-PAYGO)	.....	408	395	406	416	426	440	455	470	486	503	2,051	4,405

S–8. Mandatory and Receipt Proposals—Continued
(Deficit increases (+) or decreases (–) in millions of dollars)

	2010	2011	2012	2013	2014	2015	2016	2017	2018	2019	2020	Totals 2011–2015	Totals 2011–2020
Military Retirement Fund offsetting receipts for concurrent receipt accruals (non-PAYGO)	....	–408	–395	–406	–416	–426	–440	–455	–470	–486	–503	–2,051	–4,405
Payments to Military Retirement Fund (non-PAYGO)	....	469	487	505	524	604	627	651	675	700	727	2,589	5,969
Military Retirement Fund offsetting receipts (non-PAYGO)	....	–469	–487	–505	–524	–604	–627	–651	–675	–700	–727	–2,589	–5,969
Provide additional accrual payments to Medicare/Eligible Retiree Health Care Fund (non-PAYGO)	....	–143	....	....	....	....	....	....	....	....	....	–143	–143
Total, Defense	....	74	346	435	511	531	541	550	560	570	581	1,897	4,699
Education:													
Make Pell Grant funding mandatory and increase and index maximum awards	2	825	2,603	2,942	6,581	5,183	6,616	8,154	9,818	11,873	14,031	18,134	68,626
Eliminate entitlements for financial intermediaries under the Family Federal Education Loan Program	–2,266	–8,034	–6,527	–4,458	–3,098	–2,975	–3,184	–3,414	–3,636	–3,840	–4,129	–25,092	–43,294
Expand income-based repayment options for Federal student loans	1,692	448	512	551	586	644	708	774	842	1,158	1,265	2,741	7,487
Extend mandatory funding for Historically Black Colleges and Universities and other Minority-Serving Institutions	13	186	232	255	255	255	255	255	255	255	255	1,183	2,458
Create a new Graduation Promise Grants program to strengthen high schools	20	140	260	380	260	140	....	....	....	....	....	1,180	1,180
Create a new Early Learning Challenge Fund	31	456	588	899	966	1,000	1,000	1,000	1,000	1,000	1,000	3,909	8,909
Create a new Access and Completion Fund program	117	583	700	700	700	583	117	....	....	....	....	3,266	3,383
Provide mandatory funding for community colleges to support the American Graduation Initiative	3	541	991	765	958	793	950	950	950	950	950	4,046	8,796
Modernize Perkins loans	....	–736	–709	–614	–563	–583	–589	–539	–468	–396	–274	–3,205	–5,471
Total, Education	–388	–5,592	–1,351	1,420	6,645	5,039	5,873	7,180	8,761	11,000	13,098	6,162	52,074
Energy:													
Repeal ultra-deepwater oil and gas research and development program	....	–20	–40	–50	–50	–30	–10	....	....	....	....	–190	–200
Environmental Protection Agency:													
Enact pesticide and pre-manufacture notification (PMN) fees	....	–50	–54	–80	–83	–89	–89	–92	–92	–95	–95	–356	–819
Health and Human Services (HHS):													
Expand child care entitlement to States	....	502	753	961	1,115	1,106	1,142	1,226	1,314	1,403	1,493	4,437	11,015

S–8.   Mandatory and Receipt Proposals—Continued

(Deficit increases (+) or decreases (-) in millions of dollars)

	2010	2011	2012	2013	2014	2015	2016	2017	2018	2019	2020	Totals 2011–2015	Totals 2011–2020
Extend ARRA child support enforcement incentive match provision	....	555	114	....	....	....	....	....	....	....	....	669	669
Create a LIHEAP trigger	....	1,460	1,475	1,115	690	373	285	258	250	250	250	5,113	6,406
Continue child welfare study	....	3	2	1	....	....	....	....	....	....	....	6	6
Expand CMS program integrity authority	....	–109	–213	–1,121	–1,250	–1,418	–1,564	–1,660	–1,784	–1,912	–2,047	–4,111	–13,078
Extend TANF supplemental grants	....	251	64	4	....	....	....	....	....	....	....	319	319
Establish Fatherhood, Marriage, and Families Innovation Fund	....	–118	220	148	100	....	....	....	....	....	....	350	350
Improve child support enforcement tools	....	1	–2	–2	–2	–2	–2	–2	–2	–2	–2	–7	–17
Outyear costs of extending TANF supplemental grants	....	....	251	315	319	319	319	319	319	319	319	1,204	2,799
Reauthorize the Court Improvement Program	....	1	4	16	18	20	19	16	4	2	....	59	100
Support teen pregnancy prevention	....	20	42	48	49	50	50	50	50	50	50	209	459
Total, HHS	....	2,566	2,710	1,485	1,039	448	249	207	151	110	63	8,248	9,028
Homeland Security:													
Eliminate grants to manufacturers of worsted wool	....	5	5	5	5	....	....	....	....	....	....	20	20
Housing and Urban Development:													
Provide funding for the Affordable Housing Trust Fund	....	20	140	250	250	240	100	....	....	....	....	900	1,000
Interior:													
Increase fees for migratory bird hunting and conservation stamps[2]	....	–4	....	....	....	....	....	....	....	....	....	–4	–4
Increase return from minerals on Federal lands:													
End Abandoned Mine Lands (AML) payments to certified States	....	–115	–171	–177	–176	–97	–72	–75	–123	–140	–95	–736	–1,241
Impose fee on nonproducing oil and gas leases	....	–8	–22	–38	–53	–67	–80	–97	–114	–132	–149	–188	–760
Repeal Energy Policy Act fee prohibition and mandatory permit funds		....	–22	–22	–21	–20	....	....	....	....	....	–85	–85
Reauthorize Federal land sales/acquisition law (FLTFA)	....	–4	–6	–11	–12	–3	....	....	....	....	....	–36	–36
Repeal geothermal payments to counties under EPAct	....	–8	–8	–8	–8	–8	–8	–8	–8	–8	–8	–40	–80
Return to net receipts sharing for energy minerals	....	....	–45	–45	–47	–51	–50	–51	–51	–54	–56	–188	–450
Reserve funds for insular affairs assistance	....	21	21	21	21	16	16	16	16	16	15	100	179
Total, Interior	....	–118	–253	–280	–296	–230	–194	–215	–280	–318	–293	–1,177	–2,477

S–8. Mandatory and Receipt Proposals—Continued

(Deficit increases (+) or decreases (-) in millions of dollars)

	2010	2011	2012	2013	2014	2015	2016	2017	2018	2019	2020	Totals 2011–2015	Totals 2011–2020
Labor:													
Implement unemployment insurance integrity legislation:[2,9]													
PAYGO	.....	.....	–190	–218	–162	–164	–179	–202	–114	–199	–214	–734	–1,642
Non-PAYGO	.....	.....	–74	–148	–138	–117	–34	83	–377	26	71	–477	–708
Reform FECA program	.....	–10	–14	–7	–10	–20	–29	–39	–50	–60	–71	–61	–310
Extend foreign labor certification fees	.....	.....	.....	1	17	18	18	20	20	20	21	36	135
Reform Trade Adjustment Assistance	.....	145	564	796	1,044	948	884	846	832	847	879	3,497	7,785
Total, Labor	.....	135	286	424	751	665	660	708	311	634	686	2,261	5,260
State:													
Change retention policy for consular fees (receipt effect)[2]		782	810	825	840	857	873	891	909	927	946	4,114	8,660
Treasury:													
Levy payments to Federal contractors with delinquent tax debt:													
Authorize post-levy due process (receipt effect)[2]	.....	–77	–115	–119	–124	–109	–113	–118	–122	–127	–132	–544	–1,156
Increase levy authority to 100 percent for vendor payments (receipt effect)[2]	.....	–61	–87	–86	–90	–78	–82	–85	–88	–92	–96	–402	–845
Revise terrorism risk insurance program[2]	.....	–26	–42	–102	–134	–74	55	134	–39	–9	–12	–378	–249
Offset tax refunds to collect deliquent taxes for out-of-state residents	.....	.....	.....	.....	.....	.....	.....	.....	.....	.....	.....	.....	.....
Establish FMS debt collection fee	.....	.....	.....	.....	.....	.....	.....	.....	.....	.....	.....	.....	.....
Restructure assistance to New York City (NYC): Provide tax incentives for transportation infrastructure (receipt effect)[2]	.....	200	200	200	200	200	200	200	200	200	200	1,000	2,000
Total, Treasury	.....	36	–44	–107	–148	–61	60	131	–49	–28	–40	–324	–250
Veterans Affairs:													
Implement concurrent receipt policy:													
Effect on Veterans disability payments	.....	47	49	51	53	54	54	54	53	53	52	254	520
Extend VBA pension limitation	.....	.....	–559	–571	–584	–597	–611	.....	.....	.....	.....	–2,311	–2,922
Medicaid impact	.....	.....	313	326	339	353	367	.....	.....	.....	.....	1,331	1,698
Reform criteria for special monthly pension	.....	–3	–6	–10	–13	–16	–20	–23	–27	–30	–33	–48	–181
Extend VBA authority for use of HHS data	.....	.....	2	1	.....	–1	–2	–3	–4	–5	–5	2	–17
Extend veterans income verification	.....	.....	20	–7	–13	–20	–27	.....	.....	.....	.....	–20	–47
Provide authority for vendee loan pooling	.....	.....	–86	–99	–5	.....	.....	.....	.....	.....	.....	–190	–190
Total, Veterans Affairs	.....	44	–267	–309	–223	–227	–239	28	22	18	14	–982	–1,139

S–8. Mandatory and Receipt Proposals—Continued

(Deficit increases (+) or decreases (–) in millions of dollars)

	2010	2011	2012	2013	2014	2015	2016	2017	2018	2019	2020	Totals 2011–2015	Totals 2011–2020
Federal Communications Commission:													
Auction domestic satellite spectrum	.....	–100	–75	–25	.....	.....	.....	.....	.....	.....	.....	–200	–200
Provide permanent auction authority	.....	.....	.....	–200	–200	–200	–200	–200	–200	–200	–200	–600	–1,600
Enact spectrum license user fee	–50	–200	–300	–425	–550	–550	–550	–550	–550	–550	–550	–2,025	–4,775
Eliminate Telecommunications Development Fund	–3	–7	–7	–7	–6	–6	–6	–6	–6	–6	–6	–33	–63
Total, Federal Communications Commission	–53	–307	–382	–657	–756	–756	–756	–756	–756	–756	–756	–2,858	–6,638
Social Security Administration:													
Require States and localities to provide pension information (non-PAYGO)	.....	.....	.....	.....	–172	–375	–492	–523	–478	–452	–417	–547	–2,909
Revert to Quarterly Wage Reporting (non-PAYGO)	.....	20	30	100	.....	150	.....	.....	.....	.....	.....	150	150
Total, Social Security Administration	.....	20	30	100	–172	–375	–492	–523	–478	–452	–417	–397	–2,759
Other Independent Agencies:													
Reform financial regulatory system	.....	867	1,595	2,204	2,583	2,893	3,052	2,397	1,855	1,433	1,141	10,142	20,020
Reflect discrimination claims settlement (non-PAYGO)	690	230	230	.....	.....	.....	.....	.....	.....	.....	.....	460	460
Total, other independent agencies	690	1,097	1,825	2,204	2,583	2,893	3,052	2,397	1,855	1,433	1,141	10,602	20,480
Multi-Agency:													
Fund Cobell settlement costs:													
PAYGO	100	400	400	200	200	200	200	200	100	.....	.....	1,400	1,900
Non-PAYGO	1,412	.....	.....	.....	.....	.....	.....	.....	.....	.....	.....	.....	.....
Implement program integrity allocation adjustments (non-PAYGO)[2]	.....	–1,864	–4,555	–7,005	–9,452	–12,507	–15,807	–17,939	–19,448	–21,138	–22,506	–35,383	–132,221
Exclude refundable tax credits from means-tested programs	26	26	26	25	25	25	24	23	23	22	22	127	241
Reform asset limits in means-tested programs	.....	426	813	1,145	1,090	1,027	982	965	973	986	986	4,501	9,393
Total, multi-agency	1,538	–1,012	–3,316	–5,635	–8,137	–11,255	–14,601	–16,751	–18,352	–20,130	–21,498	–29,355	–120,687
Outyear PAYGO Impact of Changes in Mandatory Programs included in Appropriations Language:													
Justice, Crime Victims Fund Obligation Delay	.....	.....	2,731	1,366	455	.....	.....	.....	.....	.....	.....	4,552	4,552
Total, mandatory and receipt proposals	**114,309**	**81,497**	**–69,867**	**–137,843**	**–137,205**	**–128,927**	**–121,145**	**–138,590**	**–152,488**	**–165,698**	**–178,834**	**–392,346**	**–1,149,100**

Note: For receipt effects, positive figures indicate lower receipts. For outlay effects, positive figures indicate higher outlays. For net costs, positive figures indicate higher deficits.

Note: Figures displayed in the table do not reflect the impact of any recommendations from the Fiscal Commission.

S-8. Mandatory and Receipt Proposals—Continued

(Deficit increases (+) or decreases (−) in millions of dollars)

¹ The estimates for this proposal include effects on outlays. The outlay effects included in the totals above are listed below:

	2010	2011	2012	2013	2014	2015	2016	2017	2018	2019	2020	2011–2015	2011–2020
Extend making work pay tax credit in 2011	.....	703	21,265	.....	.....	.....	.....	.....	.....	.....	.....	21,968	21,968
Extend COBRA health insurance premium assistance	319	524	23	.....	.....	.....	.....	.....	.....	.....	.....	547	547
Extend option for grants to States in lieu of housing tax credits	2,435	1,815	.....	.....	.....	.....	.....	.....	.....	.....	.....	1,815	1,815
Expand earned income tax credit	.....	83	1,667	1,635	1,628	1,622	1,634	1,659	1,689	1,726	1,762	6,635	15,105
Expand child and dependent care tax credit	.....	.....	399	406	403	398	403	406	408	407	409	1,606	3,639
Provide for automatic enrollment in IRAs and double the tax credit for small employer plan startup costs	.....	.....	83	146	149	158	177	200	223	250	281	536	1,667
Expand saver's credit	.....	570	3,715	1,402	1,369	1,366	1,349	1,337	1,339	1,340	1,353	8,422	15,140
Provide American opportunity tax credit	.....	.....	2,941	3,058	3,146	3,268	3,441	3,363	3,330	3,310	3,302	12,413	29,159
Continue certain expiring provisions through calendar year 2011	66	91	23	.....	.....	.....	.....	.....	.....	.....	.....	114	114
Eliminate advanced earned income tax credit	.....	−120	−72	−70	−69	−68	−69	−69	−72	−74	−77	−399	−760
Reform and extend build America bonds	.....	266	1,216	2,630	4,108	5,608	7,105	8,595	10,078	11,554	13,023	13,828	64,183
Total outlay effects of receipt proposals	2,820	3,932	31,260	9,207	10,734	12,352	14,040	15,491	16,995	18,513	20,053	67,485	152,577

² The estimates for this proposal include effects on receipts. The receipt effects included in the totals above are listed below:

	2010	2011	2012	2013	2014	2015	2016	2017	2018	2019	2020	2011–2015	2011–2020
Provide $250 economic recovery payments	38	−1,959	.....	.....	.....	.....	.....	.....	.....	.....	.....	−1,959	−1,959
Jobs initiatives allowance	12,000	25,000	8,000	3,000	2,000	.....	.....	.....	.....	.....	.....	38,000	38,000
Health insurance allowance	.....	−16,000	−17,500	−40,500	−57,000	−75,500	−89,500	−98,000	−106,500	−116,000	−126,500	−206,500	−743,000
Preserve cost-sharing of inland waterways capital costs	.....	.....	−196	−163	−187	−129	−100	−72	−70	−68	−68	−675	−1,053
Increase fees for migratory bird hunting and conservation stamps	.....	−14	−14	−14	−14	−14	−14	−14	−14	−14	−14	−70	−140
Implement unemployment insurance integrity legislation:													
PAYGO	.....	.....	−39	−40	−27	−32	−49	−72	19	−62	−73	−138	−375
Non-PAYGO	.....	.....	−3	−2	11	36	124	247	−208	200	252	42	657
Change retention policy for passport application fees	.....	782	810	825	840	857	873	891	909	927	946	4,114	8,660
Authorize post-levy due process	.....	−77	−115	−119	−124	−109	−113	−118	−122	−127	−132	−544	−1,156
Increase levy authority to 100 percent for vendor payments	.....	−61	−87	−86	−90	−78	−82	−85	−88	−92	−96	−402	−845
Revise terrorism risk insurance program	.....	.....	21	18	45	99	173	205	6	21	15	183	603

S–8. Mandatory and Receipt Proposals—Continued

(Deficit increases (+) or decreases (–) in millions of dollars)

	2010	2011	2012	2013	2014	2015	2016	2017	2018	2019	2020	2011–2015	2011–2020
Restructure assistance to NYC: Provide tax incentives for transportation infrastructure	.....	200	200	200	200	200	200	200	200	200	200	1,000	2,000
Implement program integrity allocation adjustments – IRS	.....	–385	–1,164	–2,355	–3,955	–6,015	–7,987	–9,238	–9,931	–10,378	–10,809	–13,874	–62,217
Total receipt effects of mandatory proposals ...	12,038	7,486	–10,087	–39,236	–58,301	–80,685	–96,475	–106,056	–115,799	–125,393	–136,279	–180,823	–760,825

3 Allowance reflects the average budget impacts of the House- and Senate-passed health care reform bills, extrapolated to 2020 and adjusted to remove the effects of four provisions already included explicitly as 2011 Budget proposals. The four adjustments are for proposals to require information reporting on payments to corporations, codify the economic substance doctrine, modify cellulosic biofuel producer credit, and extend FMAP relief to States.

4 A comprehensive market-based climate change policy will be deficit neutral because proceeds from emissions allowances will be used to compensate vulnerable families, communities, and businesses during the transition to a clean energy economy. Receipts will also be reserved for investments to reduce greenhouse gas emissions, including support of clean energy technologies, and in adapting to the impacts of climate change, both domestically and in developing countries.

5 Receipt effects unless otherwise noted.

6 The Administration continues to support expanding refundability of the child tax credit by lowering the refundability threshold to $3,000, as well as the expansion of the earned income tax credit for married couples by increasing the phase-out threshold by $5,000 compared to other filers. These policies are incorporated in the baseline projection of current policy.

7 This provision is estimated to have zero receipt effects under the Administration's current projections for energy prices.

8 Outlay effects unless otherwise noted.

9 Net of income offsets.

Table S–9.   Bridge Between Total Mandatory and Receipt Proposals and PAYGO Scorekeeping

Deficit increases (+) or decreases (–) in millions of dollars

	Total[1]
2011-2020 total mandatory and receipt proposals, Table S–8	–1,149,100
Plus 2010 effects: PAYGO includes a "lookback" provision to capture current-year costs	114,309
2010–2020 total mandatory and receipt proposals and climate policies, Table S–8	**–1,034,791**
Adjustments to remove costs or savings for non-PAYGO items on S–8:	
Temporary recovery measures	–266,351
Savings from not extending upper-income tax cuts	694,931
Program integrity and other savings generated by increased discretionary funding	135,838
Other non-PAYGO items	–3,847
Total, adjustments for non-PAYGO items	**561,261**
TOTAL: Net scoreable PAYGO savings in Administration's budget	**–473,530**

Note: Figures displayed in the table do not reflect the impact of any recommendations from the Fiscal Commission.
[1] Totals represent 2010-2020 unless otherwise stated.

Table S–10. Funding Levels for Appropriated ("Discretionary") Programs by Category [1]

(Budgetary resources in billions of dollars)

	2009 Actual Non-ARRA	2009 Actual ARRA[2]	2010 Enacted	2011 Request	2012	2013	2014	2015	2016	2017	2018	2019	2020	Totals 2011–2015	Totals 2011–2020
Discretionary Policy by Category:															
Security Agencies	650.1	12.0	683.7	719.2	747.5	768.7	789.7	814.0	834.6	856.5	879.0	902.7	927.6	3,839.0	8,239.4
Non-Security Agencies	407.8	253.1	446.3	441.3	446.4	446.2	459.1	472.3	478.7	488.8	501.6	517.0	537.5	2,265.2	4,788.9
Total, Base Discretionary Funding	1,057.9	265.1	1,130.0	1,160.5	1,193.9	1,214.9	1,248.8	1,286.2	1,313.3	1,345.3	1,380.6	1,419.7	1,465.1	6,104.3	13,028.3
Other Discretionary Funding (not included above):															
Overseas Contingency Operations[3]	145.9	.....	130.0	159.3	50.0	50.0	50.0	50.0	50.0	50.0	50.0	50.0	50.0	359.3	609.3
Other Supplemental/Emergency Funding	44.1	.....	0.4	.....	.....	.....	.....	.....	.....	.....	.....	.....	.....	.....	.....
Proposed 2010 Supplemental Funding[4]	.....	.....	41.1	.....	.....	.....	.....	.....	.....	.....	.....	.....	.....	.....	.....
Grand Total, Discretionary Budgetary Resources	1,248.0	265.1	1,301.5	1,319.8	1,243.9	1,264.9	1,298.8	1,336.2	1,363.3	1,395.3	1,430.6	1,469.7	1,515.1	6,463.6	13,637.6
Memorandum:															
Base Security Budget Authority adjusted for Inflation and Population	685.5	12.6	700.1	719.2	726.6	725.5	723.7	724.3	721.0	717.7	714.6	711.9	710.5	3,619.3	7,194.9
Base Non-Security Budgetary Resources adjusted for Inflation and Population	430.0	266.9	457.0	441.3	433.9	421.1	420.8	420.2	413.6	409.6	407.7	407.7	411.7	2,137.3	4,187.6
Grand Total, Discretionary Budgetary Resources adjusted for Inflation and Population	1,315.9	279.5	1,332.8	1,319.8	1,209.1	1,193.8	1,190.2	1,189.0	1,177.7	1,169.2	1,163.0	1,159.1	1,160.5	6,102.0	11,931.5
Grand Total, Discretionary Budgetary Resources as a Percent of GDP	8.8%	1.9%	8.9%	8.6%	7.7%	7.4%	7.1%	7.0%	6.8%	6.6%	6.5%	6.4%	6.3%	7.6%	7.0%

[1] Although the Budget shows discretionary funding in nominal terms, the Administration conceives of discretionary growth rates in inflation-adjusted terms. If inflation projections are revised from what is currently projected, future budgets would be expected to adjust funding levels up or down accordingly. (This statement does not apply to funding growth between 2010 and the 2011 budget year, since the appropriations process for 2011 must begin immediately and before inflation assumptions will be revisited. It also does not apply to the outyear BA for overseas contingency operations, which is a placeholder and does not represent a policy determination.)

[2] "ARRA" refers to the American Recovery and Reinvestment Act of 2009 (P.L. 111-5).

[3] The Budget includes placeholder estimates of $50 billion per year for Overseas Contingency Operations in 2012 and beyond. These estimates do not reflect any specific policy decisions.

[4] The 2010 requested supplemental includes additional funding for Overseas Contingency Operations.

Table S–11. Funding Levels for Appropriated ("Discretionary") Programs by Agency[1]
(Budgetary resources in billions of dollars)

	2009 Actual		2010 Enacted	2011 Request	2012	2013	2014	2015	Totals	
	Non-ARRA	ARRA[2]							2011–2015	2011–2020
Base Discretionary Resources by Agency:										
Security Agencies:										
Defense (DOD)	513.2	7.4	530.8	548.9	566.4	581.8	597.8	616.0	2,910.9	6,255.3
Energy - National Nuclear Security Administration	9.1	....	9.9	11.2	11.6	11.9	12.4	12.9	60.0	126.6
Homeland Security (DHS)[3]	42.1	2.8	39.4	43.6	44.2	44.8	45.3	46.7	224.6	481.4
Veterans Affairs[4]	47.6	1.4	53.1	57.0	59.7	61.3	63.0	64.7	305.6	659.7
State and Other International Programs[5]	38.1	0.4	50.6	58.5	65.7	69.0	71.2	73.6	337.9	716.4
Subtotal, Security Agencies	**650.1**	**12.0**	**683.7**	**719.2**	**747.5**	**768.7**	**789.7**	**814.0**	**3,839.0**	**8,239.4**
Non-Security Agencies:										
Agriculture[5]	22.6	6.9	25.0	23.9	24.6	24.5	25.2	26.0	124.2	266.2
Commerce	9.4	7.8	13.9	8.9	9.1	8.8	8.5	8.8	44.2	101.0
Census Bureau	*3.1*	*1.0*	*7.2*	*1.3*	*1.1*	*1.2*	*1.3*	*1.5*	*12.1*	*23.9*
Education[6]	41.4	81.1	46.8	49.7	50.1	50.2	51.4	52.7	254.1	537.5
Energy (excluding National Nuclear Security Administration)	16.9	36.7	16.5	17.1	17.1	17.2	17.7	18.3	87.5	186.2
Health and Human Services (HHS)[7]	77.6	22.4	84.1	83.5	82.4	80.7	83.1	85.5	415.1	881.1
Housing and Urban Development	40.0	13.6	43.6	41.6	41.3	42.0	44.1	45.3	214.3	464.1
Interior	11.3	3.0	12.2	12.0	11.9	11.8	12.2	12.5	60.3	126.6
Justice	26.0	4.0	27.5	24.1	28.5	28.0	29.0	29.9	139.5	291.8
Labor	12.9	4.8	14.3	14.0	13.5	13.1	13.3	13.5	67.4	138.4
State and Other International Programs[5]	0.1	0.2	0.1	0.1	0.1	0.1	0.1	0.1	0.6	1.3
Transportation	70.5	48.1	76.0	77.6	79.2	80.6	82.1	84.7	404.2	824.5
Budget Authority (BA)	*16.8*	*48.1*	*21.8*	*22.8*	*70.0*	*33.8*	*39.0*	*41.2*	*206.6*	*418.1*
Obligation Limitations	*53.7*	*....*	*54.2*	*54.8*	*9.3*	*46.8*	*43.1*	*43.6*	*197.6*	*406.4*
Treasury	12.6	0.3	13.6	13.9	14.1	14.5	15.1	15.9	73.6	158.9
Corps of Engineers	5.3	4.6	5.4	4.9	4.7	4.6	4.7	4.8	23.6	49.3
Environmental Protection Agency	7.6	7.2	10.3	10.0	9.4	8.8	8.6	8.5	45.4	89.0
General Services Administration	0.6	5.9	0.6	0.7	0.6	0.6	0.6	0.7	3.2	6.8
National Aeronautics and Space Administration	17.8	1.0	18.7	19.0	19.4	20.0	20.6	21.0	100.0	212.7
National Science Foundation	6.5	3.0	6.9	7.4	7.8	8.3	8.9	9.5	41.9	96.9
Small Business Administration	0.6	0.7	0.8	1.0	1.0	0.9	0.9	1.0	4.8	9.9
Social Security Administration[7]	8.5	1.1	9.3	10.1	10.5	10.9	11.4	11.7	54.7	117.6
Corporation for National and Community Service	0.9	0.2	1.2	1.4	1.7	2.0	2.3	2.6	10.0	26.9
Other Agencies	18.6	0.3	19.4	20.2	19.2	18.6	19.1	19.5	96.6	202.0
Subtotal, Non-Security Discretionary Budget Authority	**354.1**	**253.1**	**392.1**	**386.4**	**437.1**	**399.4**	**416.0**	**428.7**	**2,067.6**	**4,382.5**

Table S–11. Funding Levels for Appropriated ("Discretionary") Programs by Agency[1]—Continued

(Budgetary resources in billions of dollars)

	2009 Actual		2010 Enacted	2011 Request	2012	2013	2014	2015	Totals	
	Non-ARRA	ARRA[2]							2011-2015	2011-2020
Subtotal, Non-Security Discretionary Budgetary Resources	407.8	253.1	446.3	441.3	446.4	446.2	459.1	472.3	2,265.2	4,788.9
Other Discretionary Funding (not included above):										
Overseas Contingency Operations[8]	145.9	.....	130.0	159.3	50.0	50.0	50.0	50.0	359.3	609.3
Defense	*145.7*	.....	*129.6*	*159.1*	*50.0*	*50.0*	*50.0*	*50.0*	*359.1*	*609.1*
Homeland Security	*0.3*	.....	*0.2*	*0.3*	.....	.....	.....	.....	*0.3*	*0.3*
Justice	.....	.....	*0.1*	.....	.....	.....	.....	.....	.....	.....
Other Enacted Supplemental or Emergency Funding ...	44.1	.....	0.4	.....	.....	.....	.....	.....	.....	.....
Agriculture	*1.4*		*0.4*							
Energy	*7.9*									
Health and Human Services	*10.5*									
State and Other International Programs	*13.8*									
Department of Transportation	*3.0*									
Corps of Engineers-Civil Works	*6.6*		***							
Other Agencies	*0.9*									
Proposed 2010 Supplemental Funding	.....	.....	41.1	.....	.....	.....	.....	.....	.....	.....
Defense (includes Overseas Contingency Operations)			*33.0*							
Homeland Security			*3.6*							
State and Other International Programs			*4.5*							
Grand Total, Discretionary Budget Authority	1,194.2	265.1	1,247.3	1,265.0	1,234.6	1,218.1	1,255.7	1,292.6	6,266.0	13,231.2
Grand Total, Discretionary Budgetary Resources	1,248.0	265.1	1,301.5	1,319.8	1,243.9	1,264.9	1,298.8	1,336.2	6,463.6	13,637.6

* $50 million or less.

[1] Although the Budget shows discretionary funding in nominal terms, the Administration conceives of discretionary growth rates in inflation-adjusted terms. If inflation projections are revised from what is currently projected, future budgets would be expected to adjust funding levels up or down accordingly. (This statement does not apply to funding growth between 2010 and the 2011 budget year, since the appropriations process for 2011 must begin immediately and before inflation assumptions will be revisited. It also does not apply to the outyear BA for overseas contingency operations, which is a placeholder and does not represent a policy determination.)

[2] "ARRA" refers to the American Recovery and Reinvestment Act of 2009 (P.L. 111-5).

[3] The DHS level includes $1.8 billion for BioShield in 2009 and a -$3.0 billion transfer in 2010 of BioShield balances to HHS.

[4] The Veterans Affairs total is net of medical care collections.

[5] The Security category for State and Other International Programs is comprised entirely of International Function 150. This includes funding for International Food Aid programs in the Department of Agriculture.

[6] Adjusted for advance appropriations, 2009 funding for the Department of Education is $46.2 billion. All numbers exclude funding for Pell Grants.

[7] Funding from the Hospital Insurance and Supplementary Medical Insurance trust funds for administrative expenses incurred by the Social Security Administration that support the Medicare program are included in the HHS total and not in the Social Security Administration total. Additionally, the HHS total includes $0.4 billion and $3.0 billion in 2009 and 2010, respectively, for transfer of the BioShield program in DHS.

[8] The Budget includes placeholder estimates of $50 billion per year for Overseas Contingency Operations in 2012 and beyond. These estimates do not reflect any specific policy decisions.

Table S–12.　Market Valuation and Balance Sheet of Fannie Mae and Freddie Mac
(In billions of dollars)

	2008	2009	2010	2011	2012	2013	2014	2015	2016	2017	2018	2019	2020	Totals 2011-2015	Totals 2011-2020
Transactions between Treasury and Fannie Mae/Freddie Mac:															
Senior Preferred Liquidity Payments to Fannie Mae/Freddie Mac	.....	96	69	23	.....	.....	.....	.....	.....	.....	.....	.....	.....	23	23
Senior Preferred Dividend Payments from Fannie Mae/Freddie Mac	.....	–4	–12	–18	–7	–7	–7	–7	–7	–7	–7	–7	–7	–44	–78
Net Payments	.....	91	57	5	–7	–7	–7	–7	–7	–7	–7	–7	–7	–21	–55
Market Valuation of Fannie Mae and Freddie Mac:															
Market Value of Net Liability	–18	–18													
Value of Private Equity Shares	–3	–3													
Net Position of Fannie Mae and Freddie Mac:															
Assets:															
U.S. Treasury Securities	.....	12													
Other Financial Assets	1,524	1,579													
Cash	115	110													
Other	63	54													
Liabilities:															
Debt Outstanding	1,615	1,607													
Other Financial Liabilities	90	155													
Equity:															
Treasury Senior Preferred Stock	.....	96													
Private Equity	–4	–101													
Net Position	–4	–5													

Table S–13.   Economic Assumptions
(Calendar years)

	2008 Actual	2009	2010	2011	2012	2013	2014	2015	2016	2017	2018	2019	2020
								Projections					
Gross Domestic Product (GDP):													
Nominal level, billions of dollars	14,441	14,252	14,768	15,514	16,444	17,433	18,446	19,433	20,408	21,373	22,329	23,312	24,323
Percent change, nominal GDP, year/year	2.6	–1.3	3.6	5.1	6.0	6.0	5.8	5.3	5.0	4.7	4.5	4.4	4.3
Real GDP, percent change, year/year	0.4	–2.5	2.7	3.8	4.3	4.2	4.0	3.6	3.2	2.8	2.6	2.5	2.5
Real GDP, percent change, Q4/Q4	–1.9	–0.5	3.0	4.3	4.3	4.2	3.9	3.4	3.1	2.7	2.6	2.5	2.5
GDP chained price index, percent change, year/year	2.1	1.2	0.9	1.2	1.6	1.7	1.7	1.7	1.8	1.8	1.8	1.8	1.8
Consumer Price Index[1], percent change, year/year	3.8	–0.3	1.9	1.5	2.0	2.0	2.0	2.0	2.0	2.1	2.1	2.1	2.1
Unemployment rate, civilian, percent[2]	5.8	9.3	10.0	9.2	8.2	7.3	6.5	5.9	5.5	5.3	5.2	5.2	5.2
Interest rates, percent:													
91-day Treasury bills[3]	1.4	0.2	0.4	1.6	3.0	4.0	4.1	4.1	4.1	4.1	4.1	4.1	4.1
10-year Treasury notes	3.7	3.3	3.9	4.5	5.0	5.2	5.3	5.3	5.3	5.3	5.3	5.3	5.3

Note: A more detailed table of economic assumptions is in Chapter 2, "Economic Assumptions," in the *Analytical Perspectives* volume of the Budget, Table 2–1.
[1] Seasonally adjusted CPI for all urban consumers.
[2] Annual average.
[3] Average rate, secondary market (bank discount basis).

Table S–14. Federal Government Financing and Debt
(In billions of dollars)

	2009	Estimate										
		2010	2011	2012	2013	2014	2015	2016	2017	2018	2019	2020
Financing:												
Unified budget deficit	1,413	1,556	1,267	828	727	706	752	778	778	785	908	1,003
Other transactions affecting borrowing from the public:												
Changes in financial assets and liabilities:[1]												
Change in Treasury operating cash balance[2]	-96	-5	-200	.....	.....	.....	.....	.....	.....	.....	.....	.....
Net disbursements of credit financing accounts:												
Direct loan accounts	293	210	143	135	118	108	99	70	85	79	91	91
Guaranteed loan accounts	7	-7	8	12	12	6	4	3	1	-2	-4	-6
Troubled Asset Relief Program (TARP) equity purchase accounts	105	1	-15	-*	-2	-5	-5	-5	-9	-11	-26	-16
Net purchases of non-Federal securities by the National Railroad Retirement Investment Trust (NRRIT)	-3	-1	-1	-1	-1	-1	-1	-1	-1	-1	-1	-1
Net change in other financial assets and liabilities[3]	22	.....	.....	.....	.....	.....	.....	.....	.....	.....	.....	.....
Subtotal, changes in financial assets and liabilities	329	198	-66	146	127	109	98	67	76	65	60	69
Seigniorage on coins	-*	-*	-*	-1	-1	-1	-1	-1	-1	-1	-1	-1
Total, other transactions affecting borrowing from the public	329	197	-66	145	126	108	97	67	75	64	59	68
Total, requirement to borrow from the public (equals change in debt held by the public)	1,742	1,753	1,201	974	854	814	849	844	853	849	967	1,071
Changes in Debt Subject to Statutory Limitation:												
Change in debt held by the public	1,742	1,753	1,201	974	854	814	849	844	853	849	967	1,071
Change in debt held by Government accounts	148	158	157	218	264	265	302	309	321	337	285	256
Change in other factors	4	-2	-1	1	1	1	1	1	1	1	1	-*
Total, change in debt subject to statutory limitation	1,893	1,909	1,357	1,193	1,119	1,079	1,152	1,155	1,176	1,187	1,253	1,327
Debt Subject to Statutory Limitation, End of Year:												
Debt issued by Treasury	11,850	13,760	15,117	16,308	17,426	18,505	19,656	20,809	21,984	23,171	24,424	25,751
Adjustment for discount, premium, and coverage[4]	3	2	2	4	5	6	7	8	8	9	9	9
Total, debt subject to statutory limitation[5]	11,853	13,762	15,119	16,312	17,431	18,511	19,662	20,817	21,993	23,180	24,433	25,760
Debt Outstanding, End of Year:												
Gross Federal debt:[6]												
Debt issued by Treasury	11,850	13,760	15,117	16,308	17,426	18,505	19,656	20,809	21,984	23,171	24,424	25,751
Debt issued by other agencies	26	27	27	27	27	28	28	28	27	26	26	26
Total, gross Federal debt	11,876	13,787	15,144	16,336	17,453	18,532	19,683	20,837	22,011	23,197	24,450	25,777
Held by:												
Debt held by Government accounts	4,331	4,489	4,646	4,864	5,128	5,393	5,695	6,004	6,325	6,663	6,948	7,204
Debt held by the public[7]	7,545	9,298	10,498	11,472	12,326	13,139	13,988	14,833	15,686	16,535	17,502	18,573

Table S–14. Federal Government Financing and Debt—Continued
(In billions of dollars)

	2009	Estimate										
		2010	2011	2012	2013	2014	2015	2016	2017	2018	2019	2020
Debt Held by the Public Net of Financial Assets:												
Debt held by the public	7,545	9,298	10,498	11,472	12,326	13,139	13,988	14,833	15,686	16,535	17,502	18,573
Less financial assets net of liabilities:												
Treasury operating cash balance[2]	275	270	70	70	70	70	70	70	70	70	70	70
Credit financing account balances:												
Direct loan accounts	489	700	842	977	1,095	1,204	1,303	1,373	1,458	1,537	1,628	1,719
Guaranteed loan accounts	-35	-42	-34	-22	-10	-4	*	3	5	2	-2	-7
TARP equity purchase accounts	105	106	91	91	89	84	80	75	66	55	29	13
Government-sponsored enterprise preferred stock	65	102	115	115	115	115	115	115	115	115	115	115
Non-Federal securities held by NRRIT	22	21	20	19	18	17	16	14	13	12	11	10
Other assets net of liabilities	-24	-24	-24	-24	-24	-24	-24	-24	-24	-24	-24	-24
Total, financial assets net of liabilities	898	1,133	1,080	1,227	1,353	1,462	1,560	1,627	1,703	1,768	1,827	1,896
Debt held by the public net of financial assets	6,647	8,164	9,418	10,246	10,972	11,677	12,428	13,205	13,983	14,767	15,675	16,677

Note: Figures displayed in the table do not reflect the impact of any recommendations from the Fiscal Commission.

* $500 million or less.

[1] A decrease in the Treasury operating cash balance (which is an asset) is a means of financing a deficit and therefore has a negative sign. An increase in checks outstanding (which is a liability) is also a means of financing a deficit and therefore also has a negative sign.

[2] Includes assumed Supplementary Financing Program balance of $200 billion on September 30, 2010, and zero on September 30, 2011, and beyond.

[3] Besides checks outstanding, includes accrued interest payable on Treasury debt, uninvested deposit fund balances, allocations of special drawing rights, and other liability accounts; and, as an offset, cash and monetary assets (other than the Treasury operating cash balance), other asset accounts, and profit on sale of gold.

[4] Consists mainly of debt issued by the Federal Financing Bank (which is not subject to limit), debt held by the Federal Financing Bank, the unamortized discount (less premium) on public issues of Treasury notes and bonds (other than zero-coupon bonds), and the unrealized discount on Government account series securities.

[5] The statutory debt limit is $12,394 billion, as enacted on December 28, 2009.

[6] Treasury securities held by the public and zero-coupon bonds held by Government accounts are almost all measured at sales price plus amortized discount or less amortized premium. Agency debt securities are almost all measured at face value. Treasury securities in the Government account series are otherwise measured at face value less unrealized discount (if any).

[7] At the end of 2009, the Federal Reserve Banks held $769.2 billion of Federal securities and the rest of the public held $6,775.5 billion. Debt held by the Federal Reserve Banks is not estimated for future years.

OMB CONTRIBUTORS TO THE 2011 BUDGET

The following personnel contributed to the preparation of this publication. Hundreds, perhaps thousands, of others throughout the Government also deserve credit for their valuable contributions.

A

Katherine D. Aaby
Andrew Abrams
Chandana Achanta
Karl Agcaoili
Brenda Aguilar
Shagufta I. Ahmed
Steven D. Aitken
Jameela Raja Akbari
Robert Alderfer
David Alekson
Lois E. Altoft
Scott J. Anchin
Lucas J. Anderson
Robert B. Anderson
Kevin Archer
Anna R. Arroyo
Katherine T. Astrich
Lisa L. August
Laura G. Auletta
Renee Austin
Shawn D. Azman

B

Peter Babb
Kenneth S. Baer
Elizabeth A. Bafford
Paul W. Baker
Carol Bales
Preeta D. Bansal
John W. Barkhamer
Patti Barnett
Carl Barrick
Jody Barringer
Tali Bar-Shalom

Mary C. Barth
Julie Basile
Nancy B. Beck
Jennifer Wagner Bell
Stuart Bender
Lindsey R. Berman
Elizabeth Bernhard
Boris Bershteyn
Catherine Bloniarz
Mathew C. Blum
James Boden
Melissa B. Bomberger
Debra Bond
Dan Bonesteel
Edward P. Borrego
David S. Bortnick
Constance J. Bowers
Bill Boyd
Wyatt Boyd
Chantel M. Boyens
Betty I. Bradshaw
Joshua J. Brammer
Shannon Bregman
Xavier D. Briggs
Brooke Brody-Waite
Mark Brooks
Charles H. Brown
Dustin S. Brown
James A. Brown
Jennifer E. Brown
Kelly D. Brown
Emily P. Brownlow
Michael Brunetto
Ryan J. Bubb
Paul Bugg
Joshua Bull
Tom D. Bullers

Robert B. Bullock
Benjamin Burnett
John D. Burnim
John C. Burton
Rachel A. B. Burton
Mark Bussow

C

Kathleen Cahill
Steven Cahill
Philip T. Calbos
Mark F. Cancian
Anna Canfield
Christa Capozzola
Kara K. Cardinale
Eric D. Cardoza
J. Kevin Carroll
Randy J. Caruso
Mary I. Cassell
David Cassidy
Benjamin Chan
Daniel E. Chandler
Alan Chao
James Chase
Anita Chellaraj
Lingjiao Chen
Shawn Choy
Michael C. Clark
Allison Leah Cole
John J. Colleran
Debra M. Collins
Nicole E. Comisky
David C. Connolly
Ryan H. Cooper
Matthew Coryell
Daniel Costello

Kelly T. Coylar
Catherine Crato
Joseph Crilley
Rosemarie C. Crow
Michael F. Crowley
Craig Crutchfield
Edna T. Falk Curtin
C. Tyler Curtis
William P. Curtis

D

Michael D'Amato
Veronica Daigle
Neil Danberg
J. Michael Daniel
Kristy L. Daphnis
Michael P. Darling
A. James Daumit
Joanne Davenport
Garrick Davis
Margaret B. Davis-
    Christian
Anne M. Decesaro
Deanna DeMott
Carol R. Dennis
Alyssa Denzer
G. Edward DeSeve
Samantha L.
    Deshommes
Cynthia Diamond
John H. Dick, Jr.
Frank DiGiammarino
Angela Donatelli
Paul Donohue
Bridget C. E. Dooling
Shamera Dorsey

181

Vishal D. Doshi
Audrey L. Duchesne
Laura Duke
Van Duong
Louise Dyer

E

Jacqueline A. Easley
Eugene M. Ebner
Mabel E. Echols
Jeanette Edwards
Emily M. Eelman
Katherine A. Eltrich
Zeke Emanuel
Gene Emmans
Noah Engelberg
Michelle A. Enger
Leandra English
Elizabeth Erickson
Kristofor Erickson
Sally Ericsson
Dinée Eriksen
Giannina Espichan
Victoria Espinel
Suzann K. Evinger
Rowe Ewell

F

Chris Fairhall
Robert S. Fairweather
Michael C. Falkenheim
Kim Farington
Kara Farley-Cahill
Dick Feezle
Nicole A. Fernandes
Patricia A. Ferrell
Lesley A. Field
Jessica Finkel
Alyssa D. Fisher
E. Holly Fitter
Mary E. Fitzpatrick
Michael A. Fitzpatrick
Darlene B. Fleming
Michael P. Flood
Tera Fong
Keith Fontenot
Kim Ford

James Ford-Fleming
Emily Fort
Peggy Fouts
Nicholas A. Fraser
Farrah Freis
Nathan J. Frey
Michael Friedberg

G

Marc Garufi
Thomas E. Gavin
Darcel D. Gayle
Jennifer Gera
Bassam F. Gergi
Michael D. Gerich
Brian W. Gill
Brian Gillis
David Glaudemans
Joshua Glazer
Kimberly Glenn
Adam Goldberg
Robert Goldberg
Jeffrey Goldstein
Oscar Gonzalez
Dan Gordon
Robert M. Gordon
Andrew Grandison
Melissa Green
Richard E. Green
Aron Greenberg
Lisa Greenwood
Fumie Y. Griego
Hester Grippando
Rebecca Grusky

H

Michael B. Hagan
Susan Haggerty
Christopher C. Hall
Kathleen D. Hamm
Eric V. Hansen
Linda W. Hardin
Dionne M. Hardy
David Harmon
Patsy Harris
Brian Harris-Kojetin

Nicholas R. Hart
Luke Hartig
Paul Harvey
David J. Haun
Florence Hawald
Mark H. Hazelgren
Pamela L. Heijmans
Gregory G. Henry
Kevin W. Herms
Jessica R. Hertz
Michael Hickey
Beth Higa
Cortney J. Higgins
Mary Lou Hildreth
Jeffrey C. Hilliard
Leslie K. Hinchman
Andrew Hire
Jennifer Hoef
Joanne Cianci Hoff
Adam Hoffberg
Stuart Hoffman
Michael J. Howell
Grace Hu
Kathy M. Hudgins
Carrie A. Hug
Tammy S. Hughes
Jeremy D. Hulick
James Hundt
Alexander T. Hunt
Lorraine D. Hunt
James C. Hurban
Jaki Mayer Hurwitz
Kristen D. Hyatt

I

Tae H. Im

J

Laurence R. Jacobson
Dana M. James
Carol D. Jenkins
Christopher S. Johns
Barbara A. Johnson
Carol Johnson
Kim A. Johnson
Kim I. Johnson
Kristen Johnson

Michael D. Johnson
Bryant A. Jones
Denise B. Jones
Lisa M. Jones
Scott W. Jones
James F. Jordan
James J. Jukes
Hee K. Jun

K

Julie A. Kalishman
David C. Kamin
Amy Kaminski
Jacob H. Kaplan
Irene B. Kariampuzha
Jenifer Karwoski
Regina Kearney
Matthew J. Keeneth
John W. Kelly
Kenneth S. Kelly
Ann H. Kendrall
Nancy Kenly
Paul E. Kilbride
Timothy Kim
Barry D. King
Heidi R. King
Kelly Kinneen
Carole Kitti
Ben Klay
Sarah B. Klein
Melissa A. Kline
Richard L. Kogan
Emily M. Kornegay
Steve M. Kosiak
Constantine Koulouris
John Kraemer
Lori A. Krauss
Caroline Krency
Kristi Kubista-Hovis
Divya Kumaraiah
Vivek Kundra
Joydip Kundu
Christine J. Kymn

L

Leonard L. Lainhart
James A. Laity

Chad A Lallemand
Lawrence L. Lambert
Daniel LaPlaca
Eric P. Lauer
Kristen Lauer
Jessie LaVine
Michael Lazzeri
Amanda I. Lee
David Lee
Jane K. Lee
Jessica Lee
Nicholas Lee
Richard Lee
Sarah S. Lee
Sun H. Lee
Susan Leetmaa
M. Bryan Legaspi
Christine M. Leininger
Stuart Levenbach
Ariel D. Levin
Shoshana M. Lew
Sheila D. Lewis
Wendy Liberante
Richard A.
   Lichtenberger
Jeffrey B. Liebman
Elizabeth K. Lien
Suzanne Lightman
Tung-Yen Lin
Lin C. Liu
Patrick G. Locke
Aaron M. Lopata
Marta M. Lopez
Adrienne C. Erbach
   Lucas
Kimberley Luczynski
Sarah Lyberg
Randolph M. Lyon

M

Debbie Macaulay
Ryan MacMaster
John S. Macneil
Anish Mahajan
Natalia Mahmud
Neale A. Mahoney
Mikko Makarainen
Margaret A. Malanoski

Dominic J. Mancini
Kate Mann
Meagan Mann
Sharon Mar
Celinda A. Marsh
Brendan A. Martin
Kathryn Martin
Rochelle Wilkie
   Martinez
Surujpat J. Adrian
   Mathura
Karen Yoshiko
   Matsuoka
Shelly McAllister
Karen R. McBride
Emily M. McCartan
Erin McCartney
Alexander J.
   McClelland
Anthony W. McDonald
Christine McDonald
Katrina A. McDonald
Renford McDonald
Carl McGruder
Matthew McKearn
Christopher McLaren
Robin J. McLaughry
Alex McPhillips
William J. McQuaid
William J. Mea
Andrew Medley
Inna L. Melamed
Karen C. Melanson
Gordon B. Mermin
Richard A. Mertens
Steven M. Mertens
Margaret M. Mesaros
Justin R. Meservie
P. Thaddeus
   Messenger
Shelley Metzenbaum
Julie V. Middleton
Laurie A. Mignone
Joanna Mikulski
Caitlyn Miller
Julie L. Miller
Kimberly Miller
Joe Montoni
Jeremy L. Moon

Jamesa C. Moone
David A. Morris
Jonathan D. Morse
Jane T. Moy
Jennifer W. Murray
Chris Music

N

Robert L. Nabors
Jennifer Nading
Jeptha E. Nafziger
Larry Nagl
Barry Napear
Erica Navarro
Michael A. Negron
Kimberly Nelson
Betsy Newcomer
John Newman
Kimberly A. Newman
Kevin F. Neyland
Teresa Nguyen
Abigail P. Norris
Douglas A. Norwood

O

Erin O'Brien
Kathleen E. O'Connell
Erin M. O'Keefe
Marvis G. Olfus
Farouk Ophaso
Peter R. Orszag
Jared Ostermiller
Tyler J. Overstreet
Pearson Owens

P

Ben Page
Brandye N. Page
Rasik Pandey
Louis Pappas
Sangkyun Park
Joel R. Parriott
John Pasquantino
Arati Patel
Melissa N. Patterson
Kshemendra N. Paul

Terri B. Payne
Jacqueline M. Peay
Falisa L. Peoples-Tittle
Kathleen Peroff
Andrew B. Perraut
Andrea M. Petro
John R. Pfeiffer
Stacey Que-Chi Pham
Carolyn R. Phelps
Karen A. Pica
Joseph T. Pika
Joseph G. Pipan
Alisa M. Ple-Plakon
Ruxandra I. Pond
Celestine M. Pressley
Jamie Price Pressly
Marguerite Pridgen
Robert B. Purdy
Michael J. Pyle

Q

John P. Quinlan

R

Lucas R. Radzinschi
Latonda Glass Raft
Ganeshkumar B. Raju
Maria Raphael
Peter J. Ray
McGavock D. Reed
Paul B. Rehmus
Thomas M. Reilly
Richard J. Renomeron
Keri A. Rice
M. David Rice
Renee Richburg
Shannon Richter
Earl W. Rilington, Jr.
Crystal Roach
Benjamin Roberts
John S. Roberts
Donovan O. Robinson
Marshall Rodgers
Teresa Canton Rojas
Meredith Romley
Dan T. Rosenbaum
Adam J. Ross

David Rostker
David Rowe
Mario D. Roy
Jonathan Rupp
Ross A. Rutledge
Rexon Y. Ryu

S

Fouad P. Saad
John Asa Saldivar
Dominic K. Sale
Erika Saleski
Hana Sarsour
Narahari Sastry
Ryan J. Schaefer
Erik K. Scheirer
Caryn Schenewerk
Jill Schiller
Evan Schlom
Tricia Schmitt
Andrew M. Schoenbach
Ingrid M. Schroeder
Margo Schwab
Candice M. Schwartz
Nancy Schwartz
Jasmeet K. Seehra
Nirav Shah
Shahid N. Shah
Emily L. Sharp
Dianne Shaughnessy
Paul Shawcross
Kathryn D. Sheehey
Rachel C. Shoemate
R. Jacob Shuler
Mary Jo Siclari
Sarah S. Siddiqui
Matthew J. Siegel
Sara R. Sills
Angela M. Simms
Robin Sinquefield

Jack A. Smalligan
Curtina O. Smith
Gayle E. Smith
Jan Smith
Jennifer Smookler
Joanne Snow
Silvana Solano
Leo Sommaripa
Lillian S. Spuria
Kathryn B. Stack
Scott Stambaugh
Andrea M. Staron
Henry Stawski
Nora Stein
Charlie Stern
Catherine L. Stewart
Gary Stofko
Carla B. Stone
Justin Streufert
Shannon Stuart
Tom Suarez
Alice Suh
Stephen Suh
Kevin J. Sullivan
Jessica Sun
Cass R. Sunstein

T

Teresa A. Tancre
Benjamin K. Taylor
Richard P. Theroux
LaTina Thomas
Payton Thomas
Courtney B.
   Timberlake
Bruce D. Timman
Thomas Tobasko
Richard Toner
Anne M. Toomey
Gilbert Tran

Gregg Treml
Susan M. Truslow
Gretchen Trygstad
Donald L. Tuck
Grant Turner

U

Darrell J. Upshaw

V

Matthew J. Vaeth
Ofelia M. Valeriano
Cynthia A. Vallina
Uday Varadarajan
Areletha L. Venson
Alexandra Ventura
Mark Vinkenes
Patricia Vinkenes
Dean Vonk
Kathy Voorhees
Ann M. Vrabel

W

James A. Wade
Emily Waechter
Ted Wainwright
Richard K. Wall
Martha A. Wallace
Katherine K. Wallman
Heather V. Walsh
Ali Wardle
LaTonya R. Ware
Sharon A. Warner
Gary S. Washington
Gary Waxman
Mark A. Weatherly
Bessie M. Weaver
Jean Weinberg

Jeffrey A. Weinberg
Maggie Weiss
Philip R. Wenger
Daniel Werfel
Arnette C. White
Kamela White
Kim S. White
Sherron R. White
Sarah Widor
Mary Ellen Wiggins
Debra L. Williams
Monique C. Williams
Tommy Williams
Jennifer Winkler
Brian C. Winseck
Melanie Winston
Julia B. Wise
Julie A. Wise
Daryl Womack
Chantale Wong
Daren Wong
Raymond Wong
Lauren Wright
Sophia Wright

X

Xiao Ling Xu

Y

Melany N. Yeung

Z

Ali A. Zaidi
Jeff Zients
Gail S. Zimmerman
Rachel Zinn

U.S. GOVERNMENT PRINTING OFFICE
KEEPING AMERICA INFORMED

Budget of the U.S. Government, FY 2011
Stock number: 041-001-00671-1
ISBN number: 978-0-16-084795-0
Price: $37.00

Appendix-Budget of the U.S. Government, FY 2011
Stock number: 041-001-00672-9
ISBN number: 978-0-16-084796-7
Price: $73.00

Historical Tables-Budget of the U.S. Government, FY 2011
Stock number: 041-001-00673-7
ISBN number: 978-0-16-084797-4
Price: $49.00

Analytical Perspectives-Budget of the U.S. Government, FY 2011
Stock number: 041-001-00674-5
ISBN number: 978-0-16-084798-1
Price: $52.00

The Federal Budget on CD-ROM-Budget of the U.S. Government, FY 2011
Stock number: 041-001-00675-3
ISBN number: 978-0-16-084799-8
Price: $25.00

U.S. GOVERNMENT PRINTING OFFICE
KEEPING AMERICA INFORMED

Order Processing Code: 3555

Easy Secure Internet: bookstore.gpo.gov

Toll Free: 866 512–1800
DC Area: 202 512–1800
Fax: 202 512–2104

Mail: US Government Printing Office
P.O. Box 979050
St. Louis, MO 63197–9000

Qty	Stock Number	ISBN Number	Publication Title	Unit Price	Total Price
	041-001-00671-1	978-0-16-084795-0	Budget of the U.S. Government, FY 2011	$37.00	
	041-001-00672-9	978-0-16-084796-7	Appendix-Budget of the U.S. Government, FY 2011	$73.00	
	041-001-00673-7	978-0-16-084797-4	Historical Tables-Budget of the U.S. Government, FY 2011	$49.00	
	041-001-00674-5	978-0-16-084798-1	Analytical Perspectives-Budget of the U.S. Government, FY 2011	$52.00	
	041-001-00675-3	978-0-16-084799-8	The Federal Budget on CD-ROM-Budget of the U.S. Government, FY 2011	$25.00	
			Total Order		

Personal Name _____ (Please type or Print)

Company Name _____

Street Address _____

City, State, Zip Code _____

Daytime Phone Including Area Code _____

Check Method of Payment

VISA   MasterCard   DISCOVER NOVUS   American Express

☒ Check payable to *Superintendent of Documents*

☒ SOD Deposit Account [ ][ ][ ][ ][ ][ ][ ]—[ ]

☒ VISA ☒ MasterCard ☒ Discover/NOVUS ☒ American Express

[ ][ ][ ][ ][ ][ ][ ][ ][ ][ ][ ][ ][ ][ ][ ][ ]

[ ][ ][ ][ ] (EXPIRATION DATE)

Thank you for your order!

AUTHORIZING SIGNATURE

01/10

U.S. GOVERNMENT PRINTING OFFICE
KEEPING AMERICA INFORMED

Budget of the U.S. Government, FY 2011
Stock number: 041-001-00671-1
ISBN number: 978-0-16-084795-0
Price: $37.00

Appendix-Budget of the U.S. Government, FY 2011
Stock number: 041-001-00672-9
ISBN number: 978-0-16-084796-7
Price: $73.00

Historical Tables-Budget of the U.S. Government, FY 2011
Stock number: 041-001-00673-7
ISBN number: 978-0-16-084797-4
Price: $49.00

Analytical Perspectives-Budget of the U.S. Government, FY 2011
Stock number: 041-001-00674-5
ISBN number: 978-0-16-084798-1
Price: $52.00

The Federal Budget on CD-ROM-Budget of the U.S. Government, FY 2011
Stock number: 041-001-00675-3
ISBN number: 978-0-16-084799-8
Price: $25.00

U.S. GOVERNMENT PRINTING OFFICE
KEEPING AMERICA INFORMED

Order Processing Code: 3555

Easy Secure Internet: bookstore.gpo.gov

Toll Free: 866 512–1800
DC Area: 202 512–1800
Fax: 202 512–2104

Mail: US Government Printing Office
P.O. Box 979050
St. Louis, MO 63197–9000

Qty	Stock Number	ISBN Number	Publication Title	Unit Price	Total Price
	041-001-00671-1	978-0-16-084795-0	Budget of the U.S. Government, FY 2011	$37.00	
	041-001-00672-9	978-0-16-084796-7	Appendix-Budget of the U.S. Government, FY 2011	$73.00	
	041-001-00673-7	978-0-16-084797-4	Historical Tables-Budget of the U.S. Government, FY 2011	$49.00	
	041-001-00674-5	978-0-16-084798-1	Analytical Perspectives-Budget of the U.S. Government, FY 2011	$52.00	
	041-001-00675-3	978-0-16-084799-8	The Federal Budget on CD-ROM-Budget of the U.S. Government, FY 2011	$25.00	
			Total Order		

Check Method of Payment

Personal Name _____ (Please type or Print)

Company Name _____

Street Address _____

City, State, Zip Code _____

☒ Check payable to *Superintendent of Documents*

☒ SOD Deposit Account ☐☐☐☐☐☐☐—☐

☒ VISA ☒ MasterCard ☒ Discover/NOVUS ☒ American Express

☐☐☐☐☐☐☐☐☐☐☐☐☐☐☐☐

☐☐☐☐ (EXPIRATION DATE)

Thank you for your order!

Daytime Phone Including Area Code _____

AUTHORIZING SIGNATURE

01/10

WITHDRAWN

ISBN 978-0-16-084795-0

90000